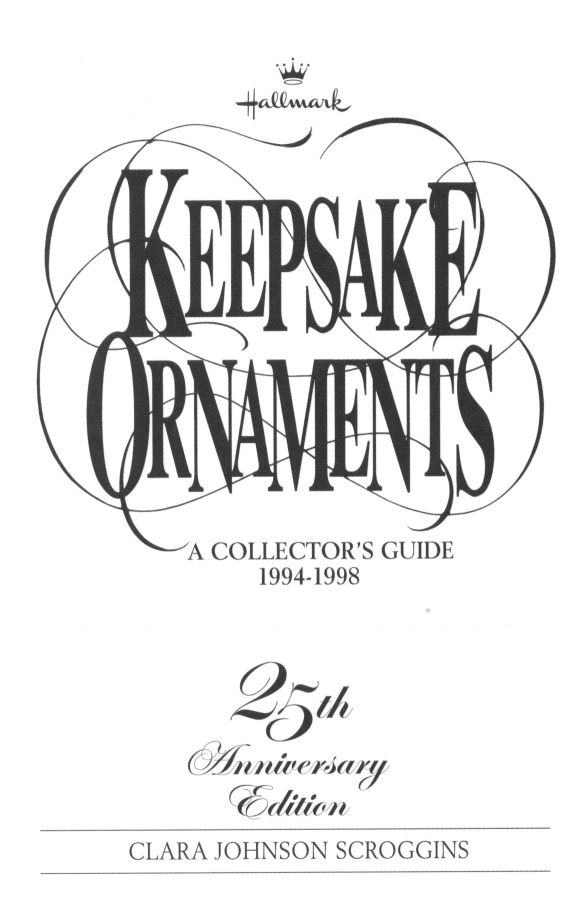

Hallmark

KEEPSAKE ORNAMENTS

A COLLECTOR'S GUIDE
1994-1998

25th Anniversary Edition

CLARA JOHNSON SCROGGINS

Hallmark
Cards

Dear Collectors,

When Hallmark introduced its first Keepsake Ornament in 1973, we had no idea
what a phenomenon ornament collecting would become.

I am, at times, overwhelmed by the enthusiasm of today's ornament collectors,
and I am very proud of our company's leadership in creativity, quality and craftsmanship, which makes Keepsake Ornaments so highly prized.

From the earliest days of our company, Hallmark has created products that enrich
people's lives and enhance their relationships. And it seems to me that the impor-
tance of relationships is never more evident than during a holiday. Not only are holidays the times when friends get in touch and families come together, but they are
the times when we tend to blend the past with the present.

Each year, when my wife Adele and I decorate our Christmas tree, we display very
old ornaments that belonged to Adele's parents next to new Hallmark Keepsake
Ornaments that delight our grandchildren. Year after year, our Christmas ornaments
help celebrate important family events and serve as memories of past delights.

Today, my three children are grown and have families of their own, and they can't
always join Adele and me to trim the tree. But we always set aside three special ornaments—one for Don, one for Margi and one for Dave—so that each of them can
hang the ornaments when they arrive. These aren't necessarily the most elaborate
ornaments nor the most expensive, but they are the ornaments that mean the most
to each of our children.

I'm sure many of you share similar traditions and family memories. I hope this
collector's guide will further the joy you get from these traditions and will be a use-
ful addition to your Hallmark Keepsake Ornament collection.

Whether you are a new collector or have been collecting ornaments for a quarter
of a century, I'm sure you will find that this 25th anniversary edition will give you
greater knowledge about the ornaments you collect and bring you closer to the people who create them.

On behalf of my family and the many Hallmark artists who have created
Hallmark Keepsake Ornaments throughout the years, I thank you for your dedication
and enthusiasm. May the next 25 years—and all the years to come after those—be
filled with the joy of the holidays and the relationships that are strengthened as you
share the tradition of ornament collecting with others.

Don Hall

Don Hall
Chairman and son of the founder
Hallmark Cards, Inc.

Thanks for
telling the
story of
Hallmark
Keepsake
Ornaments

Don Hall.

First Edition
Library of Congress Catalog
Number: 97-78254
ISBN 0-87529-750-1
© 1998 Hallmark Cards, Inc.
© 1998 Clara Johnson Scroggins

Author
Clara Johnson Scroggins

Publisher
Hallmark Cards, Inc.

Editorial Director
Linda Fewell
Senior Editor
Hallmark Cards, Inc.

Meredith Integrated Marketing

Editor
Pamela Johnson

Contributing Editor
Laura Holtorf Collins

Design Director
Jann Williams

Contributing Designer
Lori Tursi Grote

Editor-in-Chief
Don Johnson

Managing Editor
Deb Gore Ohrn

Production Director
Ivan McDonald

Marketing Director
Pam Kenyon

Publisher & General Manager
Jack Griffin

Published by Meredith Integrated
Marketing, 1912 Grand Avenue,
Des Moines, Iowa 50309-3379.
Printed in the USA.

Contents

DEDICATION
Clara Johnson Scroggins

To my family—all of the Johnsons—with a special memorial dedication to Vicki L. Johnson Ross, the "baby" of our family and my youngest sibling, who passed away in March 1997.

To my husband, Joe; to my son, Michael; and to Kathy, Michelle, Terrence, Alexzandra, Chaise and great-granddaughter Micaela.

To Lynn Wylie, Tex Ann Kraft, Linda Fewell and the entire Keepsake Ornament staff (especially the artists).

To my fellow collectors, especially those from the early days.

And, finally, to "my" clubs—the NASA Noelers, the Tampa Bay Tree Trimmers, Hooked on Heirlooms and The More the Merrier clubs.

Photos of lapel pins that have been designed and created by local chapters of the Hallmark Keepsake Ornament Collector's Club can be found throughout this book. The pins pictured are a sample from my collection, and were given to me by collectors and local clubs across the country. By including a sampling of local club pins, it is my intent to honor all local clubs. If your club pin is not represented in these pages, please know that your club's place in my heart and your collecting passion are represented.

Thank you, one and all, for the beautiful memories.

Love,
Clara

About the Author

Clara Johnson Scroggins

For more than 25 years, Clara Johnson Scroggins has shared her passion for ornament collecting and has enriched the hobby for people worldwide.

Clara's journey into the world of collecting ornaments began in December 1972, after the sudden death of her husband. During what, for her, was a sad holiday season, the young widow saw in a jewelry shop what was to become the first ornament in her collection—the second-edition Reed & Barton silver cross. In a flash of emotion, a spark of light reflected off the cross's surface and touched her heart—connecting Clara, her husband and God—and reminding her that loving faith can live forever. That belief in enduring love formed Clara's collecting philosophy, and it's a philosophy that has not wavered. You'll still hear Clara encouraging her fellow ornament enthusiasts to "collect what you love."

Clara's love of collecting, of course, did not end with that silver cross. She was propelled into a nationwide search for the first edition. By the time the 1971 cross was hers, so were 90 percent of all Christmas ornaments made by silver companies, as well as those issued by museums, mints and department stores in the United States and abroad. When Hallmark Keepsake Ornaments debuted in 1973, she immediately recognized them as collectible and added every single one of them to her growing treasury.

Clara's first edition of *Hallmark Keepsake Ornaments: A Collector's Guide* captivated collectors. Its publication in 1983 remains a watershed moment in the evolution of what, today, collecting

authorities point to as the most sought-after ornaments in the industry. She also authored a guide about silver ornaments before writing six consecutive editions of *Hallmark Keepsake Ornaments: A Collector's Guide.* The seventh and most recent edition, which celebrates the 25th anniversary of Keepsake Ornaments, is in your hands today.

Clara now has more than 500,000 ornaments in her collection and is considered the premiere contemporary ornament authority. A meticulous historian, she has been the subject of cover stories for the *Franklin Mint* and *The Plate Collector* and has been featured in the Life section of *USA Today*, as well as in feature stories in *Better Homes and Gardens, Southern Living, Equestrian Magazine* and *The New York Times* magazine. She also has been interviewed by newspapers and television talk shows, including "Today" and "Good Morning, America." She travels year-round on the lecture circuit.

Clara and husband, Joe Scroggins Jr., divide their time between homes in Tampa, Fla., and Washington, D.C. Although Joe can't match Clara's passion for collecting, he recognizes that Clara simply would not be Clara without ornaments! Clara also shares her love of collecting with her son, Michael, daughter-in-law Kathy, grandchildren Chaise, Michelle, Terrence and Alexzandra, and great-grandchild Micaela.

Then, of course, there's Clara's second family—the family of collectors who welcomes her warmly wherever they meet.

Dear Collecting Friends,

Twenty-five years ago, Hallmark launched a new division called Trim-A-Home to "help people decorate for Christmas." No one anticipated this would evolve into a creative team dedicated to bringing collectors "the very best" in ornaments, nor that, in 1998, membership in the Hallmark Keepsake Ornament Collector's Club would number more than a quarter-million people. Twenty-five years ago, I couldn't have imagined that I would author seven editions of *Hallmark Keepsake Ornaments: A Collector's Guide.* But a box containing four ball ornaments and a letter—a cherished part of my Hallmark collection—reveals a connection between these ornaments and me that was meant to be.

The date was December 13, 1972. In Kansas City, people at Hallmark were sending corrugated boxes, each containing four ball ornaments, to drugstore operators across the nation. Into each box went a letter asking the store operators to evaluate the ornaments with the thought that they might become a new product line. On that very same date in Stamford, Conn., I buried my first husband.

I didn't realize the coincidence until I attended the 1996 national Hallmark Keepsake Ornament Premiere in suburban Detroit and met a lady who had one of those boxes. I bought it and, upon returning home, decided to sit down and re-read the letter. I picked up the box and saw the metered postage stamp with the date—December 13, 1972! My sister, Precious, told me later that as God was closing the door on one part of my life, he was opening another.

Now, so many years after that December date, I think Hallmark Keepsake Ornaments—which officially debuted in 1973—became popular and collectible because they don't just "help people decorate." They help us remember, cherish and celebrate. The Keepsake Ornament artists somehow tap into our collective memories of holidays, home, special times and wonderful people.

That's what this book is about—memories. And it's about the joy and passion of collecting, too. This 1994–1998 edition is designed as a companion to the Sixth Edition, which chronicles the first 20 years of Keepsake Ornaments and is being reprinted during this 25th anniversary year. It's my hope that these guides will answer your questions, pique your interest and enrich your Hallmark hobby.

It's been a remarkable first 25 years! Happy anniversary to Hallmark Keepsake Ornaments, and to all of us who are collecting and loving it!

Clara Johnson Scroggins

Here's the postage stamp that reveals a connection between Hallmark Keepsake Ornaments and me. In the photo on page 4, I'm holding the letter and one of the four ornaments that came inside the box dated December 13, 1972.

From Clara
with love

Linda Sickman

When asked about creating Keepsake Ornaments, Linda says she delves into childhood memories. She is best known for her **Rocking Horse** and **Tin Locomotive** series. Linda likes the tin ornaments best because they are nostalgic and different from other ornaments on the market. She joined Hallmark in 1965 and, for a few years, created hand lettering for greeting cards and designed gift wrap and other gift products. She began designing Hallmark ornaments before the Keepsake Ornament studio existed. Her first creations were the six Nostalgia Ornaments that appeared in 1975 (the first year that the Keepsake Ornament line included handcrafted ornaments). Among those six, the first that Linda sculpted was **Rocking Horse.** Linda officially joined the Keepsake Ornament studio in 1976, and today, she has hundreds of Keepsake Ornament designs to her credit.

Originally from Toronto, Canada, Ed began as a carpenter, studied at Florida's Ringling Art School, then joined Hallmark in 1968. After five years, he became convinced that his talent—and his heart—were in three-dimensional work.

Perhaps that's why he says that sculpting Keepsake Ornaments was wonderful right from the start. Ed joined the Keepsake Ornament studio full time in 1980, and his **Frosty Friends** and **Tender Touches** creations soon identified him with collectors. Ed's favorite Keepsake Ornament is the 1996 **North Pole Volunteers** into which he incorporated elements he loves: Santa, a puppy and a fire truck. Ed also is known for his mini mice—whimsical critters doing "people things." Now that he has created more than 200 Keepsake Ornament designs, he says it's difficult to express how important collectors are to his work.

Ed Seale

Bob Siedler

Bob joined Hallmark in 1979 to help create catalogs and other promotional items for the Hallmark sales force. His talent for sculpting was discovered when he began creating three-dimensional "pinch art" during his lunch hours.

Since joining the Keepsake Ornament studio as a duplicate painter in 1981, Bob has sculpted hundreds of Keepsake Ornaments, including **Owliver, Reindeer Champs,** and ornaments based on licensed properties.

When asked about his favorite Keepsake Ornament, Bob couldn't identify just one. "It's like choosing your favorite movie or song. To quote a country singer, 'It's the one I'm singing now.'"

In his years with the studio, Bob has enjoyed meeting with collectors and is glad to be part of the 25th anniversary.

"I have a mind for putting things together," Ken explains. He classifies his work as "little boy, juvenile," although people of all ages are attracted to his moving creations. Pull the string on **Mistletoad,** for instance, and the festive amphibian grins and "ribbits." Ken engineered the workings himself. Before coming to Hallmark in 1979, Ken wanted to be an editorial cartoonist or a Disney animator. He says work at Hallmark is much more satisfying. "I can use my own ideas and style and animate my own characters," he says. That's been especially true since he joined the Keepsake Ornament studio in 1983. Ken's favorite ornament is the 1995 **Our Little Blessings** because he modeled it after his own son and daughter, Paul (then 4 years old) and Michelle (then 2). Ken says he has a special memory of a blind collector who smiled from the heart when she "saw" his Santa ornament through the touch of her fingertips.

Ken Crow

Here's your chance to meet the Keepsake Ornament artists whose creations are featured in this book and who still are at work in the studio creating Keepsake Ornaments today. The artists are listed in chronological order, according to the year in which each joined the Keepsake Ornament studio.

Sharon Pike

It's a toss-up which Sharon enjoys more—collecting or creating. (Sharon herself has a room full of Keepsake Ornaments that make up her personal collection!) In any case, her work gives away her enthusiasm.

A part of Hallmark since 1963, Sharon has designed products for eight different Hallmark departments. "I've always been an artist," she explains, "mostly in flat art, drawing anything I could." She began to sculpt when she joined the Keepsake Ornament studio in 1983 and has become known for a character based on her own cat, Skunk, who passed away in 1996. "He was my baby," she remembers. "I wanted to make him live on in memory." She hopes to reach collectors who share her passion for cats.

LaDene's admiration for Beatrix Potter began in childhood and now is evident in Keepsake Ornaments for which LaDene has become known. She translates two-dimensional drawings from Beatrix Potter books into lively three-dimensional characters.

LaDene originally set her sights on fashion design and admits she never dreamed of being a Keepsake Ornament artist. She first joined Hallmark in the 1960s, then moved to California for eight years, and finally returned to Hallmark to design greeting cards in 1973. She joined the Keepsake Ornament studio in 1983, and she says the things that are most important in her life are reflected in her work. "I love to capture the special mystical qualities we associate with angels," she says.

LaDene Votruba

Joyce Lyle

Joyce feels particularly fortunate to be a Keepsake Ornament artist. Mother to five children, her only drawing experience was for her family and her church.

Joyce first joined Hallmark in 1979. Soon, she began to accept freelance assignments from a department that then was called Trim-a-Home (now called Keepsake Ornaments). At that time, she painted duplicate ornament molds used in production. In 1984, she joined the Keepsake Ornament studio and quickly proved her talent as she sculpted angels, Victorian figures and roly-poly Santas.

"I enjoy making things that are meaningful," Joyce explains. She sculpted the 1995 **Rejoice!** while sitting in a Tulsa hospital, praying for her failing mother-in-law. "It became her ornament and represented the beautiful life she lived," says Joyce.

Duane could retire, but he says he continues to work because he enjoys it so much. A Keepsake Ornament artist since 1984 and part of Hallmark since 1979, Duane still dreams up new designs. "I like to use colors that are particularly beautiful against a tree," he says. That's why he draped **Magical Unicorn,** a limited-edition ornament that he sculpted for the 1986 line, in pink and mint-green ribbons. Before joining Hallmark, Duane was a high school football coach and biology teacher—and a sculptor. He created a series of limited-edition bronze sculptures (of which several were inspired by his five children) that were sold through Kansas City's Halls Crown Center department store. Hallmark design managers noticed his artistry and offered him free-lance assignments, which led to full-time work in the Keepsake Ornament studio. Today, he has 19 grandchildren and scores of Keepsake Ornament designs to his credit.

Duane Unruh

Artists' Gallery

John "Collin" Francis

John went to school to become an engineer, but he graduated an artist. He began his Hallmark career in 1966 as an engraver, and during the next 19 years, created candles, bath items, party-ware, gift wrap and other Hallmark gift products.

Since joining the Keepsake Ornament studio in 1985, John has become known among co-workers and collectors for sculpting cute little animals. "My love of animals and the outdoors —especially my native Wyoming—are my inspiration," he says. More recently, his detailed Keepsake Ornaments based on Madame Alexander® dolls have become favorites. "I think that Madame Alexander dolls are so popular because of their beautiful faces," John says. "It's an honor for me to re-create that beauty."

Patricia subscribes to the adage "Time flies when you're having fun." She's worked at Hallmark since 1976 and hardly can believe that Keepsake Ornaments already are celebrating 25 years!

Patricia first worked as an engraver, then joined the Keepsake Ornament studio in 1987. She enjoys creating ornaments based on real people and has crafted images of several movie stars, including **Marilyn Monroe, Humphrey Bogart** and Vivien Leigh as **Scarlett O'Hara.** Many collectors call Patricia "the BARBIE™ lady." She has sculpted most of the Keepsake Ornaments based on Mattel's doll. Patricia is in awe of collectors' reaction to Keepsake Ornaments. She met one woman at a 1993 Hallmark Keepsake Ornament Collector's Club convention who was dressed as an ornament that Patricia had sculpted. Since then, they've built a valued friendship. Patricia is married to Dill Rhodus, another Keepsake Ornament artist.

Patricia Andrews

Robert Chad

"I love the idea that after I'm gone my ornaments will remain," says Chad, a sculptor since 1987 in the Keepsake Ornament studio. "They may be passed down through families for generations."

After studying at the Kansas City Art Institute, and with previous animation experience, Chad worked for Hallmark on a freelance basis. He began sculpting pewter pieces, designing stuffed animals and creating other licensed properties that were developed by Hallmark.

He may be best known for his **Mary's Angels** ornaments, which he sculpts from sketches by Hallmark Master Artist Mary Hamilton. Chad also creates many Keepsake Ornaments based on licensed designs from Warner Bros. and others.

Lynn joined Hallmark in 1966 as a greeting card diemaker, creating metal molds used to emboss greeting cards.

He first became involved with helping to create Keepsake Ornaments in 1975 (a dozen years before he actually joined the Keepsake Ornament studio in 1987), and he says it was fun to see how different artists approached sculpting. "Some were using clay and wax; I was work-ing with metal and machine tools," he recalls.

Lynn's favorite ornament is 1997's **The Flight at Kitty Hawk,** first in the The Sky's the Limit historical aircraft series; he lobbied for five years to get to sculpt it. He may be best known for sculpting starship ornaments based on STAR TREK® ships.

Lynn Norton

Don joined Hallmark in 1967 and sculpted Hallmark figurines before Keepsake Ornaments made their appearance.

When he joined the Keepsake Ornament studio in 1987, Don noticed the line was geared toward women. The result was his creation of the Classic American Car series and subsequent series suited for men. "Men love cars, and through these ornaments, they can own cars they've dreamed of," he remarks. As the design and research consultant for and primary sculptor of Kiddie Car Classics, Don extends his love of cars into other Hallmark collectibles.

Don gives this advice to collectors: "Collect what you enjoy—things that add fun to your life. If you do that, you'll feel the kind of joy that we associate with childhood."

Don Palmiter

"I had a real baseball in my crib," says Dill, explaining his lifelong passion for sports and the inspiration for many of the sports-themed Keepsake Ornaments. His dad played minor-league baseball, so it makes sense that Dill's favorite Keepsake Ornament is **Nolan Ryan,** which he sculpted for the 1996 line. (He has one that was signed by Ryan himself!)

Dill says he feels lucky to have been at Hallmark since 1966. He joined the Keepsake Ornament studio in 1987 and sculpted the **Cat Naps** series and several STAR WARS® ornaments, among others. At signing events, Dill is astounded by how much collectors like what he does. He remembers signing a book for one older collector who told him: "Every day that I am blue, I look at your picture and—what you do—it makes me feel good." Dill is married to Patricia Andrews, another Keepsake Ornament artist.

Dill Rhodus

When Hallmark rejected Anita's two-dimensional portfolio, she didn't take no for an answer. She met another artist who encouraged her to try three-dimensional work, and that began her career in sculpting. After freelancing for two years, Anita joined the Keepsake Ornament studio full-time in 1987. She may be best known for her **Puppy Love** series, as well as for ornaments based on the Beatles, STAR TREK® characters and other licensed figures.

Anita's favorite ornament is **Holiday Teatime,** which she designed to honor a teatime tradition she shared with her best friend. When Anita gave the ornament to her friend, the tears and hugs made it all the more meaningful.

Anita says every meeting with collectors is special. "They're all great people," she adds.

Anita Marra
Rogers

Diana is the Keepsake Ornament decorating expert. Since joining the studio as a technical artist in 1991, she has generated hundreds of ideas for using Keepsake Ornaments on trees, wreaths, garlands, topiaries and more. A tree that she decorated in 1995 for *Collector Edition* magazine was pictured on a 1997 Hallmark Christmas card!

Joining Hallmark 20-plus years ago, Diana began as a book production artist. She now manages Keepsake Ornament "work behind the scenes"—coordinating artists' work and completing technical drawings.

Among the hundreds of Keepsake Ornaments in her personal ornament collection, Diana's favorite is the 1986 **Cookies for Santa,** which she sculpted based on her special memory of a family tradition.

Diana McGehee

Artists' Gallery

Sue Tague

"It's rewarding to create products that help people celebrate important relationships and events," says Sue about her Hallmark career, which began in 1964. She has designed greeting cards, stuffed animals, figurines and other products. While her children were growing up, Sue worked for Hallmark from home. For seven years, she was among the artists who drew the "Charmers by Hallmark" cartoon that was syndicated in newspapers, and she has created many Merry Miniatures® figurines. Although Sue did not join the Keepsake Ornament studio full-time until 1994, she designed the artwork that appeared on one of the first Hallmark ball ornaments. The artwork captured tiny Christmas elves sledding and skating in a whimsical winter wonderland. Sue created the Thimble and Bell Ringers series, but is most proud of **Pansy** in the Language of Flowers series.

Nina credits her career path to co-worker, John "Collin" Francis, who inspired her to try her hand at sculpting. Recruited from the Kansas City Art Institute in 1981, Nina joined Hallmark as a specialty artist for gift products. She sat next to John, and watching as he sculpted Merry Miniatures®, she decided to create some three-dimensional art. Those creations earned her the opportunity to begin sculpting Merry Miniatures®, and she's sculpted more than 100 to date. Nina may be best known for her Bashful Boy and Girl characters, based on her experience with a shy boyfriend. From 1987 to 1995, Nina worked as a freelance artist, continuing to sculpt for the Keepsake Ornament studio. Since joining the studio full-time in 1995, she remains inspired by how much collectors care. "Keepsake Ornaments aren't just knickknacks that hang on the tree," she says. "They're about honoring memories that mean something to people."

Nina Aubé

Katrina Bricker

"You have to be a sponge and absorb things around here," says Katrina about the Keepsake Ornament studio. Arriving at Hallmark in 1994 as a designer of gift products, then joining the Keepsake Ornament studio in 1995, Katrina remains amazed by the talent around her.

She collaborated with Kathy Johnson, a Hallmark greeting card artist, to create an ethnic ornament called **Tamika** and also designed several ornaments based on licensed characters.

Katrina grew up in Erie, Pa., and graduated from the Columbus College of Art and Design in Ohio. She considers her experience in the Keepsake Ornament studio as more educational than graduate school!

After joining Hallmark in 1981, Joanne spent 14 years creating specialty products such as gift wrap, bags and party goods. Her subsequent work on Merry Miniatures® figurines turned her on to the idea of sculpting. So, following a short stint as a greeting card designer, Joanne put her heart into sculpting.

Since joining the Keepsake Ornament studio in 1995, several of her Keepsake Ornament creations have been based on licensed characters. People have described her work as sweet and charming, with detail, texture and animation.

Joanne originally hails from the Boston area and graduated from Southeastern Massachusetts University (now Amherst University).

Joanne Eschrich

Steve Goslin

Since joining Hallmark in 1978, Steve has done nearly everything from operating a forklift to sales and security, but sculpting is by far his favorite. Coming from a family of Hallmark artists, he joined the Keepsake Ornament studio in 1995, where his first memorable project was **The Lone Ranger,** a 1997 tin lunch box ornament.

Steve's favorite Keepsake Ornament, which was sculpted by Ed Seale, is the 1985 **Santa's Ski Trip.** It lends testimony to Steve's attitude that life should be fun. "Santa deserves a vacation, too!" Steve declares.

As he continues to build his own repertoire, Steve looks forward to meeting with collectors to "stay in touch with what they like."

Whether a waving **Howdy Doody** leans from a TV or Disney characters share a dance, Tracy incorporates action into his designs. Tracy is trained in two-dimensional painting and illustration, which he says enhances his three-dimensional figures. In 1988, he began illustrating Hallmark greeting cards inspired by licensed characters. When he joined the Keepsake Ornament studio in 1995, he applied that experience to Keepsake Ornaments. He has painted backgrounds for other artists' ornaments, too. Tracy and his wife collect Keepsake Ornaments—they purchased their first to commemorate their first wedding anniversary—and now they share the collection with their children.

Tracy Larsen

Nello Williams

Since joining Hallmark and the Keepsake Ornament studio in 1995, Nello has sculpted more than 30 ornaments, including many based on licensed characters.

Originally from Safford, Ariz., and a University of Arizona graduate in commercial illustration, Nello was inspired to begin sculpting by a 1992 Keepsake Ornament called **Please Pause Here.** He saw it and said, "I can do that," and began creating ornaments for friends and family members.

Nello is inspired by collectors' enthusiasm and still cannot believe how excited people get about the work he so enjoys.

When she was 5 years old, Tammy told her mom that she wanted to work at Hallmark. Now, after refining her talent at the Kansas City Art Institute, Tammy says it's as wonderful as she dreamed. She joined Hallmark in 1988 and began by designing gift wrap and albums. In 1996, she joined the Keepsake Ornament studio.

She prefers to sculpt cute animals and children, as opposed to more serious subjects. "I try to give as much life and personality as I can to the figures I create," Tammy adds. Much of her recent work tends to resemble her young son, Zachary.

Tammy Haddix

Kristina Kline

Growing up in small-town Iowa, Kristina doesn't remember hearing much about Keepsake Ornaments. Now, she's on the inside track as one of the studio's newest members. Recruited by Hallmark from the Kansas City Art Institute, Kristina continues to learn about new tools and materials. She joined the Keepsake Ornament studio full-time in 1996, and one of her first projects was to work with Joanne Eschrich to sculpt **Mrs. Claus's Story,** a 1997 Artists on Tour event-exclusive ornament. "I hope that people will pick up something I've done and laugh or smile," she says. Kristina loves meeting collectors. "Not only do I get the chance to show them what I do, but I learn from them, too," she says. "To see the excitement on their faces makes my job so much more rewarding."

Collecting Hallmark Keepsake Ornaments

At heart, Wayne Ingalls probably was a collector "of things" anyway. But one day in 1979, he walked into a store, fell in love with a Keepsake Christmas Ornament and started a collection that now includes about 2,000 Hallmark ornaments.

Wayne's story is common among the nearly 250,000 members of the national Hallmark Keepsake Ornament Collector's Club. Many began their hobby with one sentimental purchase long before there were organized clubs, conventions or official membership kits.

"I just liked the way Hallmark ornaments were made and what they meant to me," says Wayne.

Within a few years after Hallmark began creating Keepsake Ornaments in 1973, consumers had recognized the ornaments as collectible. So many people were joining together to buy, trade and enjoy its creations that, in 1987, Hallmark launched the national Hallmark Keepsake Ornament Collector's Club in response to collectors' requests. As the Club gained in popularity, official appearances that Keepsake Ornament artists made at Hallmark stores to sign their ornaments gradually evolved into annual Artists On Tour signing events that, by 1997, included stops in 10 cities.

Artist Duane Unruh remembers being amazed at a signing in Hawaii one August. "I was impressed that there was so much enthusiasm that time of year in that climate for Christmas ornaments!" he says.

But Kathy Kwiatkowski is not surprised. She has witnessed collectors crying with joy in hotel elevators because they got to meet a Keepsake Ornament artist or get an artist's signature on a special ornament. To her, meeting collecting comrades from around the country is one of the main reasons for Club membership. "Not only does national Club membership provide opportunities to meet collectors in other cities, it also gives us exclusive access to Membership and Club Edition Ornaments that are for members only."

It was "collecting camaraderie" that drew more than 700 collectors to Kansas City, Mo., site of the international headquarters of Hallmark Cards, Inc., for the first national Hallmark Keepsake Ornament Collector's Club convention in 1991. In 1993—the 20th anniversary of Keepsake Ornaments—two conventions were needed to accommodate collectors' interest.

The next year, the first Hallmark Keepsake Ornament traveling EXPO visited eight cities. And in 1998, collectors will travel to Kansas City for the 25th Anniversary Celebration of Hallmark Keepsake Ornaments, a Club-exclusive event. Meanwhile, Keepsake Ornament artists continue to be amazed at the magic surrounding the collection connection.

At an Artists On Tour signing in San Francisco, a young couple asked Keepsake Ornament Artist LaDene Votruba to sign a **Baby's First Christmas** ornament for

"*I just liked the way Hallmark ornaments were made and what they meant to me.*"

their baby daughter. The baby's name, Violet Lily, also was the name of LaDene's recently deceased mother. "At moments like that, the meaning of our work is crystal clear," says LaDene. "The other artists and I really enjoy meeting people who want our signatures on ornaments to enhance the personal meaning that the ornaments hold."

The personal meaning of collecting also is clear in the almost 400 local chapters of the Hallmark Keepsake Ornament Collector's Club. Each local club was started by collectors at the hometown level. Many local clubs, including the Keepsake Patrollers of Rochester Hills, Mich., have expanded their interest to include community-service projects such as an annual "Toys for Tots" party at Christmastime.

"Monthly local club meetings also are a chance to exchange information and ideas," adds Carol Lawrimore of the Northeast Atlanta Collector's local club. "We've had dinners and parties together, and we talk about how to decorate with ornaments at times other than

(Above) Members of Lundy's Keepers Klub, a local club in Des Moines, Iowa, get together with Clara to talk about favorite Keepsake Ornaments.

Christmas." Carol made an arrangement of Keepsake Ornaments as the centerpiece for her son's birthday party!

So why has collecting Keepsake Ornaments become so popular with so many people? For Chris Shea of Greenville, R.I., a charter member of the national Club, Keepsake Ornament collecting is about memories of **Angel Delight,** a tiny angel in a walnut shell that graced the small tree in her first apartment. For Brad and Linda Cresto of Marseilles, Ill., it means classic car ornaments reminiscent of their first date at a drive-in theater more than 25 years ago

For others, it means a warmth and love that keep Christmas alive year-round. "I love the whole meaning of Christmas. That's why I'm drawn to Keepsake Ornaments," Kathy says. "To me, the idea of Christmas is giving, as well as re-living memories from your childhood or your kids' childhoods. At Hallmark, I find ornaments that relate to that. That's *special.*"

25 Memories
for 25 Years

"It's dated!" That was my reaction of delight as I first studied Hallmark's

Betsey Clark–First Edition ball ornament in 1973. It also was adorned with

art—American art! It was packaged in its own box, complete with stock num-

ber, company name and other data. No need for laborious research about this

ornament's age or country of origin—it was a collector's dream (and an orna-

ment-industry first from Hallmark)! I immediately wanted the Betsey Clark

ornament and any others issued with it. (You could buy one of each of the 18

ornaments Hallmark issued that year for a total of $29.75!) That's my first

Hallmark Keepsake Ornament memory. By now, I must have millions of

memories associated with Hallmark. In honor of Keepsake

Ornaments' 25th Anniversary, I've chosen 25 Keepsake

Ornaments—one from each of the line's first 25 years—to

represent my memories. Are these the Keepsake Ornaments that are most

highly sought after by all collectors? Perhaps not. Rather, they are designs

that touched me with their beauty, humor or whimsy. Here are my 25 best-

loved memories for 25 years. What are yours?

Clara Johnson Scroggins

1973—Betsey Clark—First Edition. The first Betsey Clark design with a year date features one little girl feeding a deer and another cuddling a lamb. I love it because it's the ornament that started it all!

1974—Snowgoose. A powerful snowgoose flies above whitecapped waves with a sailboat in the background—inspired by Paul Gallico's book, *The Snowgoose*. I remember this one's beauty and color.

1975—Joy. The meaning of Christmas holds a special place in my heart and so does this ornament with its handcrafted look and Baby Jesus nestled "in joy."

1976—Bicentennial '76 Commemorative. I wanted every ornament made to commemorate the American Bicentennial. Featuring Charmers dressed in the fashion of Christmas 1776, this was among the most charming.

1977—Nativity. The star-topped stable shelters the Holy Family and animals, and it reminds us: "O Come, Let Us Adore Him." I also collect nativities, so this one is special in two collections.

1978—Panorama Ball. Through the ornament's window, we see a little boy who has fallen after skating a holiday greeting on the ice. I remember this ornament for its depth and detail (and it's dated!).

1979—SNOOPY® and Friends—First Edition. I remember thinking, when I first saw this ornament, that my beagle buddy obviously loves the holidays as much as I do.

1980—Checking It Twice. This Santa is big and absolutely beautiful. My only regret is that my name is not on his list!

1981—Christmas Fantasy. A recollection of grace, beauty and magic, this one has a real brass ribbon—a special touch that makes it a memorable favorite.

1982—Tin Locomotive—First Edition. I love the tin, the colors, the design and the size. And I wouldn't dream of missing a first edition!

1983—Tin Locomotive—Second Edition. A tribute to an ornament series that I adored from start to finish.

1984—Nostalgic Houses and Shops—First Edition. I remember this Victorian dollhouse for its detail, right down to the wallpaper and Christmas tree inside.

1985—Night Before Christmas. I don't have to remember this favorite story. Push the button on this ornament, and 30 pages depicting it flip over before my eyes! It came with a stand for off-tree display.

1986—Magical Unicorn—Limited Edition. A memory of pure elegance draped in ribbons and roses.

1987—Mistletoad. Pull the cord, and he gives a marvelously cheeky grin with a loud and croaky greeting. A make-me-smile Christmas surprise!

1988—Filled with Fudge. Is it cute or what? Bring on the chocolate!

1989—Winter Surprise—First Edition. This ornament, memorable because it was so different, introduced us to penguins who revealed winter surprises in their egg-shaped universe.

1990—Two Peas in a Pod. Now here's a uniquely happy couple! I remember this ornament because it represents how diverse ornaments have become.

1991—Heavenly Angels—First Edition. Elegant, soft and beautiful, its style helps me recall the quiet majesty of old-world masters.

1992—Turtle Dreams. This unique, colorful clip-on reminds me that I envy the turtle—he's never far from home, no matter where he travels.

1993—Holiday BARBIE™—First Edition. She's simply beautiful! She's a special memory because she helped to introduce so many new collectors to Keepsake Ornaments.

1994—Murray® Champion. The material, design and feel bring memories of bygone times rushing back.

1995—Heaven's Gift. Words fail me—it's fabulous. I remember it with fondness when I think of nativities.

1996—Come All Ye Faithful. "Here is the church, here is the steeple, open..." To me, this nativity represents the true meaning of Christmas. It's particularly memorable for me because it was my first Collector's Choice ornament (so, of course, it makes my list!).

1997—The Night Before Christmas. Wind it up, hear the music, see the movement... this is the essence of Keepsake Ornaments set to the tune of "Santa Claus is Comin' to Town," and it's my second Collector's Choice.

NOTE: The 1998 line actually is Keepsake Ornament's 26th annual release. Although I've chronicled it in this book, it's still a bit early to have "memories" of 1998 Keepsake Ornaments!

1987

1989

1995

1983

1978

1988

1977

1992

1990

1984

1975

1993

1982

1996

1979

1981

1994

Hallmark Keepsake Ornaments

Collecting

1973 Hallmark introduces six decorated ball ornaments and 12 yarn ornaments. For the first time, tree decorations aren't just glass balls!

1974 The art of Norman Rockwell and Currier & Ives appears on Keepsake Ornaments.

1975 Decorated satin ball ornaments and handcrafted ornaments debut.

1976 Twirl-Abouts (movable ornaments) debut, and it's the first Christmas for Baby's First Christmas (the industry's first commemorative ornament). A bicentennial commemorative also makes an appearance.

1977 Sewn ornaments with silk-screened designs, acrylic ornaments and ornaments with the

look of stained glass are introduced. For this year only, Hallmark offers die-cast metal snowflakes and ball ornaments with regional scenes.

1978 It's the first Christmas for 25th Christmas Together. Chrome-plated chimes make their first appearance. The art of

Joan Walsh Anglund joins the line.

1979 An ornament for teachers is introduced, and the Baby's First Christmas offering includes its first handcrafted design. For the first time, a ball ornament features a black angel. The first ornament in the Here Comes Santa series,

the longest-running Keepsake Ornament series, debuts.

1980 Pastel-colored, unbreakable "cameo" designs are introduced, and the MUPPETS™ join the line. A Baby's First Christmas ball ornament shows a black baby for the first time. Heavenly Minstrel and Checking It Twice introduce the category of Special Edition

through the years

Like children who anticipate the treasures that Santa leaves beneath the tree, we collectors anticipate the arrival of each year's Hallmark Keepsake Ornaments—we can't wait to see what the Keepsake Ornament artists (Santa's helpers in the truest sense!) have created. Somehow, year after year, they manage to capture current events and nostalgic memories in ways that are delightfully new and different. Here's a look at fabulous firsts, memorable milestones and innovative introductions to Keepsake Ornament collecting through the years.

1980

1981

1980

1982

1983

1983

1985

1886
1986
The Lady

1986

1983

1986

ornaments. The first in the long-running Frosty Friends series debuts.

1981 Photo holder ornaments are introduced along with "plush" stuffed animal ornaments. The first ornament in the Rocking Horse series gallops into view.

1982 Ornaments are made for the first time in hand-embroidered fabric, sculptured acrylic, dimensional brass and cloisonné. A tree symbol or the words, "___ in a series," printed on ornaments designates them as part of a series. The first ornament in the Tin Locomotive series joins the line.

1983 Commemorative ornaments are introduced in a new ceramic bell format. Satin ball ornaments get distinctive new caps, making them instantly recognizable by their Hallmark "crowns." Clara

Johnson Scroggins authors the first complete guide to Hallmark Keepsake Ornaments.

1984 The Keepsake Lighted Ornament Collection debuts, and  the first announced limited-edition ornament joins the line. Ball ornaments with juvenile designs appear with specially designed caps.

1985 Hallmark produces ornaments that look homemade and natural in response to collector demand. FRAGGLE ROCK™, Rainbow Brite™ and Hugga Bunch™ debut.

1986 A Keepsake Ornament commemorates the 100th birthday of the Statue of Liberty. Heathcliff and Paddington™ Bear make their first appearances. For the first time, special Keepsake Ornaments are

created for Open House events held in Hallmark stores as a festive beginning to the holiday season. Motion is added to some ornaments in the Lighted Collection. The Mr. and Mrs. Claus ornament series begins.

1987 The Hallmark Keepsake Ornament Collector's Club begins and introduces exclusive ornaments available only to members. The Holiday Lighted Magic Ornament Collection gets a new name: the Keepsake Magic Ornament Collection. The Artists' Favorites collection debuts. Bone china and lead crystal are used in ornaments.

1988 Keepsake Miniature Ornaments debut. Exclusive limited-edition ornaments are offered to Hallmark Keepsake Ornament Collector's Club members for the first time.

1988 · 1988 · 1989 · 1991 · 1993 · 1992

1989 A Keepsake Ornament commemorates the 200th anniversary of George Washington's presidential inauguration. The Keepsake Magic Collection comes alive with the sound of music.

1990 Mom-to-Be, Dad-to-Be, and Child Care Giver ornaments join the line. Seven Keepsake Magic ornaments get on/off switches. The national Hallmark Keepsake Ornament Collector's Club officially begins to support local clubs, which have been flourishing at the grassroots level for more than decade.

1991 For the first time, a special Keepsake Ornament is created to be available only during Hallmark Keepsake Ornament Premiere. An ornament called Flag of Liberty represents patriotic feelings stirred by Operation Desert Storm; with every purchase of this ornament, Hallmark contributes $1 to the American Red Cross. The first Hallmark Keepsake Ornament Collector's Club convention is held in Kansas City. The Keepsake Easter Collection debuts. With collectors' encouragement, Hallmark introduces Starship Enterprise, a Magic Ornament created to celebrate the 25th anniversary of the Star Trek® television series. The first in the Classic American Cars series rolls in.

1992 Ornaments for special dogs and cats debut, and Cheerful Santa is the first African-American figural Santa ornament. A humorous ornament called The Spirit of Christmas Stress is adapted from Hallmark's own Shoebox Greetings characters. In the Magic line, Santa greets callers on Santa's Answering Machine, and Mr. Spock greets us from Shuttlecraft Galileo™.

1993 The second Hallmark Keepsake Ornament Collector's Club convention is held in Kansas City; the first Artists' Signature Piece is available only during the convention. Four special editions are created to commemorate the 20th anniversary of the Keepsake Ornament line. Look for the Wonder, the first Keepsake Ornament "designed" by a collector, is created in honor of the Keepsake Ornament Convention's costume contest winner, Joanne Pawelek. Personalized Ornaments debut, and the Keepsake Ornament Showcase introduces four distinctive, highly stylized collections. A recordable ornament debuts in the Magic line, and the first in the Holiday BARBIE™ series appears.

1994 The LOONEY TUNES™ Collection debuts, The Beatles Gift Set marks 30 years since the Fab Four came to

1994 1995 1996 1996 1997

America, and THE WIZARD OF OZ™ COLLECTION joins the line. A Magic ornament called The Eagle Has Landed commemorates the 25th anniversary of the first lunar landing. Disney images return to the line with ornaments based on characters from *The Lion King.* The Collector's Club hits the road, visiting eight cities with Hallmark Keepsake Ornament EXPO. In honor of the 35th anniversary of BARBIE®, a new series of nostalgic ornaments begins with BARBIE™— Debut 1959.

1995 Springtime BARBIE™ debuts in the Easter collection. Characters from STAR TREK®: THE NEXT GENERATION™ join the line. Two Joe Montana ornaments—a San Francisco 49ers™ and a Kansas City Chiefs version—and the A CHARLIE BROWN CHRISTMAS

ornament collection draw collectors' interest. The art of Marjolein Bastin appears in the Showcase Collection. Lighted ornaments debut in the Miniature line. The 15th anniversary of the Rocking Horse series is celebrated with a special Anniversary Edition Pewter Rocking Horse. For the first time, photos of members of the Keepsake Ornament Collector's Club appear in photo holder ornaments that are on display in stores.

1996 In response to collector requests, EXPO becomes an eight-city artist signing event called Artists on Tour. The Olympic Spirit Collection commemorates the 1996 Centennial Olympic Games. A Keepsake Ornament marks the 50th anniversary of the premiere of *It's A Wonderful Life*™. The STAR TREK® Collection celebrates 30 years since the television show debuted, and Nolan Ryan leads off in the At the Ballpark series. The

LIONEL® Train and the Madame Alexander® series introduce new collectors to Keepsake Ornaments. STAR WARS™ appears in the Magic and Miniature lines, and a miniature GONE WITH THE WIND™ set marks 60 years since Margaret Mitchell's famous book was published. For the first time, Clara Johnson Scroggins designates an ornament—Come All Ye Faithful—as her Collector's Choice.

1997 The Easter Ornament Collection expands its focus to become the Spring Ornament Collection. From Mickey Mouse to Snow White, four new ornament collections showcase characters from classic and current Disney films. The Lone Ranger™, Marilyn Monroe, Jeff Gordon®, Howdy Doody and others keep fond memories alive. NFL and NBA collections help us cheer 40 favorite teams. BARBIE™

1998

and KEN™ are featured in a two-piece ornament set, and another ornament commemorates 50 years since Jackie Robinson integrated baseball.

1998 World of Wishes ornaments, part of the Spring line, are introduced to mark special occasions, such as birthdays. An array of 25th Anniversary ornaments, bearing a commemorative logo, and a 25th Anniversary Celebration in Kansas City for members of the Keepsake Ornament Collector's Club are among the many ways that the 25th anniversary of Hallmark Keepsake Ornaments is celebrated. The Crown Reflections Blown Glass Ornament Collection introduces centuries-old European-style craftsmanship to the line. The Noel R.R.—Locomotive 1989–98 miniature pewter ornament celebrates the 10th anniversary of the Keepsake Miniature line, and the Betsey's Prayer miniature ornament appears in tribute to the 1973 Betsey Clark ball ornament that helped start the Keepsake Ornament collecting tradition 25 years ago.

25 Years of Keepsake Ornament Santas

Throughout European history, Santa has most often been portrayed as a slim, very old, gaunt-faced man who dressed, at one time or another, in every color of the rainbow. In a few countries, the gift-bringer traditionally has been female. Only in America has Santa ranged from an elf-like fellow to a grandfatherly old gent who always has worn a red-and-white suit. And one would wonder if he also wore comfortable shoes because Santa walked throughout history until 1822, when Clement C. Moore—author of the classic poem, "The Night Before Christmas"— introduced a sleigh and eight tiny reindeer.

During the last 25 years, Keepsake Ornaments have helped the jolly old fellow make his rounds with special modes of transportation. And, encouraged by Hallmark ingenuity, my how he's changed! He's tossed the pipe, shaped up, slimmed down and become a man of the '90s!

1973—Santa with Elves shows a rather tired old guy with a jelly belly.

1974—Norman Rockwell Santa appears happier than earlier Santas, perhaps because we see him with two "good" children.

1977—In a Disney ball ornament, we see Mickey Mouse in a Santa suit!

1979—Here Comes Santa—First Edition shows Santa driving a car.

1981—In **Traditional (Black Santa)**, Santa appears as a black man—a first for Keepsake Ornaments, and in **Space Santa,** he dons a space helmet and shiny accessories.

1973

1977

1982—Jogging Santa practices for a marathon (but still looks chubby!)

1983—Hitchhiking Santa, in sunglasses and summer clothes, carries a sign that reads "Goin' South."

1984—Marathon Santa participates in a patriotic run.

1986—In **Mr. and Mrs. Claus**—First Edition, Mrs. Claus appears with mistletoe. Santa's married and loving it.

1987—We see a saxophone player and a jazzy dresser in **St. Louie Nick.**

1990—A summer softball team has drafted Santa in **Perfect Catch.**

1992—Santa helps his hometown by volunteering as a **North Pole Fire Fighter.**

1994—Grass is discovered at the North Pole, and Santa must **Keep on Mowin'**!

1995—Surfin' Santa gets a tan and shows knobby knees.

1996—In **Pinball Wonder,** Santa vies for top score.

1997—Cycling Santa looks trim and muscular!

1998—We witness **The Clauses on Vacation** as Mr. and Mrs. Claus trade their fur garments for bathing suits and, sharing a reindeer innertube, run barefoot toward the waves.

1981

1983

1986

1997

The Memories and Magic Ornament Collection

1998

It's the 25th anniversary of Hallmark Keepsake Ornaments, and a beautiful array of anniversary ornaments, several of which feature silver elements, bear a commemorative logo.

For the first time, Hallmark applies centuries-old European craftsmanship to introduce the Crown Reflections Blown Glass Ornament Collection.

New properties debut, including **The Three Stooges™**, **The Grinch**—who returns to the Keepsake Ornament line after a lengthy absence—and football great **Joe Montana** captured in his college-days Notre Dame uniform. It's the third time—and the third uniform—in which Montana has appeared in the line.

Mom and Dad are lovingly rendered with Baby in the **New Arrival** Baby's First Christmas ornament. And to my great joy, The Holy Family Blessed Nativity Collection debuts as a three-piece porcelain set that will be offered for three years; each year, a new piece will be added to the set. Another set called Friend of My Heart also debuts—one of the ornaments is designed for you to give to a friend, and you keep the other for yourself.

Pony Express Rider, first in The Old West series, is among new series firsts, and Keepsake Ornaments based on Disney characters are back.

Joyful Messenger

Angelic Flight

Tin Locomotive

Halls Station

SPECIAL ISSUES
25TH ANNIVERSARY

Joyful Messenger
ANNIVERSARY EDITION
Silver-plated medallion
▨ Dated
Artist: Joyce Lyle
4¹¹⁄₁₆" H × 4⅛" W
$18.95   1895QXI6733

Angelic Flight
ANNIVERSARY EDITION
Silver-plated and lead crystal
Limited edition of 25,000
Collector's card included
▨ Designer: Bob Haas
Artist: Patricia Andrews
3¹⁄₁₆" H × 2⁷⁄₁₆" W
$85.00   8500QXI4146

Tin Locomotive
ANNIVERSARY EDITION
Tin
▨ Dated
Artist: Linda Sickman
3¹⁄₁₆" H × 4" W
$25.00   2500QX6826

Halls Station
ANNIVERSARY EDITION
Complements the Nostalgic Houses and Shops Collector's series.
▨ Dated
Artist: Don Palmiter
4¹⁄₁₆" H × 4¾" W
$25.00   2500QX6833

NBA COLLECTION

▨ Dated
Artist: Bob Siedler
3⁵⁄₁₆" H × 2⁷⁄₁₆" W
CHARLOTTE HORNETS
▨ $9.95   995QSR1033
CHICAGO BULLS
▨ $9.95   995QSR1036
DETROIT PISTONS
▨ $9.95   995QSR1043
HOUSTON ROCKETS
▨ $9.95   995QSR1046
INDIANA PACERS
▨ $9.95   995QSR1053
LOS ANGELES LAKERS

▨ $9.95   995QSR1056
NEW YORK KNICKERBOCKERS
▨ $9.95   995QSR1063
ORLANDO MAGIC
▨ $9.95   995QSR1066
SEATTLE SUPERSONICS
▨ $9.95   995QSR1076
UTAH JAZZ
▨ $9.95   995QSR1083

NBA Collection

Collegiate Collection

NFL Collection

COLLEGIATE COLLECTION
☐ Dated
Artist: Tammy Haddix
3⅜" H × 3¹⁄₁₆" W

FLORIDA STATE SEMINOLES™
☐ $9.95   995QSR2316

MICHIGAN WOLVERINES™
☐ $9.95   995QSR2323

NORTH CAROLINA TAR HEELS™
☐ $9.95   995QSR2333

NOTRE DAME® FIGHTING IRISH™
☐ $9.95   995QSR2313

PENN STATE NITTANY LIONS™
☐ $9.95   995QSR2326

NFL COLLECTION
☐ Dated
Artist: John "Collin" Francis
2¹⁄₁₆" H × 2⁷⁄₁₆" W

CAROLINA PANTHERS™
☐ $9.95   995QSR5026

CHICAGO BEARS™
☐ $9.95   995QSR5033

DALLAS COWBOYS™
☐ $9.95   995QSR5046

DENVER BRONCOS™
☐ $9.95   995QSR5053

GREEN BAY PACKERS™
☐ $9.95   995QSR5063

KANSAS CITY CHIEFS™
☐ $9.95   995QSR5013

MIAMI DOLPHINS™
☐ $9.95   995QSR5096

MINNESOTA VIKINGS™
☐ $9.95   995QSR5126

NEW YORK GIANTS™
☐ $9.95   995QSR5143

OAKLAND RAIDERS™
☐ $9.95   995QSR5086

PHILADELPHIA EAGLES™
☐ $9.95   995QSR5153

PITTSBURGH STEELERS™
☐ $9.95   995QSR5163

ST. LOUIS RAMS™
☐ $9.95   995QSR5093

SAN FRANCISCO 49ERS™
☐ $9.95   995QSR5173

WASHINGTON REDSKINS™
☐ $9.95   995QSR5186

New Arrival

Baby's First Christmas

Baby's First Christmas

Baby's First Christmas

Baby's First Christmas

Baby's Second Christmas

Child's Third Christmas

Child's Fourth Christmas

Child's Fifth Christmas

BABY

New Arrival
Porcelain
▨ Dated
Artist: LaDene Votruba
4¼" H × 1¹³⁄₁₆" W
$18.95   1895QX6306

Baby's First Christmas
▨ Dated
Artist: Joanne Eschrich
2¼" H × 1³⁄₁₆" W
$9.95   995QX6586

Baby's First Christmas
▨ Dated
Artist: Sue Tague
3" H × 1¹⁵⁄₁₆" W
$9.95   995QX6233

Baby's First Christmas
Photo Holder
▨ Dated
Artist: Kristina Kline
2⅞" H × 2¹⁵⁄₁₆" W
$8.95   895QX6596

CHILD'S AGE COLLECTION

Baby's First Christmas
▨ Dated
Artist: John "Collin" Francis
2⁵⁄₁₆" H × 2⁵⁄₁₆" W
$7.95   795QX6603

Baby's Second Christmas
▨ Dated
Artist: Ken Crow
2⅜" H × 2" W
$7.95   795QX6606

Child's Third Christmas
▨ Dated
Artist: Ken Crow
2⁹⁄₁₆" H × 2¹⁄₁₆" W
$7.95   795QX6613

Child's Fourth Christmas
▨ Dated
Artist: Ken Crow
2¹¹⁄₁₆" H × 2⁵⁄₁₆" W
$7.95   795QX6616

Child's Fifth Christmas
▨ Dated
Artist: Ken Crow
2¹⁵⁄₁₆" H × 1¹⁵⁄₁₆" W
$7.95   795QX6623

Mom

Dad

Mom and Dad

Son

FAMILY

Mom

◻ Dated

Artist: Kristina Kline

2¾" H × 1¹¹⁄₁₆" W

$8.95   895QX6656

Dad

◻ Dated

Artist: Kristina Kline

3⅛" H × 2⁷⁄₁₆" W

$8.95   895QX6663

Mom and Dad

◻ Dated

Artist: Kristina Kline

2¼" H × 2½" W

$9.95   995QX6653

Son

Opens and closes like a

real nutcracker.

◻ Dated

Artist: Nina Aubé

2¾" H × 1⅛" W

$8.95   895QX6666

Daughter

Opens and closes like a

real nutcracker.

◻ Dated

Artist: Nina Aubé

2⅝" H × 1⁵⁄₁₆" W

$8.95   895QX6673

Mother and Daughter

Porcelain

◻ Dated

Artist: LaDene Votruba

3¼" H × 3⅝" W

$8.95   895QX6696

Sister to Sister

◻ Dated

Artist: Sharon Pike

2¹⁄₁₆" H × 2⅛" W

$8.95   895QX6693

Grandma's Memories

Photo Holder

◻ Dated

Artist: Kristina Kline

2⅜" H × 1¹⁵⁄₁₆" W

$8.95   895QX6686

Grandson

◻ Dated

Artist: John "Collin" Francis

2⁷⁄₁₆" H × 2³⁄₁₆" W

$7.95   795QX6676

Granddaughter

◻ Dated

Artist: John "Collin" Francis

2⁵⁄₁₆" H × 2¹⁄₁₆" W

$7.95   795QX6683

Daughter

Mother and Daughter

Sister to Sister

Grandma's Memories

Grandson

Granddaughter

#1 Student

Special Dog

Godchild

New Home

Friend of My Heart, set of two: Mouse with Cookie; Mouse with Cutter

Chatty Chipmunk

Forever Friends Bear

#1 Student
Photo Holder
☐ Dated
2¹³⁄₁₆" H × 2¾"W
$7.95   795QX6646

Special Dog
Photo Holder
☐ Dated
2¹⁵⁄₁₆" H × 2¹⁵⁄₁₆"
$7.95   795QX6706

Godchild
☐ Dated
Artist: Robert Chad
2¾" H × 1¹¹⁄₁₆"
$7.95   795QX6703

New Home
☐ Dated
Offered in 1998 and 1999.
Artist: Ed Seale
4" H × 2⅞" W
$9.95   995QX6713

Friend of My Heart
Set of two ornaments; one design
to give to a friend and another to
keep for yourself.
☐ Dated
Artist: Ed Seale
Mouse with Cookie:
1⁹⁄₁₆" H × 1⅞" W
Mouse with Cutter:
1⅞" H × 2¼" W
$14.95   1495QX6723

Chatty Chipmunk
☐ Dated
Artist: Ken Crow
3" H × 2¹⁄₁₆" W
$9.95   995QX6716

Forever Friends Bear
THE ANDREW
BROWNSWORD
COLLECTION
☐ Dated
Artist: Sharon Pike
2⅛" H × 1⁷⁄₁₆" W
$8.95   895QX6303

LOVE
Our First Christmas Together
HALLMARK ARCHIVES
COLLECTION
Brass and fine porcelain
☐ Dated
Designer: LaDene Votruba
3¾" H × 2¾" W
$18.95   1895QX6643

Our First Christmas Together
Photo Holder
☐ Dated
Artist: Sue Tague
4" H × 3¼" W
$8.95   895QX6636

Our First Christmas Together
Acrylic
☐ Dated
Designer: LaDene Votruba
4³⁄₁₆" H × 2¹³⁄₁₆" W
$7.95   795QX3193

A Perfect Match
☐ Dated
Artist: Dill Rhodus
2¹⁵⁄₁₆" H × 2³⁄₁₆" W
$10.95   1095QX6633

Our First Christmas Together

Our First Christmas Together

Our First Christmas Together

A Perfect Match

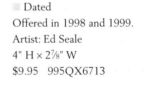

LIFESTYLES AND OCCUPATIONS

Catch of the Season
☒ Dated
Artist: Ed Seale
4⁷⁄₁₆" H × 3¼" W
$14.95 1495QX6786

Downhill Dash
☒ Dated
Artist: Ken Crow
2¾" H × 2⁹⁄₁₆" W
$13.95 1395QX6776

Holiday Camper
Compass works
☒ Dated
Artist: Ed Seale
2¹³⁄₁₆" H × 2³⁄₁₆" W
$12.95 1295QX6783

Compact Skater
☒ Dated
Artist: Sue Tague
2⁹⁄₁₆" H × 2⅜" W
$9.95 995QX6766

Good Luck Dice
☒ Dated
Artist: Tammy Haddix
2¹³⁄₁₆" H × 1¹³⁄₁₆" W
$9.95 995QX6813

Puttin' Around
☒ Dated
Artist: Dill Rhodus
3⁵⁄₁₆" H × 2⅛"
$8.95 895QX6763

Gifted Gardener
☒ Dated
Artist: Robert Chad
2¼" H × 1¼" W
$7.95 795QX6736

"Sew" Gifted
☒ Dated
Artist: Sue Tague
2¹⁄₁₆" H × 1¼" W
$7.95 795QX6743

Surprise Catch
☒ Dated
Artist: John "Collin" Francis
2¾" H × 1¾" W
$7.95 795QX6753

Polar Bowler
☒ Dated
Artist: Joanne Eschrich
2" H × 2¹⁄₁₆" W
$7.95 795QX6746

Future Ballerina
☒ Dated
Artist: Sue Tague
2¹¹⁄₁₆" H × 1½" W
$7.95 795QX6756

North Pole Reserve
☒ Dated
Artist: Ed Seale
3⅛" H × 2⁹⁄₁₆" W
$10.95 1095QX6803

Catch of the Season

Downhill Dash

Holiday Camper

Compact Skater

Good Luck Dice

Puttin' Around

Gifted Gardener

"Sew" Gifted

Surprise Catch

Polar Bowler

Future Ballerina

North Pole Reserve

National Salute

Spoonful of Love

Checking Santa's Files

Rocket to Success

Christmas Request

King Kharoof—Second King

OUR SONG, Brenda Joysmith

A Child Is Born

Feliz Navidad

Gold, Gifts for a King

Myrrh, Gifts for a King

Frankincense, Gifts for a King

LIFESTYLES AND OCCUPATIONS
National Salute
☐ Dated
Artist: Dill Rhodus
3¹⁵⁄₁₆" H × 3³⁄₈" W
$8.95   895QX6293

Spoonful of Love
☐ Dated
Artist: Sue Tague
2⅛" H × 2½" W
$8.95   895QX6796

Checking Santa's Files
☐ Dated
Artist: Sue Tague
3¾" H × 3¾" W
$8.95   895QX6806

Rocket to Success
☐ Dated
Artist: Sharon Pike
1⁷⁄₁₆" H × 3¾" W
$8.95   895QX6793

HOLIDAY TRADITIONS
ETHNIC
Christmas Request
☐ Dated
Artist: John "Collin" Francis
3¹⁄₁₆" H × 2¾" W
$14.95   1495QX6193

King Kharoof—Second King
Complements the 1997 and 1999
Legend of The Three Kings
Collection. Collector's card enclosed.
☐ Dated
Artist: Patricia Andrews
4⁷⁄₁₆" H × 2⁷⁄₁₆" W
$12.95   1295QX6186

OUR SONG
Brenda Joysmith
Ceramic. Display stand included.
☐ Designer: Brenda Joysmith
3½" H × 2½" W
$9.95   995QX6183

A Child Is Born
☐ Dated
Artist: LaDene Votruba
3⁹⁄₁₆" H × 2¹⁵⁄₁₆" W
$12.95   1295QX6176

Feliz Navidad
☐ Dated
Artist: Robert Chad
2⅜" H × 1⅞" W
$8.95   895QX6173

CROWN REFLECTIONS
BLOWN GLASS
ORNAMENT COLLECTION
Gold
Gifts for a King
THE THREE KINGS
COLLECTION
Offered in 1998 and 1999.
☐ Artist: Tracy Larsen
4½" H × 2⅜" W
$22.00   2200QBG6836

Frankincense
Gifts for a King
THE THREE KINGS
COLLECTION
Offered in 1998 and 1999.
☐ Artist: Tracy Larsen
4⁷⁄₁₆" H × 2⅜" W
$22.00   2200QBG6896

Myrrh
Gifts for a King
THE THREE KINGS
COLLECTION
Offered in 1998 and 1999.
☐ Artist: Tracy Larsen
4⁹⁄₁₆" H × 2⅜" W
$22.00   2200QBG6893

Sweet Memories

Set of eight ornaments.
☐ Designer: Kristina Kline
Star: 1¾" H × ⅞" W
Long: 3⁷⁄₁₆" H × 1³⁄₁₆" W
Ribbon: 3⁵⁄₁₆" H × 1" W
Round: 3⅛" H × 1³⁄₁₆" W
$45.00   4500QBG6933

Frosty Friends

Set of two ornaments. Inspired by
the Frosty Friends series of
Keepsake Ornaments.
☐ Dated
Designer: Ed Seale
Frosty: 5⅜" H × 3" W
Penguin: 4" H × 2¹⁄₁₆" W
$48.00   4800QBG6907

Festive Locomotive

Inspired by the 1982 Keepsake
Ornament Tin Locomotive.
☐ Dated
Designer: Sue Tague
4⅜" W × 3¹¹⁄₁₆" W
$35.00   3500QBG6903

Sugarplum Cottage

☐ Designer: Tammy Haddix
5¹⁄₁₆" H × 3⅝" W
$35.00   3500QBG6917

White Poinsettias

Complements the Holiday
Traditions series.
☐ 3½" diameter
$25.00   2500QBG6923

Pink Poinsettias

Complements the Holiday
Traditions series.
☐ 3½" diameter
$25.00   2500QBG6926

1955 Murray® Fire Truck

Inspired by the 1995 Keepsake
Ornament.
☐ Dated
Designer: Tammy Haddix
3⅝" H × 5⁵⁄₁₆" W
$35.00   3500QBG6909

RELIGIOUS
Cross of Peace

Precious metal
☐ Dated
Artist: Kristina Kline
2⁹⁄₁₆" H × 1¹³⁄₁₆" W
$9.95   995QX6856

Journey to Bethlehem

Clara Johnson Scroggins named
this design as her 1998
COLLECTOR'S CHOICE.
☐ Dated
Artist: Duane Unruh
3⁷⁄₁₆" H × 3½" W
$16.95   1695QX6223

The Holy Family

Blessed Nativity Collection.
Fine porcelain. Three-piece set.
Offered in 1998, 1999, and 2000.
Each year, a new piece will
be added.
☐ Dated
Artist: Joyce Lyle
Mary: 3⁷⁄₁₆" H × 2⅝" W
Joseph: 4⁹⁄₁₆" H × 2¹³⁄₁₆" W
Baby Jesus: 1³⁄₁₆" H × 2⁹⁄₁₆" W
$25.00   2500QX6523

Sweet Memories

Frosty Friends

Festive Locomotive

Sugarplum Cottage

White Poinsettias

Pink Poinsettias

1955 Murray® Fire Truck

Cross of Peace

Journey to Bethlehem   The Holy Family

Watchful Shepherd

African-American Holiday BARBIE™

Red Poinsettias

RELIGIOUS

Watchful Shepherd
☐ Dated
Artist: Kristina Kline
2¹³/₁₆" H × 1⅝" W
$8.95   895QX6496

Madonna and Child
☐ Dated
Artist: Anita Marra Rogers
4⁷/₁₆" H × 1⁵/₁₆" W
$12.95   1295QX6516

Miracle in Bethlehem
☐ Dated
Artist: Ed Seale
3⅝" H × 2¹¹/₁₆" W
$12.95   1295QX6513

Treetop Choir
☐ Dated
Artist: John "Collin" Francis
2¹³/₁₆" H × 3⅛" W
$9.95   995QX6506

Madonna and Child

Miracle in Bethlehem

Treetop Choir

NEW SERIES

**African-American
Holiday BARBIE™**
First in the African-American
Holiday BARBIE™ Ornament
series. Each year's design will cor-
respond to the Happy Holidays®
doll offered that season.
☐ Dated
Artist: Patricia Andrews
3¾" H × 2⅝" W
$15.95   1595QX6936

Red Poinsettias
CROWN REFLECTIONS
BLOWN GLASS ORNAMENT
COLLECTION
First in the Holiday Traditions
series
4" diameter
$35.00   3500QBG6906

Glorious Angel
First in the Madame Alexander®
Holiday Angels series
☐ Dated
Artist: John "Collin" Francis
4¼" H × 2¾" W
$14.95   1495QX6493

Cruella de Vil
First in the Unforgettable
Villains series
☐ Dated
4½" H × 2⅝" W
$14.95   1495QXD4063

A Visit From Piglet
First in the Winnie the Pooh series
☐ Dated
2½" H × 2" W
$13.95   1395QXD4086

A Pony for Christmas
First in the A Pony for
Christmas series
Features nostalgic designs inspired
by children's toy horses.
☐ Dated
Artist: Linda Sickman
3¼" H × 2¹³/₁₆" W
$10.95   1095QX6316

Joe Cool
First in the Spotlight on
SNOOPY series
☐ Dated
Artist: Bob Siedler
2⁵/₁₆" H × 1¾" W
$9.95   995QX6453

Snow Buddies
First in the Snow Buddies series
☐ Dated
Artist: Tammy Haddix
2⅝" H × 2¼" W
$7.95   795QX6853

Glorious Angel

Cruella de Vil

A Visit from Piglet

A Pony for Christmas

Joe Cool

Snow Buddies

Donald and Daisy in Venice

Pony Express Rider

Richard Petty

Mario Lemieux

Marilyn Monroe

Scarlett O'Hara™

The Clauses on Vacation

Walt Disney's *Snow White*

Minnie Plays the Flute

Princess Leia™

Ready for Christmas

Donald and Daisy in Venice
First in the Romantic
Vacations series
Donald and Daisy—or Mickey
and Minnie—visit a different,
glamorous location each year.
▨ Dated
2¹³/₁₆" H × 4¹⁵/₁₆" W
$14.95   1495QXD4103

Pony Express Rider
First in The Old West series
Features legendary characters who
shaped history in America's West.
▨ Dated
Artist: Duane Unruh
3½" H × 4½" W
$13.95   1395QX6323

ONGOING SERIES
Richard Petty
Second in the Stock Car
Champions series
Hallmark-exclusive trading
card included.
▨ Artist: Ed Seale
4⅛" H × 3⁵/₁₆" W
$15.95   1595QXI4143

Mario Lemieux
Second in the Hockey
Greats series
Hallmark-exclusive trading
card included.
▨ Dated
Artist: John "Collin" Francis
4½" H × 4¼" W
$15.95   1595QXI6476

Marilyn Monroe
Second in the Marilyn
Monroe series
▨ Dated
Artist: Patricia Andrews
4⁷/₁₆" H × 2¹¹/₁₆" W
$14.95   1495QX6333

Scarlett O'Hara™
Second in the Scarlett
O'Hara™ series
▨ Dated
Artist: Patricia Andrews
4¹¹/₁₆" H × 2⁷/₁₆" W
$14.95   1495QX6336

The Clauses on Vacation
Second in The Clauses on
Vacation series
▨ Dated
Artist: Bob Siedler
2⁵/₁₆" H × 2½" W
$14.95   1495QX6276

Walt Disney's *Snow White*
Second in The Enchanted
Memories Collection
▨ Dated
5⅛" H × 2⅛" W
$14.95   1495QXD4056

Minnie Plays the Flute
Second in the Mickey's Holiday
Parade series
▨ Dated
3⅛" H × 1⅝" W
$13.95   1395QXD4106

Princess Leia™
Second in the STAR
WARS™ series
▨ Dated
Artist: Dill Rhodus
3¾" H × 1¹/₁₆" W
$13.95   1395QXI4026

Ready for Christmas
Second in the Hallmark
Archive series
Includes collector's card.
▨ Dated
3" H × 2⅝" W
$12.95   1295QXD4006

1917 Curtiss JN-4D "Jenny"

Timber Wolves at Play

Victorian Christmas II

Pennsylvania GG-1 Locomotive

Iris Angel

Mop Top Wendy

Mexican BARBIE™

Cal Ripken Jr.

Emmitt Smith

Grant Hill

1937 Ford V-8

ONGOING SERIES

1917 Curtiss JN-4D "Jenny"
Second in the Sky's the
Limit series
☐ Dated
Artist: Lynn Norton
1¹⁄₁₆" H × 4½" W
$14.95   1495QX6286

Timber Wolves at Play
Mark Newman
Second in the Majestic
Wilderness series
☐ Dated
2" H × 2⅜" W
$12.95   1295QX6273

Victorian Christmas II
Thomas Kinkade, Painter
of Light™
Second in the Thomas
Kinkade series
Ceramic
☐ Dated
2¾" H × 3⅜" W
$10.95   1095QX6343

**Pennsylvania GG-1
Locomotive**
Third in the LIONEL®
Train series
Die-cast metal. Wheels turn.
☐ Dated
1⁵⁄₃₂" H × 4³⁄₁₆" W
$18.95   1895QX6346

Iris Angel
Third in The Language of
Flowers series
Silver-plated basket
☐ Dated
Artist: Sue Tague
3⁹⁄₁₆" H × 2¹⁄₁₆" W
$15.95   1595QX6156

Mop Top Wendy
Third in the Madame
Alexander® series
☐ Dated
Artist: John "Collin" Francis
3⅝" H × 2⅛" W
$14.95   1495QX6353

Mexican BARBIE™
Third in the "Dolls of the World"
Ornament series
☐ Dated
Artist: Anita Marra Rogers
4⁵⁄₁₆" H × 1¹⁷⁄₃₂" W
$14.95   1495QX6356

Cal Ripken Jr.
Third in the At the Ballpark series
Hallmark exclusive trading
card included.
☐ Dated
Artist: Dill Rhodus
4⅝" H × 2⅝" W
$14.95   1495QXI4033

Emmitt Smith
Fourth in the Football
Legends series
Hallmark exclusive trading
card included.
☐ Artist: Dill Rhodus
4⁵⁄₁₆" H × 2" W
$14.95   1495QXI4036

Grant Hill
Fourth in the Hoop Stars series
Hallmark exclusive trading
card included.
☐ Artist: Duane Unruh
3⁹⁄₁₆" H × 2⅞" W
$14.95   1495QXI6846

1937 Ford V-8
Fourth in the All-American
Trucks series
Wheels turn.
☐ Dated
Artist: Don Palmiter
1¾" H × 4¼" W
$13.95   1395QX6263

1955 Murray® Tractor and Trailer

Silken Flame™

Holiday BARBIE™

Puppy Love

1970 Plymouth® Hemi 'Cuda

Merry Olde Santa

Fabulous Decade

Daphne—Mary's Angels

1955 Murray® Tractor and Trailer

Fifth in the Kiddie Car
Classics series
Cast metal. Set of two ornaments.
Wheels turn.
☐ Dated
Artist: Don Palmiter
Tractor: 1¼" H × 3¼" W
Trailer: 1¼" H × 2¹³⁄₁₆" W
$16.95   1695QX6376

Silken Flame™

Fifth in the BARBIE™
Ornament series
☐ Dated
Artist: Patricia Andrews
4⁵⁄₁₆" H × 2⅛" W
$15.95   1595QXI4043

Holiday BARBIE™

Sixth in the Holiday
BARBIE™ Ornament series
☐ Dated
Artist: Patricia Andrews
3¾" H × 2⅝" W
$15.95   1595QXI4023

Puppy Love

Eighth in the Puppy Love series
Brass tag
☐ Dated
Artist: Anita Marra Rogers
2½" H × 2¹⁄₁₆" W
$7.95   795QX6163

1970 Plymouth® Hemi 'Cuda

Eighth in the Classic American
Cars series
☐ Dated
Artist: Don Palmiter
1¼" H × 4¹⁄₁₆" W
$13.95   1395QX6256

Merry Olde Santa

Ninth in the Merry Olde
Santa series
☐ Dated
Artist: Duane Unruh
4¹⁵⁄₁₆" H × 3⅞" W
$15.95   1595QX6386

Fabulous Decade

Ninth in the Fabulous
Decade series
☐ Brass date
Artist: Sharon Pike
1¹¹⁄₁₆" H × 2⅛" W
$7.95   795QX6393

Daphne—Mary's Angels

11th in the Mary's Angels series
Designer: Mary Hamilton
☐ Artist: Robert Chad
2⁷⁄₁₆" H × 1¹⁵⁄₁₆" W
$7.95   795QX6153

Grocery Store

15th in the Nostalgic Houses and
Shops series
☐ Dated
Artist: Don Palmiter
3¾" H × 2⅝" W
$16.95   1695QX6266

Frosty Friends

19th in the Frosty Friends series
☐ Dated
Artist: Ed Seale
2⁵⁄₁₆" H × 2¹¹⁄₁₆" W
$10.95   1095QX6226

Santa's Bumper Car

20th in the Here Comes
Santa series
☐ Dated
Artist: Sue Tague
3¹³⁄₁₆" H × 3¹⁄₁₆" W
$14.95   1495QX6283

Grocery Store

Frosty Friends

Santa's Bumper Car

Ricky—All God's Children®

A Celebration of Angels

Yuletide Central

Cat Naps

Bright Sledding Colors

Boba Fett™

Captain Kathryn Janeway™

Joe Montana, Notre Dame

The Grinch™

Heavenly Melody

Santa's Hidden Surprise

Bright Sledding Colors
10th and final in the
CRAYOLA® Crayon series
☐ Dated
Artist: Sue Tague
1⅞" H × 2⅝" W
$12.95   1295QX6166

SPECIAL ISSUES
Boba Fett™
STAR WARS™
☐ Artist: Dill Rhodus
4⁷⁄₁₆" H × 1⅞" W
$14.95   1495QXI4053

Captain Kathryn Janeway™
STAR TREK: *VOYAGER*™
☐ Stardated
Artist: Anita Marra Rogers
5¹³⁄₁₆" H × 3⁹⁄₁₆" W
$14.95   1495QXI4046

Joe Montana
Notre Dame
☐ Dated
Artist: Duane Unruh
4½" H × 3⅝" W
$14.95   1495QXI6843

The Grinch™
DR. SEUSS
☐ Dated
Artist: Robert Chad
4⁵⁄₁₆" H × 1½" W
$13.95   1395QXI6466

GENERAL
Heavenly Melody
HALLMARK ARCHIVES
COLLECTION
Original artwork by Hallmark
Artist Bob Haas; Masterworks
Collection, Hallmark Archives
☐ Dated
Artist: LaDene Votruba
4¼" H × 4¹¹⁄₁₆" W
$18.95   1895QX6576

Santa's Hidden Surprise
Ceramic. Santa opens at
the waist.
☐ Dated
Size: 3" H × 1½" W
$14.95   1495QX6913

FINAL EDITIONS
Ricky—All God's Children®
Martha Root
Third and final in the All God's
Children® series
☐ Dated
2⅜" H × 2¹³⁄₁₆" W
$12.95   1295QX6363

A Celebration of Angels
Fourth and final in the
A Celebration of Angels series
☐ Dated
Artist: Patricia Andrews
4" H × 3¼" W
$13.95   1395QX6366

Yuletide Central
Fifth and final in the Yuletide
Central series
Pressed tin. Wheels turn.
☐ Dated
Artist: Linda Sickman
2¹¹⁄₁₆" H × 3⅝" W
$18.95   1895QX6373

Cat Naps
Fifth and final in the Cat
Naps series
☐ Dated
Artist: Katrina Bricker
2³⁄₁₆" H × 2⁷⁄₁₆" W
$8.95   895QX6383

Santa's Flying Machine

Cruising into Christmas

Soaring with Angels

Santa's Flying Machine
Handcrafted and tin. Rotor blades
and wheels turn.
■ Dated
Artist: Ed Seale
3¹¹⁄₁₆" H × 3⁷⁄₁₆" W
$16.95   1695QX6573

Cruising into Christmas
Handcrafted and tin
■ Dated
Artist: Ken Crow
3" H × 3¹³⁄₁₆" W
$16.95   1695QX6196

Soaring with Angels
FOLK ART
AMERICANA COLLECTION
Angel has antiqued copper wings
and a stole made of beads.
■ Dated
Artist: Linda Sickman
3¹¹⁄₁₆" H × 3⁷⁄₁₆" W
$16.95   1695QX6213

Holiday Decorator
Display on your tree as any other
Keepsake Ornament, or enjoy the
special lighting effect using your
own miniature light string.
■ Dated
Artist: Nello Williams
4¹⁄₁₆" H × 1⅞" W
$13.95   1395QX6566

A Christmas Eve Story
Becky Kelly
Display on your tree as any other
Keepsake Ornament, or enjoy the
special lighting effect using your
own miniature light string.
■ Dated
Designer: Becky Kelly
Artist: Sue Tague
4" H × 2⅜" W
$13.95   1395QX6873

Mistletoe Fairy
■ Dated
Artist: Joanne Eschrich
3½" H × 3½" W
$12.95   1295QX6216

Christmas Sleigh Ride
Die-cast metal. Wheel turns.
■ Dated
Artist: Ken Crow
2¹¹⁄₁₆" H × 3⅝" W
$12.95   1295QX6556

Peekaboo Bears
Tree opens up to reveal three
bears playing peekaboo.
■ Dated
Artist: Ken Crow
4⅜" H × 2" W
$12.95   1295QX6563

Country Home
Marjolein Bastin
NATURE'S SKETCHBOOK
■ Dated
Designer: Marjolein Bastin
Artist: John "Collin" Francis
2¹⁵⁄₁₆" H × 1¹¹⁄₁₆" W
$10.95   1095QX5172

Merry Chime
Handcrafted and brass
Chimes will ring with a
little breeze.
■ Dated
Artist: Ken Crow
4½" H × 1¾" W
$9.95   995QX6692

Night Watch
■ Dated
Artist: Bob Siedler
2⅞" H × 2" W
$9.95   995QX6725

Holiday Decorator

A Christmas Eve Story

Mistletoe Fairy

Christmas Sleigh Ride

Peekaboo Bears

Country Home

Merry Chime

Night Watch

Nick's Wish List

GENERAL
Nick's Wish List
▣ Dated
Artist: Patricia Andrews
3¼" H × 2⁷⁄₁₆" W
$8.95   895QX6863

Sweet Rememberings
▣ Dated
Artist: Sue Tague
2⁷⁄₁₆" H × 1¹⁄₁₆" W
$8.95   895QX6876

Sweet Rememberings

Fancy Footwork
▣ Dated
Artist: LaDene Votruba
3" H × 2¼" W
$8.95   895QX6536

Warm and Cozy
▣ Dated
Artist: Linda Sickman
2¼" H × 3¼" W
$8.95   895QX6866

Fancy Footwork

Warm and Cozy

Guardian Angel

Purr-fect Little Deer

Writing to Santa

Memories of Christmas

Guardian Angel
▣ Dated
Artist: Joyce Lyle
2³⁄₈" H × 1½" W
$8.95   895QX6543

Purr-fect Little Deer
▣ Dated
Artist: Sharon Pike
2⁷⁄₁₆" H × 2⁹⁄₁₆" W
$7.95   795QX6526

Writing to Santa
▣ Dated
Artist: Nina Aubé
1¹⁵⁄₁₆" H × 2¹⁄₈" W
$7.95   795QX6533

Memories of Christmas
Based on a popular Hallmark greeting card.
▣ Dated
Redesigned by: Tracy Larsen
3¼" diameter
$5.95   595QX2406

DISNEY COLLECTION
Runaway Toboggan
Mickey & Co.
Set of two ornaments
▣ Dated
1¾" H × 2³⁄₁₆" W
$16.95   1695QXD4003

The Mickey and Minnie Handcar
Mickey & Co.
▣ Dated
2¾" H × 3½" W
$14.95   1495QXD4116

Mickey's Favorite Reindeer
Mickey & Co.
▣ Dated
3½" H × 3½" W
$13.95   1395QXD4013

Make-Believe Boat
Disney Babies
▣ Dated
1¹⁵⁄₁₆" H × 1½" W
$12.95   1295QXD4113

Goofy Soccer Star
▣ Dated
3¾" H × 2⁷⁄₈" W
$10.95   1095QXD4123

Runaway Toboggan

The Mickey and Minnie Handcar

Mickey's Favorite Reindeer

Make-Believe Boat

Goofy Soccer Star

Buzz Lightyear

Disney's *Toy Story*
▨ Dated
3¼" H × 4" W
$14.95   1495QXD4066

Cinderella's Coach

Disney's *Cinderella*
▨ Dated
2¹⁵⁄₁₆" H × 4⅛" W
$14.95   1495QXD4083

Woody the Sheriff

Disney's *Toy Story*
▨ Dated
5³⁄₁₆" H × 2½" W
$14.95   1495QXD4163

Simba and Nala

Disney's *Simba's Pride*
▨ Dated
2⅞" H × 3" W
$13.95   1395QXD4073

Daydreams

Ariel, *The Little Mermaid*
▨ Dated
2½" H × 3" W
$13.95   1395QXD4136

Iago, Abu and the Genie

Disney's *Aladdin*
▨ Dated
3⁷⁄₁₆" H × 3¾" W
$12.95   1295QXD4076

Princess Aurora

Disney's *Sleeping Beauty*
Set of two ornaments
▨ Dated
Sleeping Beauty: 4¼" H × 3¹⁄₁₆" W
Crown: ¹³⁄₁₆" H × 1¹³⁄₃₂" W
$12.95   1295QXD4126

Mulan, Mushu and Cri-Kee

Disney's *Mulan*
Set of two ornaments
▨ Dated
Mulan: 3¼" H × 4¹⁄₂" W
Mushu and Cri-Kee: 2" H × 2" W
$14.95   1495QXD4156

Flik

Disney's *A Bug's Life*
3½" H × 3½" W
▨ $12.95   1295QXD4153

<u>WINNIE THE POOH
COLLECTION</u>
Building a Snowman
▨ Dated
2⅝" H × 2½" W
$14.95   1495QXD4133

Bouncy Baby-sitter
▨ Dated
3¹¹⁄₁₆" H × 2" W
$12.95   1295QXD4096

<u>POP CULTURE ICONS</u>
Larry, Moe and Curly
The Three Stooges™
Set of three ornaments
▨ Dated
Artist: Tracy Larsen
Larry: 3¹³⁄₁₆" H × 2⅝" W
Moe: 4¹¹⁄₁₆" H × 2½" W
Curly: 3½" H × 2⅜" W
$27.00   2700QX6503

Buzz Lightyear

Cinderella's Coach

Woody the Sheriff

Simba and Nala

Daydreams

Iago, Abu and the Genie

Princess Aurora

Mulan, Mushu and Cri-Kee

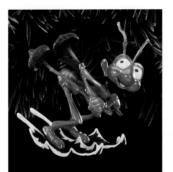
Flik

Building a Snowman

Bouncy Baby-sitter

Larry, Moe and Curly—The Three Stooges™

Tonka® Road Grader

Hot Wheels™

Munchkinland™ Mayor and Coroner

Superman™

Mrs. Potato Head®

Sweet Treat

Maxine

POP CULTURE ICONS

Tonka® Road Grader
Die-cast metal. Front section and grader pivot.
◻ Dated
1¼" H × 3¼" W
$13.95   1395QX6483

Hot Wheels™
30TH ANNIVERSARY
◻ Dated
Artist: Ken Crow
2¹³⁄₁₆" H × 3¼" W
$13.95   1395QX6436

Munchkinland™ Mayor and Coroner
THE WIZARD OF OZ™
Set of two ornaments
◻ Artist: Joyce Lyle
Mayor: 2¹¹⁄₁₆" H × 1¹⁵⁄₁₆" W
Coroner: 3³⁄₁₆" H × 2" W
$13.95   1395QX6463

Superman™
COMMEMORATIVE EDITION
Pressed tin. Opens and closes.
◻ Dated
2¹¹⁄₁₆" H × 3³⁄₁₆" W
$12.95   1295QX6423

Mrs. Potato Head®
◻ Dated
3¾" H × 4¼" W
$10.95   1095QX6886

Sweet Treat
HERSHEY'S™
◻ Dated
Artist: Kristina Kline
1⅞" H × 2⅛" W
$10.95   1095QX6433

Maxine
◻ Dated
Character designer: John Wagner
Artist: Sharon Pike
2⅜" H × 2⁵⁄₁₆" W
$9.95   995QX6446

Bugs Bunny
LOONEY TUNES
◻ Artist: Robert Chad
4⅜" H × 1⅞" W
$13.95   1395QX6443

1998 Corvette® Convertible
Wheels turn.
◻ Dated
Artist: Don Palmiter
1¹⁄₁₆" H × 3⅞" W
$13.95   1395QX6416

ARTIST'S STUDIO COLLECTION

Santa's Deer Friend
◻ Dated
Artist: Robert Chad
4¹⁄₁₆" H × 4" W
$24.00   2400QX6583

MAGIC NEW SERIES

The Stone Church
First in the Candlelight Services series
Light. Features lighted churches in a variety of architectural styles.
◻ Dated
Artist: Ed Seale
4½" H × 3⅝" W
$18.95   1895QLX7636

Bugs Bunny

1998 Corvette® Convertible

Santa's Deer Friend

The Stone Church

MAGIC ONGOING SERIES

Lighthouse Greetings

Second in the Lighthouse
Greetings series
Flashing light
☐ Dated
Artist: John "Collin" Francis
4⁷⁄₁₆" H × 2¹⁵⁄₁₆" W
$24.00   2400QLX7536

Apollo Lunar Module

Third in the Journeys into
Space series
Sound. The Lunar Module was
used to taxi U.S. astronauts from
their Apollo spacecraft to the surface of the moon and back. You
can hear a message from the 1971
Apollo 14 mission.
☐ Dated
3" H × 4⁷⁄₁₆" W
$24.00   2400QLX7543

MAGIC GENERAL

The Washington Monument

Flashing lights and sound. Light at
base of monument glows softly.
Lights flash across the sky accom-
panied by the sounds of fireworks.
☐ Dated
Artist: Ed Seale
3¾" H × 2⁷⁄₁₆" W
$24.00   2400QLX7553

1998 Corvette®

Light, blinking lights and motion.
Spotlight overhead glows. Red
"chase lights" circle the turntable.
☐ Dated
Artist: Don Palmiter
4⁵⁄₁₆" H × 2¹⁵⁄₁₆" W
$24.00   2400QLX7605

St. Nicholas Circle
**Thomas Kinkade, Painter
of Light™**

Light. Light glows softly in
the background.
☐ Dated
Artist: Duane Unruh
4¹⁄₁₆" H × 3¼" W
$18.95   1895QXI7556

Mickey's Comet

Mickey & Co.
Light and flickering light. Hatch
and "running lights" glow.
Exhaust-plume light flickers.
☐ Dated
3" H × 5½" W
$24.00   2400QXD7586

Santa's Show 'n' Tell

Light. Turn wheel on back of
ornament to create shadows
on the wall.
☐ Dated
Artist: Ken Crow
3⁷⁄₈" H × 2¹¹⁄₁₆" W
$18.95   1895QLX7566

Santa's Spin Top

Motion. Santa and his reindeer
circle the striped pole.
☐ Dated
Artist: Sue Tague
4¹⁵⁄₁₆" H × 3¹¹⁄₁₆" W
$22.00   2200QLX7573

Cinderella at the Ball

Disney's *Cinderella*
Light and motion. Cinderella and
prince glide around dance floor.
Light above chandelier glows.
☐ Dated
4¹⁵⁄₁₆" H × 2¹³⁄₁₆" W
$24.00   2400QXD7576

MAGIC SPECIAL ISSUES

**U.S.S. Enterprise™
NCC-1701-E**

STAR TREK: *First Contact*™
Light. The front deflector shield,
both warp engines and the
impulse engines are lighted.
☐ Stardated
Artist: Lynn Norton
1⁵⁄₁₆" H × 6¹⁄₈" W
$24.00   2400QXI7633

X-Wing Starfighter™

STAR WARS™
Light. Lights glow from the
back of the X-Wing
Starfighter's four engine pods.
☐ Dated
Artist: Dill Rhodus
1" H × 4³⁄₈" W
$24.00   2400QXI7596

Lighthouse Greetings

Apollo Lunar Module

The Washington Monument

1998 Corvette®

St. Nicholas Circle

Mickey's Comet

Santa's Show 'n' Tell

Santa's Spin Top

Cinderella at the Ball

U.S.S. Enterprise™ NCC-1701-E

X-Wing Starfighter™

The Miniature Ornament Collection
1998

The Miniature Ornament line for 1998 is "on track" with the **Noel R.R.—Locomotive 1989–1998**, a pewter ornament, to help celebrate the 10th anniversary of Keepsake Miniature Ornaments.

A new Kiddie Car Luxury Edition series takes to the road, the 60th anniversary of the Man of Steel is commemorated with a two-piece ornament set that reproduces the character and the cover of the first Superman™ Action Comics™ book, and **Singin' in the Rain™**, another two-piece set, features Gene Kelly and a reproduction of the original 1952 lobby poster.

The **Betsey's Prayer** ornament appears in tribute to the first-in-a-series Betsey Clark ball ornament that appeared in the 1973 Keepsake Ornament line—it helped to create the Keepsake Ornament-collecting excitement.

NEW SERIES

The Nativity
First in The Nativity series
As the series continues, visitors arrive to celebrate the birth of Baby Jesus. Fine pewter.
- Dated
Artist: Duane Unruh
1 3/16" H × 1" W
$9.95   995QXM4156

1937 Steelcraft Auburn
First in the Miniature Kiddie Car Luxury Edition series
Pedal cars based on Luxury Edition models from the popular Hallmark collection of Kiddie Car Classics. Die-cast metal. Wheels turn.
- Dated
Artist: Don Palmiter
9/16" H × 1 3/16" W
$6.95   695QXM4143

Winter Fun with SNOOPY®
First in the Winter Fun with SNOOPY® series
- Dated
Artist: Tracy Larsen
1 1/4" H × 1 1/4" W
$6.95   695QXM4243

Snowflake Ballet

ONGOING SERIES

Welcome Friends
Second in the Welcome Friends series
- Dated
Artist: Sharon Pike
1 3/8" H × 1" W
$6.95   695QXM4153

Antique Tractors
Second in the Antique Tractors series
Die-cast metal
- Dated
Artist: Linda Sickman
15/16" H × 1 1/2" W
$6.95   695QXM4166

Snowflake Ballet
Second in the Snowflake Ballet series
- Dated
Artist: Patricia Andrews
1 9/16" H × 13/16" W
$5.95   595QXM4173

The Nativity

1937 Steelcraft Auburn

Winter Fun with SNOOPY®

Welcome Friends

Antique Tractors

Teddy-Bear Style
Second in the Teddy-Bear
Style series
Arms and legs move.
▢ Dated
Artist: Duane Unruh
1¼" H × ¹³⁄₁₆" W
$5.95   595QXM4176

Nutcracker
Third in The Nutcracker
Ballet series
▢ Dated
Artist: LaDene Votruba
1½" H × ¹¹⁄₁₆" W
$5.95   595QXM4146

Murray Inc.® Dump Truck
Fourth in the Miniature Kiddie
Car Classics series
Die-cast metal
▢ Dated
Artist: Don Palmiter
⅝" H × 1¼" W
$6.95   695QXM4183

Miniature Clothespin Soldier
Fourth in the Miniature
Clothespin Soldier series
Arms move back and forth.
▢ Artist: Linda Sickman
1" H × ⁵⁄₁₆" W
$4.95   495QXM4193

Christmas Bells
Fourth in the Christmas
Bells series
Handcrafted and metal
▢ Dated
Artist: Ed Seale
1⅛" H × ⅞" W
$4.95   495QXM4196

Nutcracker Guild
Fifth in the Nutcracker
Guild series
Opens and closes like a
real nutcracker.
▢ Dated
Artist: Linda Sickman
1⁷⁄₁₆" H × ¹¹⁄₁₆" W
$6.95   695QXM4203

Centuries of Santa
Fifth in the Centuries of
Santa series
▢ Dated
Artist: Linda Sickman
1¼" H × ⅞" W
$5.95   595QXM4206

FINAL EDITIONS
Cheshire Cat
Fourth and final in the Alice in
Wonderland series
▢ Dated
Artist: Patricia Andrews
1¼" H × ¹¹⁄₁₆" W
$6.95   695QXM4186

On the Road
Sixth and final in the On the
Road series
Pressed tin
▢ Dated
Artist: Linda Sickman
⁷⁄₁₆" H × 1¼" W
$5.95   595QXM4213

Caboose
10th and final in the Noel
R.R. series
▢ Dated
Artist: Linda Sickman
1¹⁄₁₆" H × 1¼" W
$6.95   695QXM4216

Teddy-Bear Style

Nutcracker

Murray Inc.® Dump Truck

Miniature Clothespin Soldier

Christmas Bells

Nutcracker Guild

Centuries of Santa

Cheshire Cat

On the Road

Caboose

Noel R.R.—Locomotive 1989–1998   Angel Chime

Ewoks™

Glinda, The Good Witch; Wicked Witch of the West™

Singin' in the Rain™

Superman™

"Coca-Cola®" Time

ANNIVERSARY EDITION
Noel R.R.—Locomotive 1989–1998
10 Years of Collecting Memories
Fine pewter
This ornament was redesigned in fine pewter from the 1989 first in the Noel R.R. series to commemorate the 10th anniversary of Keepsake Miniature Ornaments.
Dated
Artist: Linda Sickman
1" H × 1¼" W
$10.95   1095QXM4286

PRECIOUS EDITION
Angel Chime
Dated
Artist: Sue Tague
1⅛" H × ⅞" W
$8.95   895QXM4283

SPECIAL ISSUE
Ewoks™
STAR WARS™
Set of three Miniature Ornaments
Artist: Katrina Bricker
Ewok with baby: 1¼" H × 11/16" W
Ewok with horn: 1¼" H × ¾" W
Ewok with spear: 1¼" H × ⅞" W
$16.95   1695QXI4223

POP CULTURE ICONS
Glinda, The Good Witch™
Wicked Witch of the West™
THE WIZARD OF OZ™
Set of two ornaments
Artist: Joyce Lyle
Good Witch: 2 1/16" H × 1 7/16" W
Wicked Witch: 2" H × 2¼" W
$14.95   1495QXM4233

Singin' in the Rain™
Set of two ornaments
This miniature set features Gene Kelly and a reproduction of the original 1952 lobby poster.
Dated
Artist: Patricia Andrews
Gene Kelly: 2⅛" H × 1 7/16" W
Poster: 3⅛" H × 2" W
$10.95   1095QXM4303

Superman™
COMMEMORATIVE EDITION
Set of two ornaments
Commemorates the Man of Steel's incredible career. Includes a reproduction of his debut appearance in Action Comics #1.
Dated
Artist: Robert Chad
Superman: 2" H × 2 5/16" W
Poster: 3" H × 2" W
$10.95   1095QXM4313

"Coca-Cola®" Time
Artist: Duane Unruh
1 7/16" H × 1⅜" W
$6.95   695QXM4296

GENERAL
Holly-Jolly Jig
Legs dangle.
◻ Dated
Artist: Sue Tague
1" H × $^{11}/_{16}$" W
$6.95   695QXM4266

Fishy Surprise
◻ Dated
Artist: Joanne Eschrich
$^{7}/_{8}$" H × $^{13}/_{16}$" W
$6.95   695QXM4276

Peaceful Pandas
Complements "Noah's Ark"
Special Edition set introduced
in 1994.
◻ Artist: Linda Sickman
$^{5}/_{8}$" H × 1" W
$5.95   595QXM4253

Pixie Parachute
◻ Dated
Artist: Joanne Eschrich
$1^{3}/_{8}$" H × $^{7}/_{8}$" W
$4.95   495QXM4256

Sharing Joy
Rodney Reindeer
◻ Dated
$^{7}/_{8}$" H × $^{15}/_{16}$" W
$4.95   495QXM4273

Betsey's Prayer
BETSEY CLARK
◻ Dated
Artist: Kristina Kline
1" H × $^{11}/_{16}$" W
$4.95   495QXM4263

WINNIE THE POOH
COLLECTION
Tree Trimmin' Time
Set of three Miniature Ornaments
◻ Dated
Pooh: $1^{3}/_{4}$" H × $^{13}/_{16}$" W
Tigger: $1^{15}/_{16}$" H × $1^{5}/_{8}$" W
Piglet and tree: $1^{7}/_{16}$" H × $1^{1}/_{4}$" W
$19.95   1995QXD4236

Holly-Jolly Jig

Fishy Surprise

Peaceful Pandas

Pixie Parachute

Sharing Joy

Betsey's Prayer

Tree Trimmin' Time

The Spring Ornament Collection
1998

The 1998 Spring Collection includes the first-ever Spring Preview event-exclusive ornament, **Tigger in the Garden.** A Mickey & Co. design called **Practice Swing** introduces Donald Duck to the line, the Midge™ doll celebrates her 35th anniversary, and a STAR WARS™ design appears on a pressed-tin lunch box ornament. The new World of Wishes group—**Precious Baby, Wedding Memories, Sweet Birthday, Happy Diploma Day!** and **Special Friends**—arrive. They are ornaments that we can give to commemorate special occasions that may occur at any time during the year.

1931 Ford Model A Roadster

Based on the BARBIE® as Little Bo-Peep Doll

1939 Mobo Horse

NEW SERIES
1931 Ford Model A Roadster
First in the Vintage
Roadsters series
Die-cast metal
☐ Dated
Artist: Don Palmiter
1½" H × 1⅝" W
$14.95   1495QEO8416

ONGOING SERIES
Based on the BARBIE® as Little Bo-Peep Doll
Second in the Children's
Collector Barbie Ornament series
☐ Dated
Artist: Anita Marra Rogers
3½" H × 1⅞" W
$14.95   1495QEO8373

1939 Mobo Horse
Second in the Sidewalk
Cruisers series
Die-cast metal
☐ Dated
2⅝" H × 2⅝₁₆" W
$12.95   1295QEO8393

Benjamin Bunny™
Third in the Beatrix
Potter™ series
☐ Dated
Artist: LaDene Votruba
2½" H × 1¼" W
$8.95   895QEO8383

Benjamin Bunny™

Passenger Car

Joyful Angels

Garden Club

Passenger Car
Third in the Cottontail
Express series
☐ Dated
Artist: Ken Crow
1¹⁵⁄₁₆" H × 1⅛" W
$9.95   995QEO8376

FINAL EDITIONS
Joyful Angels
Third and final in the Joyful
Angels series
☐ Dated
Artist: Joyce Lyle
4" H × 2⅝" W
$10.95   1095QEO8386

Garden Club
Fourth and final in the Garden
Club Series
☐ Dated
Artist: Sharon Pike
1⁹⁄₁₆" H × 1¹⁄₁₆" W
$7.95   795QEO8426

POP CULTURE ICONS
Practice Swing—Donald Duck
Mickey & Co.
☐ Dated
3½" H × 2⅜" W
$10.95   1095QEO8396

Midge™—35th Anniversary
☐ Dated
Artist: Patricia Andrews
4¾" H × 2" W
$14.95   1495QEO8413

Forever Friends
THE ANDREW
BROWNSWORD
COLLECTION
☐ Dated
Artist: Sharon Pike
2¹¹⁄₁₆" H × 2" W
$9.95   995QEO8423

Practice Swing—Donald Duck   Midge™—35th Anniversary   Forever Friends

STAR WARS™

Pressed tin. Lunch box opens.
☐ Dated
Designer: Steve Goslin
2¹¹⁄₁₆" H × 3³⁄₁₆" W
$12.95   1295QEO8406

Going Up?
CHARLIE BROWN—
PEANUTS®

☐ Dated
Artist: Sharon Pike
2" H × 2⅞" W
$9.95   995QEO8433

The Garden of Piglet and Pooh

Winnie the Pooh
Set of two ornaments
☐ Dated
Piglet: 1⁹⁄₁₆" H × 1¼" W
Pooh: 2⅜" H × 1¼" W
$12.95   1295QEO8403

SEASONAL CELEBRATION
Bashful Gift

Set of two ornaments
☐ Dated
Artist: Nina Aubé
Each: 2¹⁄₁₆" H × 1⅛" W
$11.95   1195QEO8446

What's Your Name?

☐ Dated
Artist: Kristina Kline
1⅞" H × 1½" W
$7.95   795QEO8443

Victorian Cross

Fine pewter
☐ Dated
Artist: Duane Unruh
2¼" H × 1⅜" W
$8.95   895QEO8453

Bouquet of Memories

☐ Dated
Artist: Sue Tague
2½" H × 1" W
$7.95   795QEO8456

WORLD OF WISHES
Precious Baby

Fine porcelain
☐ Dated
Artist: Sue Tague
2⅝" H × 2¹³⁄₁₆" W
$9.95   995QEO8463

Wedding Memories

Fine porcelain
"Dreams have a way of coming
true more beautifully when
dreamed by two."
☐ Dated
Artist: LaDene Votruba
4½" H × 3" W
$9.95   995QEO8466

Special Friends

Spoonful of Stars
"The very best way to share a day
is to spend it with a friend."
☐ Dated
Designer: Becky Kelly
Artist: LaDene Votruba
2⅞" H × 2⅜" W
$12.95   1295QEO8523

Sweet Birthday

☐ Dated
Artist: Kristina Kline
2¼" H × 1½" W
$7.95   795QEO8473

Happy Diploma Day!

☐ Dated
Artist: Tammy Haddix
2⅛" H × 1¾" W
$7.95   795QEO8476

Tigger in the Garden

Winnie the Pooh
☐ First Spring Preview event-
exclusive ornament
1⅝" H × 1¹⁵⁄₁₆" W
$9.95   995QEO8436

STAR WARS™

Going Up?

The Garden of Piglet and Pooh

Bashful Gift

What's Your Name?

Victorian Cross

Bouquet of Memories

Precious Baby

Wedding Memories

Special Friends

Sweet Birthday

Happy Diploma Day!

Tigger in the Garden

The Memories and Magic Ornament Collection
1997

This year, the Hockey Greats series skated in with **Wayne Gretzky. Darth Vader™** looked awe-inspiring, BARBIE™ and KEN™ made it to the altar, and **Jeff Gordon®** led the Stock Car Champions series.

We bid farewell to several series, too, including Turn of the Century Parade, Christmas Visitors, Mother Goose, and Chris Mouse, a little creature we'd loved for 13 years. The Baseball Heroes series also retired as it saluted **Jackie Robinson,** who integrated Major League Baseball 50 years ago.

The Disney characters join the line! Four new collections of Keepsake Ornaments—Mickey & Co., Classic Movies, New Movies and Winnie the Pooh—celebrate Disney's beloved creations.

The Lone Ranger™ (love that lunch box!), **Howdy Doody™,** and **Mr. Potato Head®** were among great, new licensed properties. NFL blimps were joined by 10 NBA plaques, complete with team stats.

Madonna and Child led a marvelous array of religious ornaments, including **King Noor,** the first black king in a new legend about following the star.

BARBIE™ and KEN™ Wedding Day

BARBIE™ and KEN™ Wedding Day
Set of two ornaments
This commemorative set complements the BARBIE™ Keepsake Ornaments in the Collector's Series. Mattel offered this BARBIE™ bridal gown from 1959 to 1962 and introduced the KEN® tuxedo in 1961.
░ Dated
BARBIE™ artist: Patricia Andrews
KEN™ artist: Don Palmiter
BARBIE™: 4⁹⁄₁₆" H × 2³⁄₁₆" W
KEN™: 4¹⁵⁄₁₆" H × 1½" W
$35.00   3500QXI6815

After the 1997 NFL Collection was produced, but before it debuted in stores, the HOUSTON OILERS™ became the TENNESSEE OILERS™. No TENNESSEE OILERS™ ornaments were produced.

NFL Collection

NFL COLLECTION
░ Dated
Artist: Bob Siedler
2⅛" H × 2¹³⁄₁₆" W
ARIZONA CARDINALS™
░ $9.95   995QSR5505
ATLANTA FALCONS™
░ $9.95   995QSR5305
BALTIMORE RAVENS™
░ $9.95   995QSR5352
BUFFALO BILLS™
░ $9.95   995QSR5312
CAROLINA PANTHERS™
░ $9.95   995QSR5315
CHICAGO BEARS™
░ $9.95   995QSR5322
CINCINNATI BENGALS™
░ $9.95   995QSR5325
DALLAS COWBOYS™
░ $9.95   995QSR5355
DENVER BRONCOS™
░ $9.95   995QSR5362
DETROIT LIONS™
░ $9.95   995QSR5365
GREEN BAY PACKERS™
░ $9.95   995QSR5372
HOUSTON OILERS™
░ $9.95   995QSR5375
INDIANAPOLIS COLTS™
░ $9.95   995QSR5411
JACKSONVILLE JAGUARS™
░ $9.95   995QSR5415
KANSAS CITY CHIEFS™
░ $9.95   995QSR5302
MIAMI DOLPHINS™
░ $9.95   995QSR5472
MINNESOTA VIKINGS™
░ $9.95   995QSR5475
NEW ENGLAND PATRIOTS™
░ $9.95   995QSR5482
NEW ORLEANS SAINTS™
░ $9.95   995QSR5485

SPECIAL ISSUES
Commander Data™
STAR TREK®: THE NEXT GENERATION™
Stardated
░ Artist: Anita Marra Rogers
4⅛" H × 3⅝" W
$14.95   1495QXI6345

Commander Data™

Yoda™
STAR WARS™
░ Artist: Katrina Bricker
2³⁄₁₆" H × 1½" W
$9.95   995QXI6355

Yoda™

Dr. Leonard H. McCoy™
STAR TREK™
Stardated
░ Artist: Anita Marra Rogers
5⁷⁄₁₆" H × 1¹³⁄₁₆" W
$14.95   1495QXI6352

Dr. Leonard H. McCoy™

1997 CORVETTE
Wheels turn.
░ Dated
Artist: Don Palmiter
1³⁄₁₆" H × 3¹⁵⁄₁₆" W
$13.95   1395QXI6455

1997 Corvette

NFL Collection continued

NEW YORK GIANTS™
☐ $9.95 995QSR5492
NEW YORK JETS™
☐ $9.95 995QSR5495
OAKLAND RAIDERS™
☐ $9.95 995QSR5422
PHILADELPHIA EAGLES™
☐ $9.95 995QSR5502
PITTSBURGH STEELERS™
☐ $9.95 995QSR5512
ST. LOUIS RAMS™
☐ $9.95 995QSR5425
SAN DIEGO CHARGERS™
☐ $9.95 995QSR5515
SAN FRANCISCO 49ERS™
☐ $9.95 995QSR5522
SEATTLE SEAHAWKS™
☐ $9.95 995QSR5525
TAMPA BAY
    BUCCANEERS™
☐ $9.95 995QSR5532
WASHINGTON
    REDSKINS™
☐ $9.95 995QSR5535

Baby's First Christmas

Baby's Second Christmas

Child's Third Christmas

Child's Fourth Christmas

Child's Fifth Christmas

Baby's First Christmas

CHILD'S AGE COLLECTION
Baby's First Christmas
☐ Dated
Artist: Ken Crow
2³⁄₁₆" H × 1⅝" W
$7.95 795QX6495

Baby's Second Christmas
☐ Dated
Artist: Ken Crow
2⅜" H × 2" W
$7.95 795QX6502

Child's Third Christmas
☐ Dated
Artist: Ken Crow
2⁹⁄₁₆" H × 2¹⁄₁₆" W
$7.95 795QX6505

Child's Fourth Christmas
☐ Dated
Artist: Ken Crow
2¹¹⁄₁₆" H × 2⁵⁄₁₆" W
$7.95 795QX6512

Child's Fifth Christmas
☐ Dated
Artist: Ken Crow
2¹⁵⁄₁₆" H × 1¹⁵⁄₁₆" W
$7.95 795QX6515

BABY
Baby's First Christmas
Harlem Textile Works™
☐ Dated
Artist: Patricia Andrews
1⁵⁄₁₆" H × 2¹³⁄₁₆" W
$9.95 995QX6492

Baby's First Christmas
Photo Holder
☐ Dated
4⁹⁄₁₆" H × 2⅛" W
$7.95 795QX6482

Baby's First Christmas
Fine porcelain
☐ Dated
Artist: LaDene Votruba
2¹¹⁄₁₆" H × 3" W
$14.95 1495QX6535

Baby's First Christmas
☐ Dated
Artist: LaDene Votruba
3¹⁄₁₆" H × 2½" W
$9.95 995QX6485

FAMILY
Mom and Dad
☐ Dated
Artist: Bob Siedler
4⁵⁄₁₆" H × 1¹³⁄₁₆" W
$9.95 995QX6522

Mom
☐ Dated
Artist: Bob Siedler
2½" H × 2⅜" W
$8.95 895QX6525

Dad
☐ Dated
Artist: Bob Siedler
2⁹⁄₁₆" H × 2⁹⁄₁₆" W
$8.95 895QX6532

Baby's First Christmas

Baby's First Christmas

Baby's First Christmas

Mom and Dad

Mom

Dad

Son

Book of the Year

Sister to Sister

Grandma

Daughter

FAMILY
Son
Pressed tin
☐ Dated
Designer: Katrina Bricker
3¹³⁄₁₆" H × 2½" W
$7.95   795QX6605

Daughter
Pressed tin
☐ Dated
Designer: Katrina Bricker
3¹³⁄₁₆" H × 2½" W
$7.95   795QX6612

Book of the Year
Photo Holder
☐ Dated
Artist: Katrina Bricker
2⁷⁄₁₆" H × 3¹⁄₁₆" W
$7.95   795QX6645

Sister to Sister
☐ Dated
Artist: Sharon Pike
2⁹⁄₁₆" H × 2⁷⁄₁₆" W
$9.95   995QX6635

Grandma
☐ Dated
Artist: Sharon Pike
1¹⁵⁄₁₆" H × 1¾" W
$8.95   895QX6625

Granddaughter
☐ Dated
Artist: Sue Tague
2⁷⁄₁₆" H × 1½" W
$7.95   795QX6622

Grandson
☐ Dated
Artist: Sue Tague
2³⁄₈" H × 1⁹⁄₁₆" W
$7.95   795QX6615

Friendship Blend
☐ Dated
Artist: Ed Seale
Illustrator: Tracy Larsen
3¹¹⁄₁₆" H × 2⁵⁄₁₆" W
$9.95   995QX6655

Godchild
☐ Dated
Artist: Katrina Bricker
1⁹⁄₁₆" H × 1½" W
$7.95   795QX6662

New Home
☐ Dated
Artist: Sharon Pike
3⁵⁄₁₆" H × 2¼" W
$8.95   895QX6652

Special Dog
Photo Holder
☐ Dated
Artist: Katrina Bricker
3¹⁄₁₆" H × 2¹¹⁄₁₆" W
$7.95   795QX6632

LOVE
Our First Christmas Together
Acorn home swings to and fro.
☐ Dated
Artist: Ed Seale
3¹⁄₁₆" H × 2⁹⁄₁₆" W
$10.95   1095QX6465

Our Christmas Together
Fine pewter
☐ Dated
2¾" H × 3⅞" W
$16.95   1695QX6475

Granddaughter

Grandson

Friendship Blend

Godchild

New Home

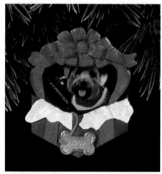
Special Dog

Our First Christmas Together

Our Christmas Together

Our First Christmas Together

Our First Christmas Together

Cycling Santa

Santa's Ski Adventure

Our First Christmas Together
Acrylic
☐ Dated
3⁵⁄₁₆" H × 3³⁄₁₆" W
$7.95   795QX3182

Our First Christmas Together
Photo Holder
☐ Dated
Artist: Sharon Pike
2⁵⁄₁₆" H × 3" W
$8.95   895QX6472

LIFESTYLES AND
OCCUPATIONS
Cycling Santa
Wheels turn.
☐ Dated
Artist: Nello Williams
3⁷⁄₈" H × 3¹³⁄₁₆" W
$14.95   1495QX6425

Santa's Ski Adventure
☐ Dated
Artist: Robert Chad
3⁵⁄₈" H × 2³⁄₈" W
$12.95   1295QX6422

All-Round Sports Fan
☐ Dated
Artist: Nello Williams
2³⁄₈" H × 1¼" W
$8.95   895QX6392

Elegance on Ice
☐ Dated
Artist: Joyce Lyle
4³⁄₁₆" H × 2¹¹⁄₁₆" W
$9.95   995QX6432

All-Weather Walker
☐ Dated
Artist: Nello Williams
3⅛" H × 1¾" W
$8.95   895QX6415

Clever Camper
☐ Dated
Artist: Robert Chad
3¹⁄₁₆" H × 1⁹⁄₁₆" W
$7.95   795QX6445

What a Deal!
☐ Dated
Artist: Sharon Pike
1¹⁵⁄₁₆" H × 3" W
$8.95   895QX6442

Catch of the Day
☐ Dated
Artist: Sue Tague
2½" H × 2⁵⁄₁₆" W
$9.95   995QX6712

Santa's Ski Adventure

All-Round Sports Fan

Elegance on Ice

All-Weather Walker

Clever Camper

What a Deal!

Catch of the Day

LIFESTYLES AND OCCUPATIONS

Bucket Brigade
Dated
Artist: John "Collin" Francis
2¹³⁄₁₆" H × 2³⁄₁₆" W
$8.95   895QX6382

Expressly for Teacher
Dated
Artist: Sue Tague
1⁷⁄₁₆" H × 2½" W
$7.95   795QX6375

Tomorrow's Leader
BOY SCOUTS OF AMERICA
Ceramic
Artwork by Norman Rockwell
Dated
3½" H × 2½" W
$9.95   995QX6452

Christmas Checkup
Dated
Artist: Bob Siedler
2³⁄₈" H × 1¾" W
$7.95   795QX6385

Snow Bowling
Dated
Artist: Nello Williams
2⁷⁄₈" H × 2⁷⁄₁₆" W
$6.95   695QX6395

Love to Sew
Dated
Artist: Sue Tague
1¹³⁄₁₆" H × 1¹³⁄₁₆" W
$7.95   795QX6435

ETHNIC

Stealing a Kiss
Dated
Artist: Sue Tague
2¾" H × 2¹¹⁄₁₆" W
$14.95   1495QX6555

Feliz Navidad
Dated
Artist: Ed Seale
1½" H × 2½" W
$8.95   895QX6665

Snowgirl
Dated
Artist: Sue Tague
2⁷⁄₁₆" H × 1¼" W
$7.95   795QX6562

King Noor—First King
Legend of Three Kings Collection
The legend begins this year. Other
kings will follow. Collector's
card enclosed.
Dated
Artist: Patricia Andrews
5" H × 2¹⁵⁄₁₆" W
$12.95   1295QX6552

Bucket Brigade

Expressly for Teacher

Tomorrow's Leader

Christmas Checkup

Snow Bowling

Stealing a Kiss

Feliz Navidad

Snowgirl

King Noor—First King

Love to Sew

Praise Him

Madonna del Rosario

ETHNIC
Praise Him
☐ Dated
Artist: Linda Sickman
3³⁄₁₆" H × 2¹³⁄₁₆" W
$8.95   895QX6542

Madonna del Rosario
Bartolomé Esteban Murillo
☐ Dated
Frame artist: Linda Sickman
3³⁄₈" H × 2½" W
$12.95   1295QX6545

RELIGIOUS
Heavenly Song
HALLMARK ARCHIVES
COLLECTION
Acrylic
Original artwork by Hallmark
Artist Bob Hass, Masterworks
Collection, Hallmark Archives
Stylist: LaDene Votruba
☐ 3¼" H × 2¼" W
$12.95   1295QX6795

Classic Cross
Precious metal
☐ Dated
Artist: LaDene Votruba
2⁵⁄₁₆" H × 1¾" W
$13.95   1395QX6805

God's Gift of Love
Bisque porcelain
☐ Dated
Artist: Joyce Lyle
4¹⁄₁₆" H × 3⅝" W
$16.95   1695QX6792

Juggling Stars
☐ Dated
Artist: Sue Tague
3¹⁄₁₆" H × 2" W
$9.95   995QX6595

Playful Shepherd
☐ Dated
Artist: Sue Tague
2¹¹⁄₁₆" H × 2¼" W
$9.95   995QX6592

The Spirit of Christmas
Collector's plate
Display stand included.
☐ Dated
Designer: Tracy Larsen
3³⁄₁₆" diameter
$9.95   995QX6585

Nativity Tree
☐ Dated
Artist: Duane Unruh
4¹⁄₁₆" H × 2¼" W
$14.95   1495QX6575

Lion and Lamb
☐ Dated
Artist: Nello Williams
1⅜" H × 2⁵⁄₁₆" W
$7.95   795QX6602

Heavenly Song

Classic Cross

God's Gift of Love

Juggling Stars

Playful Shepherd

The Spirit of Christmas

Nativity Tree

Lion and Lamb

Swinging in the Snow

NBA Collection

NBA COLLECTION
The team's official logo appears on the front of each plaque, while the team's statistics and highlights are detailed on the back. Display stand included. Ceramic.
◻ Dated
2½" H × 3½" W
CHARLOTTE HORNETS™
◻ $9.95   995QSR1222
CHICAGO BULLS™
◻ $9.95   995QSR1232
DETROIT PISTONS™
◻ $9.95   995QSR1242
HOUSTON ROCKETS™
◻ $9.95   995QSR1245
INDIANA PACERS™
◻ $9.95   995QSR1252
LOS ANGELES LAKERS™
◻ $9.95   995QSR1262
NEW YORK KNICKERBOCKERS™
◻ $9.95   995QSR1272
ORLANDO MAGIC™
◻ $9.95   995QSR1282
PHOENIX SUNS™
◻ $9.95   995QSR1292
SEATTLE SUPERSONICS™
◻ $9.95   995QSR1295

GENERAL
Swinging in the Snow
Handcrafted and glass
◻ Dated
Artist: Sue Tague
3⁹⁄₁₆" H × 2½" W
$12.95   1295QX6775

Prize Topiary
Clip-on
◻ Dated
Artist: Ed Seale
2¹⁵⁄₁₆" H × 2⁹⁄₁₆" W
$14.95   1495QX6675

Sweet Dreamer
◻ Dated
Artist: Katrina Bricker
1½" H × 2½" W
$6.95   695QX6732

Breezin' Along
◻ Dated
Artist: Ed Seale
1¹⁵⁄₁₆" H × 1⅞" W
$8.95   895QX6722

Downhill Run
Reindeer rock from side to side.
◻ Dated
Artist: Ken Crow
1½" H × 3¼" W
$9.95   995QX6705

Leading the Way
FOLK ART
AMERICANA COLLECTION
◻ Dated
Artist: Linda Sickman
3¹³⁄₁₆" H × 4⅜" W
$16.95   1695QX6782

Santa's Merry Path
FOLK ART
AMERICANA COLLECTION
◻ Dated
Artist: Linda Sickman
4⅛" H × 2¹³⁄₁₆" W
$16.95   1695QX6785

Jingle Bell Jester
◻ Dated
Artist: Sharon Pike
4½" H × 2¹⁄₁₆" W
$9.95   995QX6695

Santa Mail
◻ Dated
Artist: Nello Williams
2" H × 2⅝" W
$10.95   1095QX6702

Santa Mail

Prize Topiary

Sweet Dreamer

Breezin' Along

Downhill Run

Leading the Way

Santa's Merry Path

Sailor Bear
◻ Dated
Artist: Duane Unruh
2⁵⁄₁₆" H × 1⅜" W
$14.95   1495QX6765

Biking Buddies
◻ Dated
Artist: Don Palmiter
3½" H × 2⅞" W
$12.95   1295QX6682

Jingle Bell Jester

Sailor Bear

Biking Buddies

Garden Bouquet

Garden Bouquet
NATURE'S SKETCHBOOK
▨ Dated
Designer: Marjolein Bastin
Artist: Joyce Lyle
3" H × 3¹⁵⁄₁₆" W
$14.95   1495QX6752

Honored Guests
NATURE'S SKETCHBOOK
▨ Dated
Designer: Marjolein Bastin
Artist: John "Collin" Francis
4¹⁄₁₆" H × 3" W
$14.95   1495QX6745

Santa's Friend
▨ Dated
Designer: Marjolein Bastin
Artist: Duane Unruh
3⁹⁄₁₆" H × 2¹⁄₁₆" W
$12.95   1295QX6685

Santa's Polar Friend
HALLMARK ARCHIVES
COLLECTION
Inspired by an original c. 1880
Victorian decorative image;
Historical Collection, Hallmark
Archives
▨ Dated
Artist: Robert Chad
3³⁄₈" H × 2⁷⁄₈" W
$16.95   1695QX6755

Meadow Snowman
Pressed tin
▨ Dated
Artist: Linda Sickman
4³⁄₁₆" H × 4¹⁄₄" W
$12.95   1295QX6715

Porcelain Hinged Box
Porcelain
Snowman opens at the waist.
▨ Dated
Artist: LaDene Votruba
2⁵⁄₁₆" H × 1¹⁄₄" W
$14.95   1495QX6772

Angel Friend
HALLMARK ARCHIVES
COLLECTION
Porcelain
Inspired by an original c. 1880
Victorian decorative image;
Historical Collection, Hallmark
Archives
▨ Dated
Artist: John "Collin" Francis
3¹³⁄₁₆" H × 2¹⁄₈" W
$14.95   1495QX6762

Honored Guests

Santa's Friend

The Flight at Kitty Hawk

NEW SERIES
The Flight at Kitty Hawk
First in the Sky's the Limit series
This series will highlight historical
aircraft and events in aviation.
▨ Dated
Artist: Lynn Norton
1¹⁄₈" H × 4¹⁄₄" W
$14.95   1495QX5574

Victorian Christmas
Thomas Kinkade, Painter
of Light™
First in the Thomas Kinkade
series
Fine porcelain
▨ Dated
2¹³⁄₁₆" H × 3³⁄₈" W
$10.95   1095QXI6135

Marilyn Monroe
First in the Marilyn Monroe series
Each ornament in this series will
recall a different, glamorous
image of Marilyn.
▨ Dated
Artist: Patricia Andrews
4³⁄₁₆" H × 1¹³⁄₁₆" W
$14.95   1495QX5704

Victorian Christmas—Thomas
Kinkade, Painter of Light™

Marilyn Monroe

Santa's Polar Friend

Meadow Snowman

Porcelain Hinged Box

Angel Friend

Santa's Magical Sleigh

The Night Before Christmas

ARTIST'S STUDIO COLLECTION
Santa's Magical Sleigh
Santa's Victorian sleigh is guided by two beautiful reindeer; a wonderful bag of toys helps make dreams come true.
▢ Dated
Artist: Duane Unruh
2¹³⁄₁₆" H × 5" W
$24.00   2400QX6672

The Night Before Christmas
Clara Johnson Scroggins named this as her 1997 COLLECTOR'S CHOICE. Plays "Santa Claus is Comin' to Town." Windup music and movement.
▢ Dated
Artist: Ken Crow
4⅝" H × 3" W
$24.00   2400QX5721

Luke Skywalker™
First in the STAR WARS™ series
▢ Dated
Artist: Dill Rhodus
4¹³⁄₁₆" H × 1⅞" W
$13.95   1395QXI5484

Scarlett O'Hara™
First in the Scarlett O'Hara™ series
This series will feature the lavish costumes from the classic 1939 film *Gone With the Wind™*.
▢ Dated
Artist: Patricia Andrews
4¼" H × 2⅛" W
$14.95   1495QX6125

Luke Skywalker™

The Clauses on Vacation
First in The Clauses on Vacation series
This series will portray Santa and Mrs. Claus enjoying a different "dream vacation" each year.
▢ Dated
Artist: Bob Siedler
2⁷⁄₁₆" H × 2½" W
$14.95   1495QX6112

Jeff Gordon®
First in the Stock Car Champions series
This series will feature a different outstanding driver and car each year. Hallmark-exclusive Classic trading card included.
▢ Artist: Ed Seale
4¼" H × 3⅝" W
$15.95   1595QXI6165

Scarlett O'Hara™

Snowshoe Rabbits in Winter
First in the Majestic Wilderness series—Mark Newman
▢ Dated
2⁷⁄₁₆" H × 2⅞" W
$12.95   1295QX5694

Wayne Gretzky
First in the Hockey Greats series
This series will feature a different outstanding hockey player each year. Hallmark-exclusive Classic trading card included.
▢ Dated
Artist: Duane Unruh
4¹³⁄₁₆" H × 4¹⁵⁄₁₆" W
$15.95   1595QXI6275

Cinderella
First in the Enchanted Memories Collection
▢ Dated
4¾" H × 2¾" W
$14.95   1495QXD4045

Donald's Surprising Gift
First in the Hallmark Archives series
▢ Dated
2⅛" H × 2⁵⁄₁₆" W
$12.95   1295QXD4025

Bandleader Mickey
First in the Mickey's Holiday Parade series
▢ Dated
3⅛" H × 2" W
$13.95   1395QXD4022

The Clauses on Vacation

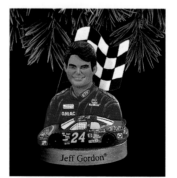
Jeff Gordon®

Snowshoe Rabbits in Winter

Wayne Gretzky

Cinderella

Donald's Surprising Gift

Bandleader Mickey

Little Red Riding Hood—1991

Nikki—All God's Children®

Snowdrop Angel

Chinese BARBIE™

1950 Santa Fe F3 Diesel Locomotive

Hank Aaron

Joe Namath

Magic Johnson

1953 GMC

A Celebration of Angels

Yuletide Central

Wedding Day 1959–1962

ONGOING SERIES

Little Red Riding Hood—1991
Second in the Madame Alexander™ series
▪ Dated
Artist: John "Collin" Francis
3⅜" H × 3" W
$14.95   1495QX6155

Nikki—All God's Children®
Martha Root
Second in the All God's Children® series
Two-piece set
▪ Dated
Nikki: 3⁹⁄₁₆" H × 1½" W
Bear: 1½" H × 1½" W
$12.95   1295QX6142

Snowdrop Angel
Second in The Language of Flowers series
Silver-plated container
▪ Dated
Artist: Sue Tague
3¹³⁄₁₆" H × 2" W
$15.95   1595QX1095

Chinese BARBIE™
Second in the "Dolls of the World" series
▪ Dated
Artist: Anita Marra Rogers
4½" H × 1⅛" W
$14.95   1495QX6162

1950 Santa Fe F3 Diesel Locomotive
Second in the LIONEL® Train series
Die-cast metal. Wheels turn.
▪ Dated
1⅛" H × 4" W
$18.95   1895QX6145

Hank Aaron
Second in the At the Ballpark series
Hallmark-exclusive Classic trading card included.
▪ Artist: Dill Rhodus
4³⁄₁₆" H × 2½" W
$14.95   1495QXI6152

Joe Namath
Third in the Football Legends series
Hallmark-exclusive Classic trading card included.
▪ Artist: Dill Rhodus
4⁹⁄₁₆" H × 2¼" W
$14.95   1495QXI6182

Magic Johnson
Third in the Hoop Stars series
Hallmark-exclusive Classic trading card included.
▪ 5½" H × 2¼" W
$14.95   1495QXI6832

1953 GMC
Third in the All-American Trucks series
Wheels turn.
▪ Dated
Artist: Don Palmiter
1⅝" H × 4⅜" W
$13.95   1395QX6105

A Celebration of Angels
Third in A Celebration of Angels series
▪ Dated
Artist: Patricia Andrews
4¹⁵⁄₁₆" H × 2⅝" W
$13.95   1395QX6175

Yuletide Central
Fourth in the Yuletide Central series
Pressed tin. Wheels turn and doors of car slide open.
▪ Dated
Artist: Linda Sickman
2⁵⁄₁₆" H × 3½" W
$18.95   1895QX5812

Wedding Day 1959–1962
Fourth in the BARBIE™ Ornament series
▪ Dated
Artist: Patricia Andrews
4⁹⁄₁₆" H × 2³⁄₁₆" W
$15.95   1595QXI6812

Cat Naps

Murray® Dump Truck

Holiday BARBIE™

1969 Hurst Oldsmobile 442

Puppy Love

Fabulous Decade

Merry Olde Santa

Bright Rocking Colors

Daisy—Mary's Angels

Cafe

ONGOING SERIES

Cat Naps
Fourth in the Cat Naps series
Dated
Artist: Katrina Bricker
2½" H × 2¼" W
$8.95   895QX6205

Murray® Dump Truck
Fourth in the Kiddie Car
Classics series
Cast metal. Movable tailgate and
dumping mechanism.
Dated
Artist: Don Palmiter
2¹⁄₁₆" H × 4" W
$13.95   1395QX6195

Holiday BARBIE™
Fifth in the Holiday BARBIE™
Ornament series
Dated
Artist: Patricia Andrews
3⁹⁄₁₆" H × 3" W
$15.95   1595QXI6212

1969 Hurst Oldsmobile 442
Seventh in the Classic American
Cars series
Wheels turn.
Dated
Artist: Don Palmiter
1¼" H × 4⅛" W
$13.95   1395QX6102

Puppy Love
Seventh in the Puppy Love series
Brass tag
Dated
Artist: Anita Marra Rogers
1¹⁵⁄₁₆" H × 2³⁄₁₆" W
$7.95   795QX6222

Fabulous Decade
Eighth in the Fabulous
Decade series
Brass date
Artist: Sharon Pike
1⅞" H × 2" W
$7.95   795QX6232

Merry Olde Santa
Eighth in the Merry Olde
Santa series
Dated
Artist: Joyce Lyle
4⁷⁄₁₆" H × 2⅝" W
$14.95   1495QX6225

Bright Rocking Colors
Ninth in the CRAYOLA®
Crayon series
Dated
Artist: Sue Tague
3¾" H × 4¼" W
$12.95   1295QX6235

Daisy—Mary's Angels
10th in the Mary's
Angels series
Designer: Mary Hamilton
Artist: Robert Chad
2⁹⁄₁₆" H × 1¾" W
$7.95   795QX6242

Cafe
14th in the Nostalgic Houses and
Shops series
Dated
Artist: Don Palmiter
3⁹⁄₁₆" H × 2⅞" W
$16.95   1695QX6245

Frosty Friends

The Claus-Mobile

Kolyada

Santa Claus

Jackie Robinson

Little Boy Blue

Mickey's Long Shot

New Pair of Skates

Mickey's Snow Angel

Goofy's Ski Adventure

Frosty Friends
18th in the Frosty Friends series
⬜ Dated
Artist: Ed Seale
5" H × 3 1/16" W
$10.95   1095QX6255

The Claus-Mobile
19th in the Here Comes
Santa series
Wheels turn.
⬜ Dated
Artist: Sue Tague
2 1/8" H × 3 3/4" W
$14.95   1495QX6262

FINAL EDITIONS
Kolyada
Third and final in the
Christmas Visitors series
⬜ Dated
Artist: LaDene Votruba
4 3/8" H × 2 1/16" W
$14.95   1495QX6172

Santa Claus
Third and final in the Turn-of-
the-Century Parade series
Die-cast metal and brass. Wheels
turn and bell rings.
⬜ Dated
Artist: Ken Crow
3 3/16" H × 3 9/16" W
$16.95   1695QX1215

Jackie Robinson
50th Anniversary 1947–1997
Fourth and final in the Baseball
Heroes series
⬜ Dated
Artist: Dill Rhodus
3 3/8" diameter
$12.95   1295QX6202

Little Boy Blue
Fifth and final in the Mother
Goose series
Book opens to display verse.
⬜ Dated
Artist: Ed Seale
Illustrator: LaDene Votruba
2 1/2" H × 2 1/16" W
$13.95   1395QX6215

DISNEY COLLECTION
Mickey's Long Shot
⬜ Dated
3 1/8" H × 2 1/8" W
$10.95   1095QXD6412

New Pair of Skates
⬜ Dated
2 3/4" H × 2 3/4" W
$13.95   1395QXD4032

Mickey's Snow Angel
⬜ Dated
2 1/2" H × 2 3/8" W
$9.95   995QXD4035

Goofy's Ski Adventure
⬜ Dated
2 7/8" H × 3 1/8" W
$12.95   1295QXD4042

Two-Tone

DISNEY COLLECTION

Two-Tone
101 Dalmatians
▨ 3¹⁄₁₆" H × 1⅝" W
$9.95   995QXD4015

Gus and Jaq
Cinderella
▨ Dated
2³⁄₁₆" H × 1¼" W
$12.95   1295QXD4052

Timon and Pumbaa
The Lion King
▨ Dated
2⅜" H × 1⅞" W
$12.95   1295QXD4065

Jasmine and Aladdin
Aladdin and the King of Thieves
▨ Dated
2½" H × 2¹¹⁄₁₆" W
$14.95   1495QXD4062

Phoebus and Esmeralda
*The Hunchback of
Notre Dame*
▨ 4¾" H × 1⅝" W
$14.95   1495QXD6344

**Snow White, Anniversary
Edition**
Set of two ornaments
▨ Dated
Snow White:
2¾" H × 2⅛" W
Dopey: 3" H × 11½" W
$16.95   1695QXD4055

Ariel
The Little Mermaid
▨ 4½" H × 3³⁄₁₆" W
$12.95   1295QXI4072

Hercules
▨ 4⅝" H × 4" W
$12.95   1295QXI4005

Megara and Pegasus
Hercules
▨ 3¹⁄₁₆" H × 4½" W
$16.95   1695QXI4012

**Waitin' on Santa—Winnie
the Pooh**
▨ 2⅝" H × 2¹⁄₁₆" W
$12.95   1295QXD6365

Gus and Jaq

Timon and Pumbaa

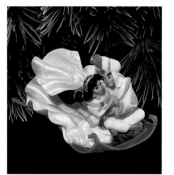

Jasmine and Aladdin

Phoebus and Esmeralda

Snow White, Anniversary Edition

Ariel

Hercules

Megara and Pegasus

Waitin' on Santa—Winnie the Pooh

POP CULTURE ICONS

Michigan J. Frog
LOONEY TUNES™
▨ Artist: Robert Chad
3³⁄₈" H × 1³⁄₈" W
$9.95   995QX6332

Miss Gulch
THE WIZARD OF OZ™
Bicycle wheels turn.
▨ Artist: Joyce Lyle
4⁷⁄₁₆" H × 4¹⁄₈" W
$13.95   1395QX6372

Tonka® Mighty Front Loader
Die-cast metal. Front bucket
assembly pivots and wheels turn.
▨ Dated
1½" H × 3¼" W
$13.95   1395QX6362

The Lone Ranger™
Pressed tin. Lunch box opens
and closes.
▨ Dated
Designer: Steve Goslin
2¹¹⁄₁₆" H × 3³⁄₁₆" W
$12.95   1295QX6265

Sweet Discovery
HERSHEY'S™
▨ Dated
Artist: Linda Sickman
3⁷⁄₁₆" H × 2⁷⁄₈" W
$11.95   1195QX6325

Mr. Potato Head®
▨ Dated
Design: Bob Siedler
3½" H × 3½" W
$10.95   1095QX6335

Howdy Doody™
ANNIVERSARY EDITION
50 Years of "It's Howdy
Doody™ Time!"
▨ Dated
Artist: Tracy Larsen
3½" H × 2³⁄₁₆" W
$12.95   1295QX6272

Taking a Break
"Coca-Cola®" Santa
▨ Dated
Artist: Duane Unruh
3⁵⁄₈" H × 2⁷⁄₁₆" W
$14.95   1495QX6305

The Incredible Hulk®
▨ 3¼" H × 3½" W
$12.95   1295QX5471

Marbles Champion
Norman Rockwell Art. Inspired
by *The Saturday Evening Post*
Cover: September 2, 1939.
▨ Dated
Artist: Duane Unruh
3¾" H × 2¾" W
$10.95   1095QX6342

Michigan J. Frog

Miss Gulch

Tonka® Mighty Front Loader

The Lone Ranger™

Sweet Discovery

Mr. Potato Head®

Howdy Doody™

Taking a Break

The Incredible Hulk®

Marbles Champion

Glowing Angel

Madonna and Child

SNOOPY Plays Santa

Decorator Taz

MAGIC RELIGIOUS
Glowing Angel
Halo and wings have a soft glow.
▢ Dated
Artist: LaDene Votruba
4⅝" H × 2⁷⁄₁₆" W
$18.95   1895QLX7435

Madonna and Child
Clouds are softly highlighted
with light.
▢ Dated
Artist: Joyce Lyle
3⅞" diameter
$19.95   1995QLX7425

MAGIC GENERAL
SNOOPY Plays Santa
PEANUTS®
Doghouse sleigh circles
home below.
▢ Dated
Artist: Anita Marra Rogers
4⅛" H × 3⁹⁄₁₆" W
$22.00   2200QLX7475

Decorator Taz
LOONEY TUNES™
Taz spins and circles the lighted
Christmas tree.
▢ Dated
Artist: Robert Chad
4½" H × 3¼" W
$30.00   3000QLX7502

The Lincoln Memorial
Light and music. Plays "America
the Beautiful." Includes
collector's card.
▢ Dated
Artist: Ed Seale
4½" H × 2⁹⁄₁₆" W
$24.00   2400QLX7522

Santa's Showboat
MAGIC SPECIAL EDITION
Plays "Jingle Bells." Paddle wheel
turns and running lights
operate. Light flickers above
steamboat's chimneys and
portholes glow constantly.
▢ Dated
Artist: Ken Crow
3⁷⁄₁₆" H × 5⅝" W
$42.00   4200QLX7465

The Lincoln Memorial

Darth Vader™

MAGIC SPECIAL ISSUES
Darth Vader™
STAR WARS™
His lightsaber glows, and he
says, "The Force is with you,
young Skywalker. But you are
not a Jedi yet!"
▢ Dated
Artist: Dill Rhodus
5" H × 2¹³⁄₁₆" W
$24.00   2400QXI7531

**The Warmth of Home
Thomas Kinkade, Painter
of Light™**
Light glows softly in
mountain background.
▢ Dated
Artist: Tracy Larsen
3⅝" H × 3¼" W
$18.95   1895QXI7545

U.S.S. Defiant™
STAR TREK: Deep Space Nine
Light and blinking lights
▢ Stardated
Artist: Lynn Norton
⁹⁄₁₆" H × 4 ¾" W
$24.00   2400QXI7481

Santa's Showboat—MAGIC SPECIAL EDITION

The Warmth of Home—Thomas
Kinkade, Painter of Light™

U.S.S. Defiant™

Motorcycle Chums

Teapot Party

Joy to the World

Santa's Secret Gift

Holiday Serenade

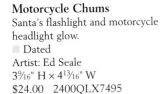

Motorcycle Chums
Santa's flashlight and motorcycle
headlight glow.
☐ Dated
Artist: Ed Seale
3⁹/₁₆" H × 4¹³/₁₆" W
$24.00   2400QLX7495

Teapot Party
Light inside teapot glows.
☐ Dated
Artist: Sue Tague
3¹⁵/₁₆" H × 4⅞" W
$18.95   1895QLX7482

Joy to the World
Globe glows softly.
☐ Dated
Artist: Sue Tague
3½" H × 4¼" W
$14.95   1495QLX7512

Santa's Secret Gift
Plays "Jolly Old St. Nicholas."
Santa holds a gift bag that can
hold a small gift or message.
☐ Dated
Artist: Robert Chad
4½" H × 2¾" W
$24.00   2400QLX7455

Holiday Serenade
Light glows from inside
birdhouse, and the cardinals sing.
☐ Dated
Artist: John "Collin" Francis
2¹⁵/₁₆" H × 3⁵/₁₆" W
$24.00   2400QLX7485

MAGIC NEW SERIES
Lighthouse Greetings
First in the Lighthouse
Greeting series
This series will depict styles of
lighthouses from various loca-
tions. Beacon light flashes, and
light glows inside home and on
Christmas tree.
☐ Dated
Artist: John "Collin" Francis
4¾" H × 3" W
$24.00   2400QLX7442

MAGIC ONGOING SERIES
Friendship 7
Second in the Journeys into
Space series
Commemorates the first
American manned orbital space-
flight 35 years ago. Light and
voice. Plays an original transmis-
sion from this flight.
☐ Dated
Artist: Ed Seale
2¹¹/₁₆" H × 5⅜" W
$24.00   2400QLX7532

Lighthouse Greetings

Friendship 7

MAGIC FINAL EDITION
Chris Mouse Luminaria
13th and final in the Chris
Mouse series
"Candle" glows softly.
☐ Dated
Artist: Bob Siedler
3¹¹/₁₆" H × 2¾" W
$14.95   1495QLX7525

Chris Mouse Luminaria

Miniature Ornament Collection
1997

Two Collector's Classics sets debuted for 1997—a three-piece set saluted the movie *Casablanca™*, and a four-piece set called **King of the Forest** gave us our four favorite friends from *The Wizard of Oz™* in miniature.

New series included Antique Tractors, Welcome Friends, Snowflake Ballet, and Teddy-Bear Style. Three series—Santa's Little Big Top, Village Depot, and Rocking Horse—came to an end while about a dozen series kept going.

It's easy to see how the popularity of Keepsake Miniature Ornament collecting has grown—there are 33 miniature ornaments in the 1997 line!

Herr Drosselmeyer

Miniature Clothespin Soldier

Murray, Inc. "Pursuit" Airplane

ONGOING SERIES

Herr Drosselmeyer
Second of five ornaments in The Nutcracker Ballet series
☐ Dated
Artist: LaDene Votruba
1⅝" H × ⅝" W
$5.95   595QXM4135

Miniature Clothespin Soldier
Third in the Miniature Clothespin Soldier series
Arms move back and forth.
☐ Artist: Linda Sickman
1³⁄₁₆" H × ⅝" W
$4.95   495QXM4155

White Rabbit
Third in the Alice in Wonderland series
☐ Dated
Artist: Patricia Andrews
1¹¹⁄₁₆" H × ¹¹⁄₁₆" W
$6.95   695QXM4142

Murray Inc.® "Pursuit" Airplane
Third in the Miniature Kiddie Car Classic series
Die-cast metal
☐ Dated
Artist: Don Palmiter
⅝" H × 1³⁄₁₆" W
$6.95   695QXM4132

White Rabbit

C-3PO™ AND R2-D2™ STAR WARS™
Set of two ornaments
☐ Dated
Artist: Dill Rhodus
C-3PO™: 2" H × 1" W
R2-D2™: 1¼" H × ⅞" W
$12.95   1295QXI4265

Miniature 1997 Corvette
☐ Dated
Artist: Don Palmiter
⅜" H × 1⁵⁄₁₆" W
$6.95   695QXI4322

NEW SERIES

Welcome Friends
First in the Welcome Friends series
☐ Dated
Artist: Sharon Pike
¹³⁄₁₆" H × 1" W
$6.95   695QXM4205

Snowflake Ballet
First in the Snowflake Ballet series
☐ Dated
Artist: Patricia Andrews
1½" H × ¹⁵⁄₁₆" W
$5.95   595QXM4192

Teddy-Bear Style
First in the Teddy-Bear Style series
Arms and legs move.
☐ Dated
Artist: Duane Unruh
1⁵⁄₁₆" H × ¹¹⁄₁₆" W
$5.95   595QXM4215

Antique Tractor
First in the Antique Tractors series
Wheels turn and front cross bar pivots left and right. Die-cast metal.
☐ Dated
Artist: Linda Sickman
¹³⁄₁₆" H × 1³⁄₁₆" W
$6.95   695QXM4185

Teddy-Bear Style

C-3PO™ and R2-D2™—STAR WARS™

Miniature 1997 Corvette

Welcome Friends

Snowflake Ballet

Antique Tractor

Christmas Bells
Third in the Christmas
Bells series
Handcrafted and metal
■ Dated
Artist: Ed Seale
1⁵⁄₁₆" H × 1³⁄₁₆" W
$4.95   495QXM4162

Christmas Bells

Nutcracker Guild

Centuries of Santa

Nutcracker Guild
Fourth in the Nutcracker
Guild series
Opens and closes like a
real nutcracker.
■ Dated
Artist: Linda Sickman
1³⁄₁₆" H × ⁷⁄₈" W
$6.95   695QXM4165

Centuries of Santa
Fourth in the Centuries of
Santa series
■ Dated
Artist: Linda Sickman
1³⁄₈" H × ¾" W
$5.95   595QXM4295

On the Road

Candy Car

On the Road
Fifth in the On the Road series
Pressed tin. Wheels turn.
■ Dated
Artist: Linda Sickman
⁷⁄₁₆" H × 1¼" W
$5.95   595QXM4172

FINAL EDITIONS
Santa's Little Big Top
Third and final in the Santa's
Little Big Top series
Turn knob at bottom to watch
the elephants perform.
■ Dated
Artist: Ken Crow
1⁵⁄₈" H × 1¹⁄₁₆" W
$6.95   695QXM4152

Candy Car
Ninth in the Noel R.R. series
■ Dated
Artist: Linda Sickman
¹³⁄₁₆" H × 1⁵⁄₁₆" W
$6.95   695QXM4175

Village Depot
10th and final in the Old English
Village series
■ Dated
Artist: Tracy Larsen
1³⁄₁₆" H × 1³⁄₁₆" W
$6.95   695QXM4182

Santa's Little Big Top

Village Depot

Rocking Horse
10th and final in the Rocking
Horse series
■ Dated
Artist: Linda Sickman
1⅛" H × 1³⁄₈" W
$4.95   495QXM4302

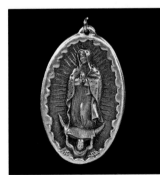
Our Lady of Guadalupe

GENERAL
He Is Born
■ Dated
Artist: LaDene Votruba
1¼" H × ¹⁵⁄₁₆" W
$7.95   795QXM4235

Rocking Horse

He Is Born

PRECIOUS EDITION
Our Lady of Guadalupe
This Keepsake Ornament honors
the patron saint of Mexico.
Fine pewter.
■ Dated
Artist: Robert Chad
1⁷⁄₁₆" H × ⁷⁄₈" W
$8.95   895QXM4275

Seeds of Joy
■ Dated
Artist: Sue Tague
1³⁄₁₆" H × 1" W
$6.95   695QXM4242

Sew Talented
■ Dated
Artist: Ed Seale
1" H × 1⁵⁄₁₆" W
$5.95   595QXM4195

Seeds of Joy

Sew Talented

Gentle Giraffes

Home Sweet Home

Shutterbug

Future Star

Heavenly Music

GENERAL
Gentle Giraffes
Complements "Noah's Ark"
Special Edition set introduced
in 1994
▨ Artist: Linda Sickman
1$\frac{7}{16}$" H × 1$\frac{3}{8}$" W
$5.95   595QXM4221

Home Sweet Home
▨ Dated
Artist: Ed Seale
1$\frac{3}{16}$" H × 1" W
$5.95   595QXM4222

Shutterbug
▨ Dated
Artist: Sue Tague
1$\frac{1}{16}$" H × $\frac{9}{16}$" W
$5.95   595QXM4212

Future Star
▨ Dated
Artist: Sharon Pike
1$\frac{3}{4}$" H × $\frac{3}{8}$" W
$5.95   595QXM4232

Heavenly Music
▨ Dated
Artist: Sue Tague
1" H × $\frac{5}{8}$" W
$5.95   595QXM4292

Tiny Home Improvers
Six-piece set
▨ Dated
Artist: Ed Seale
Master Painter: 1$\frac{1}{8}$" H × $\frac{11}{16}$" W
Dunn Workin': $\frac{9}{16}$" H × $\frac{5}{8}$" W
Pipe Dreams: $\frac{11}{16}$" H × 1$\frac{1}{8}$" W
Wally Paper: $\frac{13}{16}$" H × $\frac{3}{4}$" W
Sam Sawyer: 1" H × 1$\frac{1}{16}$" W
Art Lover: $\frac{7}{8}$" H × $\frac{3}{4}$" W
$29.00   2900QXM4282

DISNEY
**Honey of a Gift
—Winnie the Pooh**
▨ 1" H × $\frac{13}{16}$" W
$6.95   695QXD4255

Tiny Home Improvers

Honey of a Gift—Winnie the Pooh

Victorian Skater
- Dated
Artist: Duane Unruh
1³⁄₁₆" H × ⁷⁄₈" W
$5.95 595QXM4305

Peppermint Painter
- Dated
Artist: Sue Tague
1⅛" H × ¾" W
$4.95 495QXM4312

Victorian Skater

Peppermint Painter

Snowboard Bunny
- Dated
Artist: Sue Tague
1³⁄₁₆" H × ¾" W
$4.95 495QXM4315

Polar Buddies
- Dated
Artist: John "Collin" Francis
⁷⁄₈" H × ¹⁵⁄₁₆" W
$4.95 495QXM4332

Snowboard Bunny   Polar Buddies

COLLECTOR'S CLASSICS
Ice Cold Coca-Cola®
- Artist: Robert Chad
1⅛" H × ¾" W
$6.95 695QXM4252

Casablanca™
Three-piece set. This set salutes
the 1942 film classic, winner of
three Oscars. One ornament,
which reproduces the original
theater lobby poster, displays on
the back the familiar phrase,
"Here's looking at you, kid."
- Dated
Artist: Patricia Andrews
Poster: 3⅛" H × 2" W
Humphry Bogart: 2³⁄₁₆" H × ⅝" W
Ingrid Bergman: 2⅛" H × ⁹⁄₁₆" W
$19.95 1995QXM4272

King of the Forest
The Wizard of Oz™
Four-piece set
- Artist: Anita Marra Rogers
Dorothy™: 1⅝" H × 1¼" W
Scarecrow™: 1⅝" H × ⁷⁄₈" W
Cowardly Lion™:
1¹¹⁄₁₆" H × 1⁹⁄₁₆" W
Tin Man™: 1¹⁵⁄₁₆" H × ¹¹⁄₁₆" W
$24.00 2400QXM4262

Ice Cold Coca-Cola®

Casablanca™

King of the Forest, *The Wizard of Oz™*

Spring Ornament Collection
1997

Think Spring! That was the thrust in 1997 as the Easter Ornament Collection expanded its focus to become the Spring Ornament Collection. This focus, which Hallmark adopted in answer to collector requests, broadened the line beyond Easter and gave us ornaments to display throughout the season.

In other news, the **1935 Steelcraft Streamline Velocipede by Murray®** pedaled in as a first in the Sidewalk Cruisers series (it was a hit!), and the Children's Collector Series based on Mattel's children's story BARBIE® dolls debuted with **Based on the BARBIE® as Rapunzel Doll**. The Springtime Barbie™, Apple Blossom Lane, Springtime Bonnets, Collector's Plate, and Here Comes Easter series ended, and four series continued. Three ornaments celebrating the Christian Easter observance spoke to collectors' growing interest in spiritual beliefs, and a design by Marjolein Bastin graced the offering for the first time.

1935 Steelcraft Streamline Velocipede by Murray®

Based on the BARBIE® as Rapunzel doll

NEW SERIES
1935 Steelcraft Streamline Velocipede by Murray®
First in the Sidewalk Cruisers series
Die-cast metal
▪ Dated
Artist: Dill Rhodus
1¾" H × 1⅝" W
$12.95   1295QEO8632

Based on the BARBIE® as Rapunzel doll
First in the Children's Collector Ornament series
▪ Dated
Artist: Anita Marra Rogers
3½" H × 1⅝" W
$14.95   1495QEO8635

ONGOING SERIES
Colorful Coal Car
Second in the Cottontail Express series
▪ Dated
Artist: Ken Crow
1½" H × 1" W
$8.95   895QEO8652

Jemima Puddle-duck™
Second in the Beatrix Potter™ series
▪ Dated
Artist: LaDene Votruba
2½" H × 1¼" W
$8.95   895QEO8645

Joyful Angels
Second in the Joyful Angels series
▪ Dated
Artist: Joyce Lyle
3¹¹⁄₁₆" H × 1⁵⁄₁₆" W
$10.95   1095QEO8655

Garden Club
Third in the Garden Club series
▪ Dated
Artist: Katrina Bricker
1½" H × 1" W
$7.95   795QEO8665

FINAL EDITIONS
Springtime BARBIE™
Third and final in the Springtime BARBIE™ series
▪ Dated
Artist: Patricia Andrews
3½" H × 2⅛" W
$12.95   1295QEO8642

Apple Blossom Lane
Third and final in the Apple Blossom Lane series
▪ Dated
Artist: John "Collin" Francis
2⁵⁄₁₆" H × 1⅝" W
$8.95   895QEO8662

Colorful Coal Car

Jemima Puddle-duck™

Joyful Angels

Garden Club

Springtime BARBIE™

Apple Blossom Lane

Here Comes Easter
Fourth and final in the Here
Comes Easter series
☐ Dated
Artist: Ken Crow
2⅛" H × 1¼" W
$7.95   795QEO8682

Collector's Plate
"Sunny Sunday Best"
Fourth and final in the Collector's
Plate series
Hand-painted fine porcelain
☐ Dated
Artist: LaDene Votruba
2⅝" diameter
$7.95   795QEO8675

Springtime Bonnets
Fifth and final in the Springtime
Bonnets series
☐ Dated
Artist: Sharon Pike
2⁵⁄₁₆" H × 1¾" W
$7.95   795QEO8672

GENERAL
Eggs-pert Artist—
CRAYOLA® Crayon
☐ Dated
Artist: Sue Tague
1½" H × 1¼" W
$8.95   895QEO8695

Swing-Time
☐ Dated
Artist: Sue Tague
3¼" H × 1¼" W
$7.95   795QEO8705

A Purr-fect Princess
☐ Dated
Artist: Sharon Pike
2³⁄₁₆" H × 1⅝" W
$7.95   795QEO8715

Victorian Cross
Fine pewter
☐ 2¼" H × 1½" W
$8.95   895QEO8725

Gentle Guardian
Original artwork:
Scott Freeman
☐ Stylist: Tracy Larsen
3" H × 1¼" W
$6.95   695QEO8732

Digging In
☐ Dated
Artist: Ed Seale
Illustrator: LaDene Votruba
2³⁄₁₆" H × 2½" W
$7.95   795QEO8712

Garden Bunnies
Nature's Sketchbook
☐ Dated
Designer: Marjolein Bastin
Artist: Duane Unruh
3" H × ⁷⁄₁₆" W
$14.95   1495QEO8702

Bumper Crop, Tender
Touches
Set of three ornaments
☐ Dated
Artist: Ed Seale
Grade A Packer: 2" H × 1¾" W
First Taster: 1½" H × ¹³⁄₁₆" W
24-Carrot Dreams:
1⅝" H × 1⅜" W
$14.95   1495QEO8735

Here Comes Easter

Collector's Plate

Springtime Bonnets

Eggs-pert Artist—CRAYOLA® Crayon

Swing-Time

A Purr-fect Princess

Gentle Guardian

Digging In

Garden Bunnies, Nature's Sketchbook

Bumper Crop, Tender Touches

Victorian Cross

The Memories and Magic Ornament Collection
1996

In 1996, we celebrated the 100th anniversary of the modern Olympic Games with six ornaments, and we celebrated 30 years of STAR TREK® with a special anniversary set.

It was a banner year of series firsts—LIONEL® train (a series of engines), BARBIE™ "Dolls of the World," All God's Children®, and Madame Alexander™. In particular, At the Ballpark (Nolan Ryan on the mound) and The Language of Flowers (wildly popular in its first year!) were among the most delightful series firsts.

Baby Boomers' childhood nostalgia made an impact—**Olive Oyl and Swee' Pea, Tonka® Mighty Dump Truck,** and **THE JETSONS™** took us back in time. So did the first in the Journeys Into Space series, which celebrated the 35th anniversary of the first American manned spaceflight.

I felt truly honored with a first for me: Hallmark asked me to select one ornament from the 1996 line to be designated as my Collector's Choice. I picked **Come All Ye Faithful** because it tells a story and represents the true meaning of Christmas.

NFL Collection

NFL COLLECTION
☐ Dated
Artist: Duane Unruh
3" H × 1⅞" W

ARIZONA CARDINALS™
☐ $9.95   995QSR6484
ATLANTA FALCONS™
☐ $9.95   995QSR6364
BROWNS™
☐ $9.95   995QSR6391
BUFFALO BILLS™
☐ $9.95   995QSR6371
CAROLINA PANTHERS™
☐ $9.95   995QSR6374
CHICAGO BEARS™
☐ $9.95   995QSR6381
CINCINNATI BENGALS™
☐ $9.95   995QSR6384
DALLAS COWBOYS™
☐ $9.95   995QSR6394
DENVER BRONCOS™
☐ $9.95   995QSR6411
DETROIT LIONS™
☐ $9.95   995QSR6414
GREEN BAY PACKERS™
☐ $9.95   995QSR6421
INDIANAPOLIS COLTS™
☐ $9.95   995QSR6431
JACKSONVILLE JAGUARS™
☐ $9.95   995QSR6434
KANSAS CITY CHIEFS™
☐ $9.95   995QSR6361

MIAMI DOLPHINS™
☐ $9.95   995QSR6451
MINNESOTA VIKINGS™
☐ $9.95   995QSR6454
NEW ENGLAND PATRIOTS™
☐ $9.95   995QSR6461
NEW ORLEANS SAINTS™
☐ $9.95   995QSR6464
NEW YORK GIANTS™
☐ $9.95   995QSR6471
NEW YORK JETS™
☐ $9.95   995QSR6474
OAKLAND RAIDERS™
☐ $9.95   995QSR6441
OILERS™
☐ $9.95   995QSR6424
PHILADELPHIA EAGLES™
☐ $9.95   995QSR6481
PITTSBURG STEELERS™
☐ $9.95   995QSR6491
ST. LOUIS RAMS™
☐ $9.95   995QSR6444
SAN DIEGO CHARGERS™
☐ $9.95   995QSR6494
SAN FRANCISCO 49ERS™
☐ $9.95   995QSR6501
SEATTLE SEAHAWKS™
☐ $9.95   995QSR6504
TAMPA BAY BUCCANEERS™
☐ $9.95   995QSR6511
WASHINGTON REDSKINS™
☐ $9.95   995QSR6514

When the 1996 NFL Collection was produced, two teams—the BROWNS™ and the OILERS™—were in the process of name and/or location change. Therefore, the ornaments for those teams were produced without mention of city name.

Parade of Nations

Olympic Triumph

IZZY™—The Mascot

Invitation to the Games

THE OLYMPIC SPIRIT COLLECTION
Parade of Nations
Collector's plate. Display stand included. Fine porcelain.
☐ Dated
3³⁄₁₆" diameter
$10.95   1095QXE5741

Olympic Triumph
☐ Dated
Artist: Ed Seale
4¹⁄₁₆" H × 2¹³⁄₁₆" W
$10.95   1095QXE5731

IZZY™—The Mascot
☐ Dated
Artist: Don Palmiter
3¹¹⁄₁₆" H × 2¹¹⁄₁₆" W
$9.95   995QXE5724

Invitation to the Games
Set of two trading-card size plaques with commemorative copy. Ceramic. Display stands included.
☐ Dated
Stylist: Diana McGehee
3½" H × 2½" W
$14.95   1495QXE5511

CHILD'S AGE COLLECTION
Baby's First Christmas
▨ Dated
Artist: Ken Crow
2³⁄₁₆" H × 1⅝" W
$7.95   795QX5764

Baby's Second Christmas
▨ Dated
Artist: Ken Crow
2⅜" H × 2" W
$7.95   795QX5771

Child's Third Christmas
▨ Dated
Artist: Ken Crow
2⁹⁄₁₆" H × 2¹⁄₁₆" W
$7.95   795QX5774

Child's Fourth Christmas
▨ Dated
Artist: Ken Crow
2¹¹⁄₁₆" H × 2⁵⁄₁₆" W
$7.95   795QX5781

Child's Fifth Christmas
▨ Dated
Artist: Dill Rhodus
2⅜" H × 3½" W
$6.95   695QX5784

BABY
Baby's First Christmas
▨ Dated
Artist: Patricia Andrews
2⅞" H × 2½" W
$9.95   995QX5754

Baby's First Christmas
Collector's plate
Display stand included. Fine porcelain.
Painting by: Bessie Pease Gutmann
▨ Dated
3¼" diameter
$10.95   1095QX5751

The **Mom** ornament in the 1996 line was sculpted by Joyce Lyle. Although the *Dream Book* and the packaging for the ornament list Joyce's name, LaDene Votruba's name mistakenly was printed on the bottom of the ornaments. All of the **Mom** ornaments were produced this way.

Baby's First Christmas
Beatrix Potter™
Fine porcelain
▨ Dated
Artist: LaDene Votruba
3⅛" H × 2¼" W
$18.95   1895QX5744

Baby's First Christmas
Photo Holder
Opens to display photo.
▨ Dated
Artist: Ed Seale
2¹⁵⁄₁₆" H × 1³⁄₁₆" W
$7.95   795QX5761

FAMILY
Mom
▨ Dated
Artist: Joyce Lyle
3¼" H × 1⅞" W
$7.95   795QX5824

Mom-to-Be
▨ Dated
Artist: Duane Unruh
2⁵⁄₁₆" H × 1½" W
$7.95   795QX5791

Mom and Dad
▨ Dated
Artist: Dill Rhodus
3¹⁵⁄₁₆" H × 2" W
$9.95   995QX5821

Baby's First Christmas

Baby's Second Christmas

Child's Third Christmas

Child's Fourth Christmas

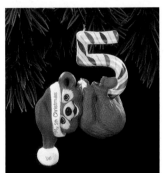

Child's Fifth Christmas

Baby's First Christmas

Baby's First Christmas

Baby's First Christmas

Baby's First Christmas

Mom

Mom-to-Be

Mom and Dad

Dad

Sister to Sister

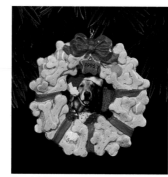

Special Dog

Son
▨ Dated
Artist: Don Palmiter
$2\frac{1}{2}$" H × $2\frac{7}{16}$" W
$8.95   895QX6079

Grandma
▨ Dated
Artist: LaDene Votruba
$2\frac{5}{8}$" H × $2\frac{1}{16}$" W
$8.95   895QX5844

Grandpa
▨ Dated
Artist: LaDene Votruba
$2\frac{9}{16}$" H × $2\frac{1}{2}$" W
$8.95   895QX5851

On My Way
Photo Holder
▨ Dated
Artist: Sue Tague
$3\frac{5}{16}$" H × $2\frac{9}{16}$" W
$7.95   795QX5861

Grandson
▨ Dated
Artist: Anita Marra Rogers
$1\frac{5}{8}$" H × $1\frac{13}{16}$" W
$7.95   795QX5699

Granddaughter
▨ Dated
Artist: Anita Marra Rogers
$1\frac{5}{8}$" H × $2\frac{3}{16}$" W
$7.95   795QX5697

Godchild
▨ Dated
Artist: Anita Marra Rogers
$2\frac{3}{16}$" H × $1\frac{13}{16}$" W
$8.95   895QX5841

Daughter

Son

<u>FAMILY</u>
Dad
▨ Dated
Artist: Bob Siedler
$2\frac{7}{8}$" H × $1\frac{5}{8}$" W
$7.95   795QX5831

Sister to Sister
▨ Dated
Artist: Joyce Lyle
$1\frac{7}{8}$" H × $1\frac{1}{8}$" W
$9.95   995QX5834

Special Dog
Photo Holder
▨ Dated
Artist: Sue Tague
$3\frac{1}{16}$" diameter
$7.95   795QX5864

Daughter
▨ Dated
Artist: Don Palmiter
$2\frac{1}{2}$" H × $1\frac{5}{16}$" W
$8.95   895QX6077

Grandma

Grandpa

On My Way (Photo Holder)

Grandson

Granddaughter

Godchild

Thank You, Santa
Photo Holder
▨ Dated
Artist: Katrina Bricker
2⁷⁄₁₆" H × 2¾" W
$7.95   795QX5854

Close-Knit Friends
▨ Dated
Artist: Katrina Bricker
2⁹⁄₁₆" H × 2⁷⁄₁₆" W
$9.95   995QX5874

New Home
▨ Dated
Artist: Ed Seale
1¹⁵⁄₁₆" H × 3⁷⁄₁₆" W
$8.95   895QX5881

LOVE
Hearts Full of Love
▨ Dated
Artist: Dill Rhodus
1¹⁵⁄₁₆" H × 2⅜" W
$9.95   995QX5814

Our Christmas Together
Swing moves back and forth.
▨ Dated
Artist: Don Palmiter
3⁹⁄₁₆" H × 2¾" W
$18.95   1895QX5794

Our First Christmas Together
Acrylic
▨ Dated
Artist: LaDene Votruba
3¼" H × 3⅛" W
$6.95   695QX3051

Our First Christmas Together
▨ Dated
Artist: Don Palmiter
3⅜" H × 3³⁄₁₆" W
$9.95   995QX5811

Our First Christmas Together
Collector's plate
Display stand included. Fine
porcelain.
▨ Dated
3¼" diameter
$10.95   1095QX5801

Our Christmas Together
Photo Holder
▨ Dated
Artist: Ken Crow
2¾" H × 2½" W
$8.95   895QX5804

It's a Wonderful Life™
ANNIVERSARY EDITION
Celebrating 50 years
Bell rings.
▨ Dated
Artist: Ken Crow
4⅜" H × 3³⁄₁₆" W
$14.95   1495QXI6531

Thank You, Santa

Close-Knit Friends

New Home

Hearts Full of Love

Our Christmas Together

Our First Christmas Together

Our First Christmas Together

Our First Christmas Together

It's a Wonderful Life™

Our Christmas Together

I Dig Golf

Bounce Pass

Happy Holi-doze

This Big!

Goal Line Glory

Fan-tastic Season

Bowl 'em Over

Polar Cycle

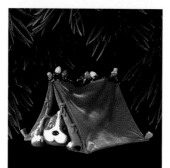

Pup-Tenting

Merry Carpoolers

Growth of a Leader—BOY SCOUTS OF AMERICA

HOBBIES AND LIFESTYLES

I Dig Golf
Clip-on
Dated
Artist: Dill Rhodus
2" H × 2¹¹/₁₆" W
$10.95   1095QX5891

Bounce Pass
Ball attached by spring to simulate bouncing.
Dated
Artist: Bob Siedler
3³/₁₆" H × 2⁵/₁₆" W
$7.95   795QX6031

Happy Holi-doze
Dated
Artist: Dill Rhodus
2¹⁵/₁₆" H × 2¹/₈" W
$9.95   995QX5904

This Big!
Dated
Artist: Ed Seale
3³/₄" H × 2¹¹/₁₆" W
$9.95   995QX5914

Goal Line Glory
Set of two ornaments
Dated
Artist: Ed Seale
Goal tender:
2³/₈" H × 2¹/₁₆" W
Penguin hitting puck:
2¹/₂" H × 2³/₁₆" W
$12.95   1295QX6001

Fan-tastic Season
Dated
Artist: Robert Chad
3⁵/₁₆" H × 2¹/₂" W
$9.95   995QX5924

Bowl 'em Over
Dated
Artist: Bob Siedler
2³/₁₆" H × 2³/₁₆" W
$7.95   795QX6014

Polar Cycle
Dated
Artist: Duane Unruh
3³/₁₆" H × 3¹/₁₆" W
$12.95   1295QX6034

Pup-Tenting
Dated
Artist: Don Palmiter
1³/₄" H × 2¹/₂" W
$7.95   795QX6011

Merry Carpoolers
Dated
Artist: Ken Crow
3³/₁₆" H × 2¹³/₁₆" W
$14.95   1495QX5884

Growth of a Leader
BOY SCOUTS
OF AMERICA
Ceramic
Artwork by Norman Rockwell
Dated
3¹/₂" H × 2¹/₂" W
$9.95   995QX5541

Antlers Aweigh!
⬜ Dated
Artist: Robert Chad
2⅝" H × 3³⁄₁₆" W
$9.95   995QX5901

Sew Sweet
⬜ Dated
Artist: Nina Aubé
2⁵⁄₁₆" H × 2" W
$8.95   895QX5921

Jackpot Jingle
⬜ Dated
Artist: Bob Siedler
2⁹⁄₁₆" H × 2" W
$9.95   995QX5911

Star of the Show
⬜ Dated
Artist: Nina Aubé
3⁵⁄₁₆" H × 2⅛" W
$8.95   895QX6004

Yuletide Cheer
⬜ Dated
Artist: LaDene Votruba
2⅝" H × 1¹³⁄₁₆" W
$7.95   795QX6054

Matchless Memories
⬜ Dated
Artist: Ken Crow
3⁷⁄₁₆" H × 2¹⁄₁₆" W
$9.95   995QX6061

Apple for Teacher
⬜ Dated
Artist: Nina Aubé
3³⁄₁₆" H × 3" W
$7.95   795QX6121

Tender Lovin' Care
⬜ Dated
Artist: Ed Seale
2⅛" H × 1½" W
$7.95   795QX6114

Hurrying Downstairs
⬜ Dated
Artist: John "Collin" Francis
3¹¹⁄₁₆" H × 1⁹⁄₁₆" W
$8.95   895QX6074

Child Care Giver
⬜ Dated
Artist: Bob Siedler
2½" H × 1¹³⁄₁₆" W
$8.95   895QX6071

Antlers Aweigh!

Sew Sweet

Jackpot Jingle

Star of the Show

Yuletide Cheer

Matchless Memories

Apple for Teacher

Tender Lovin' Care

Hurrying Downstairs

Child Care Giver

Laverne, Victor and Hugo

Quasimodo

Esmeralda and Djali

Making His Rounds
⬛ Dated
Artist: John "Collin" Francis
4³⁄₁₆" H × 2" W
$14.95   1495QX6271

Kindly Shepherd
⬛ Dated
Artist: Patricia Andrews
4¹¹⁄₁₆" H × 2¼" W
$12.95   1295QX6274

Tamika
Penda Kids™
⬛ Dated
Character designer: Cathy Johnson
Artist: Katrina Bricker
2⁵⁄₁₆" H × 1⁵⁄₁₆" W
$7.95   795QX6301

Feliz Navidad
⬛ Dated
Artist: Linda Sickman
2¹³⁄₁₆" H × 2¹¹⁄₁₆" W
$9.95   995QX6304

Madonna and Child
Stamped tin
⬛ Dated
Painting by Jusepe de Ribera
Frame artist: Linda Sickman
4⁹⁄₁₆" H × 2⁷⁄₁₆" W
$12.95   1295QX6324

Lighting the Way
⬛ Dated
Artist: Robert Chad
3⁵⁄₁₆" H × 3¹⁵⁄₁₆" W
$12.95   1295QX6124

101 Dalmatians

Making His Rounds

THE HUNCHBACK OF NOTRE DAME COLLECTION
Laverne, Victor and Hugo
⬛ 3³⁄₁₆" H × 2¾" W
$12.95   1295QXI6354

Quasimodo
⬛ 4⁹⁄₁₆" H × 2½" W
$9.95   995QXI6341

Esmeralda and Djali
⬛ 4¾" H × 2⅞" W
$14.95   1495QXI6351

SPECIAL ISSUE
101 Dalmatians
Collector's plate
Display stand included.
⬛ 3¼" diameter
$12.95   1295QXI6544

Christmas Joy
⬛ Dated
Artist: Duane Unruh
3⅛" H × 3¼" W
$14.95   1495QX6241

Precious Child
⬛ Dated
Artist: LaDene Votruba
3⅜" diameter
$8.95   895QX6251

Kindly Shepherd

Tamika

Feliz Navidad

Madonna and Child

Lighting the Way

Christmas Joy

Precious Child

Glad Tidings
☐ Dated
Artist: Joyce Lyle
4⅝" H × 2⅝" W
$14.95   1495QX6231

Prayer for Peace
☐ Dated
Artist: Joyce Lyle
2³⁄₁₆" H × 1⅜" W
$7.95   795QX6261

Welcome Him
☐ Dated
Artist: Sue Tague
3¼" H × 2⁷⁄₁₆" W
$8.95   895QX6264

Come All Ye Faithful
Clara Johnson Scroggins
named this design as her first
COLLECTOR'S CHOICE.
Church opens.
☐ Dated
Artist: Ken Crow
3¹⁵⁄₁₆" H × 2½" W
$12.95   1295QX6244

Jolly Wolly Ark
Rocks to and fro.
☐ Dated
Artist: Ken Crow
3¹⁄₁₆" H × 2³⁄₁₆" W
$12.95   1295QX6221

Woodland Santa
Pressed tin
☐ Artist: Linda Sickman
4⅝" H × 3" W
$12.95   1295QX6131

Holiday Haul
☐ Dated
Artist: Linda Sickman
2¹⁵⁄₁₆" H × 3⁷⁄₁₆" W
$14.95   1495QX6201

Maxine
10th Anniversary of
Shoebox Greetings
☐ Dated
Character designer: John Wagner
Artist: Sharon Pike
3⁵⁄₁₆" H × 2½" W
$9.95   995QX6224

High Style
☐ Dated
Artist: Robert Chad
4⅛" H × 1⅝" W
$8.95   895QX6064

Regal Cardinal
Clip-on
☐ Dated
Artist: John "Collin" Francis
2⅜" H × 3⁹⁄₁₆" W
$9.95   995QX6204

A Little Song and Dance
☐ Dated
Artist: Ken Crow
3¹⁄₁₆" H × 2¹⁵⁄₁₆" W
$9.95   995QX6211

Evergreen Santa
☐ Dated
Artist: Joyce Lyle
3¹¹⁄₁₆" H × 3" W
$22.00   2200QX5714

Glad Tidings

Prayer for Peace

Welcome Him

Come All Ye Faithful

Jolly Wolly Ark

Woodland Santa

Holiday Haul

Maxine

High Style

Regal Cardinal

Evergreen Santa

A Little Song and Dance

Commander William T. Riker™

Mr. Spock

Peppermint Surprise

Hillside Express

STAR TREK COLLECTION

Commander William T. Riker™
STAR TREK®: THE
NEXT GENERATION™
⬜ Dated
Artist: Anita Marra Rogers
4⅜" H × 3¹⁵⁄₁₆" W
$14.95   1495QXI5551

Mr. Spock
STAR TREK®
⬜ Dated
Artist: Anita Marra Rogers
4⅛" H × 3" W
$14.95   1495QXI5544

Peppermint Surprise
⬜ Dated
Artist: Sharon Pike
1¹⁵⁄₁₆" H × 1¹³⁄₁₆" W
$7.95   795QX6234

Hillside Express
⬜ Dated
Artist: Nina Aubé
1¹⁵⁄₁₆" H × 4¹⁄₁₆" W
$12.95   1295QX6134

Ziggy®

SPIDER-MAN™

WONDER WOMAN™

Foghorn Leghorn and Henery Hawk

Marvin the Martian

COLLECTOR'S CLASSICS

Ziggy®
25th ANNIVERSARY
⬜ Dated
Artist: Robert Chad
2³⁄₁₆" H × 2¹³⁄₁₆" W
$9.95   995QX6524

SPIDER-MAN™
Use the two "web-lines" when
placing him on your tree.
⬜ Artist: Robert Chad
3" H × 4¹⁄₁₆" W
$12.95   1295QX5757

WONDER WOMAN™
⬜ Artist: Anita Marra Rogers
4⁷⁄₁₆" H × 2⅞" W
$12.95   1295QX5941

**Foghorn Leghorn and
Henery Hawk**
Celebrating 50 Years
LOONEY TUNES™
Set of two ornaments
⬜ Artist: Robert Chad
Foghorn: 3¹¹⁄₁₆" H × 3¹⁄₁₆" W
Henery: 1⁵⁄₁₆" H × ⁹⁄₁₆" W
$13.95   1395QX5444

Marvin the Martian
LOONEY TUNES™
⬜ Artist: Robert Chad
2¹⁵⁄₁₆" H × 2⅛" W
$10.95   1095QX5451

Olive Oyl and Swee' Pea
▢ Artist: Robert Chad
3¹¹⁄₁₆" H × 1⁷⁄₁₆" W
$10.95   1095QX5481

Winnie the Pooh and Piglet
▢ Dated
3¼" H × 2¹⁄₁₆" W
$12.95   1295QX5454

Yogi Bear™ and Boo Boo™
▢ Artist: Anita Marra Rogers
3¼" H × 2¼" W
$12.95   1295QX5521

A Tree for SNOOPY®
Complements A Tree for
WOODSTOCK Keepsake
Miniature Ornament
▢ Dated
Artist: Bob Siedler
1⅞" H × 3¼" W
$8.95   895QX5507

Witch of the West
THE WIZARD OF OZ™
▢ Artist: Joyce Lyle
4³⁄₁₆" H × 3⅞" W
$13.95   1395QX5554

Percy the Small Engine—No. 6
THOMAS THE TANK ENGINE
& FRIENDS™
▢ Artist: Dill Rhodus
1¹¹⁄₁₆" H × 3⅛" W
$9.95   995QX6314

Welcome Guest
"Coca-Cola®" Santa
▢ Dated
Artist: Duane Unruh
4⅛" H × 2⅝" W
$14.95   1495QX5394

Tonka® Mighty Dump Truck
Die-cast metal
▢ Dated
1⅞" H × 3" W
$13.95   1395QX6321

PEZ® Snowman
▢ Dated
4⅜" H × 1½" W
$7.95   795QX6534

Little Spooners
Norman Rockwell Art
▢ Dated
Artist: Duane Unruh
3¾" H × 2¹³⁄₁₆" W
$12.95   1295QX5504

Time for a Treat
HERSHEY'S™
▢ Dated
Artist: Linda Sickman
1¾" H × 3⁷⁄₁₆" W
$11.95   1195QX5464

Christmas Snowman
▢ Dated
Designer: Marjolein Bastin
Artist: Duane Unruh
3⁵⁄₁₆" H × 2⅛" W
$9.95   995QX6214

Olive Oyl and Swee' Pea

Winnie the Pooh and Piglet

Yogi Bear™ and Boo Boo™

A Tree for SNOOPY®

Witch of the West

Percy the Small Engine—No. 6

Welcome Guest

Tonka® Mighty Dump Truck

PEZ® Snowman

Little Spooners

Time for a Treat

Christmas Snowman

Christy—All God's Children®
First in the All God's Children® series
▨ Dated
Artist: Martha Holcombe
3¹³⁄₁₆" H × 2¾" W
$12.95   1295QX5564

700E Hudson Steam Locomotive
First in the LIONEL® Train series
Die-cast metal
▨ Dated
1³⁄₁₆" H × 4¹⁄₁₆" W
$18.95   1895QX5531

Cinderella—1995
First in the Madame Alexander™ series
▨ Artist: John "Collin" Francis
3⁹⁄₁₆" H × 2½" W
$14.95   1495QX6311

Native American BARBIE™
First in the "Dolls of the World" series
▨ Dated
Artist: Patricia Andrews
4¼" H × 1⁵⁄₁₆" W
$14.95   1495QX5561

Nolan Ryan
First in the At the Ballpark series
Hallmark-exclusive trading card included.
▨ Dated
Artist: Dill Rhodus
4⁷⁄₁₆" H × 2½" W
$14.95   1495QXI5711

A Celebration of Angels
Second in A Celebration of Angels series
▨ Dated
Artist: Patricia Andrews
4½" H × 3¾" W
$12.95   1295QX5634

Christkindl
Second in the Christmas Visitors series
▨ Dated
Artist: LaDene Votruba
4⁵⁄₁₆" H × 2⅛" W
$14.95   1495QX5631

Troy Aikman
Second in the Football Legends series
Hallmark-exclusive trading card included.
▨ Artist: Dill Rhodus
5³⁄₁₆" H × 2⁷⁄₁₆" W
$14.95   1495QXI5021

Larry Bird
Second in the Hoop Stars series
Hallmark-exclusive trading card included.
▨ 6¹⁵⁄₁₆" H × 1¹⁵⁄₁₆" W
$14.95   1495QX15014

1955 Chevrolet Cameo
Second in the All-American Trucks series
▨ Dated
Artist: Don Palmiter
1¹¹⁄₁₆" H × 4⁷⁄₁₆" W
$13.95   1395QX5241

Christy—All God's Children®

700E Hudson Steam Locomotive

Cinderella—1995

Native American BARBIE™

Nolan Ryan

A Celebration of Angels

Christkindl

Troy Aikman

Larry Bird

1955 Chevrolet Cameo

Yuletide Central

Murray® Airplane

Cat Naps

Satchel Paige

Featuring the Enchanted Evening
BARBIE® Doll

Holiday BARBIE™

Mary Had a Little Lamb

Puppy Love

1959 Cadillac De Ville

Fabulous Decade

Yuletide Central
Third in the Yuletide
Central series
Pressed tin
▨ Dated
Artist: Linda Sickman
2⁵⁄₁₆" H × 3⅝" W
$18.95   1895QX5011

Murray® Airplane
Third in the Kiddie Car
Classics series
Cast metal
▨ Dated
Artist: Don Palmiter
2" H × 3⁵⁄₁₆" W
$13.95   1395QX5364

Cat Naps
Third in the Cat Naps series
▨ Dated
Artist: Dill Rhodus
1⅞" H × 3½" W
$7.95   795QX5641

Satchel Paige
Third in the Baseball
Heroes series
▨ Dated
Artist: Dill Rhodus
3⅜" diameter
$12.95   1295QX5304

**Featuring the Enchanted
Evening BARBIE® Doll**
Third in the BARBIE™
Ornament series
▨ Dated
Artist: Patricia Andrews
4⅜" H × 1¹³⁄₁₆" W
$14.95   1495QXI6541

Holiday BARBIE™
Fourth in the Holiday BARBIE™
Ornament series
▨ Dated
Artist: Patricia Andrews
3⁷⁄₁₆" H × 3¹⁄₁₆" W
$14.95   1495QXI5371

Mary Had a Little Lamb
Fourth in the Mother
Goose series
Book opens to display verse.
▨ Dated
Artist: Ed Seale
Illustrator: LaDene Votruba
2½" H × 2¹⁄₁₆" W
$13.95   1395QX5644

Puppy Love
Sixth in the Puppy Love series
Brass tag
▨ Dated
Artist: Anita Marra Rogers
2⅜" H × 1½" W
$7.95   795QX5651

1959 Cadillac De Ville
Sixth in the Classic American
Cars series
▨ Dated
Artist: Don Palmiter
1¼" H × 4¹³⁄₁₆" W
$12.95   1295QX5384

Fabulous Decade
Seventh in the Fabulous
Decade series
▨ Brass date
Artist: Ed Seale
2³⁄₁₆" H × 2⅛" W
$7.95   795QX5661

Merry Olde Santa
Seventh in the Merry Olde
Santa series
▨ Dated
Artist: Ken Crow
4⁵⁄₁₆" H × 2⅛" W
$14.95   1495QX5654

Mary's face on the inside
of the 1996 **Mary Had a
Little Lamb** ornament
is not painted. This was
an intentional design
decision, not an error.
Because the face is so
small, it was virtually
impossible to accurately
paint facial details, so the
face was left unpainted.
The face on the cover of
the ornament, however,
is painted.

Merry Olde Santa

Bright Flying Colors

Violet—Mary's Angels

Victorian Painted Lady

Frosty Friends

Santa's 4 × 4

The PEANUTS® Gang

Rocking Horse

Pansy

Uncle Sam

Caroling Angel

Mrs. Claus

Santa's Gifts

ONGOING SERIES

Bright Flying Colors
Eighth in the CRAYOLA® series
Propeller spins and wheels turn.
☐ Dated
Artist: Ken Crow
2¼" H × 2¹⁵⁄₁₆" W
$10.95   1095QX5391

Violet—Mary's Angels
Ninth in the Mary's Angels series
☐ Designer: Mary Hamilton
Artist: Robert Chad
2½" H × 1¹¹⁄₁₆" W
$6.95   695QX5664

Victorian Painted Lady
13th in the Nostalgic Houses and
Shops series
☐ Dated
Artist: Don Palmiter
3¹¹⁄₁₆" H × 2¾" W
$14.95   1495QX5671

Frosty Friends
17th in the Frosty Friends series
☐ Dated
Artist: Ed Seale
2³⁄₁₆" H × 3⁵⁄₁₆" W
$10.95   1095QX5681

Santa's 4 × 4
18th in Here Comes Santa series
☐ Dated
Artist: Ed Seale
2½" H × 4½" W
$14.95   1495QX5684

FINAL EDITIONS

The PEANUTS® Gang
Fourth and final in The
PEANUTS® Gang series
☐ Dated
Artist: John "Collin" Francis
2⁵⁄₁₆" H × 1³⁄₁₆" W
$9.95   995QX5381

Rocking Horse
16th and final in the Rocking
Horse series
☐ Dated
Artist: Linda Sickman
3" H × 4" W
$10.95   1095QX5674

SHOWCASE SERIES

Pansy
First in The Language of Flowers
series
Container is silver-plated.
☐ Dated
Artist: Sue Tague
3½" H × 3¹⁄₁₆" W
$15.95   1595QK1171

Uncle Sam
Second in the Turn-of-the-
Century Parade series
Die-cast metal with brass bell
Wheels turn and bell rings.
☐ Dated
Artist: Ken Crow
4" H × 2¹¹⁄₁₆" W
$16.95   1695QK1084

SHOWCASE COLLECTIONS

Caroling Angel
FOLK ART AMERICANA
COLLECTION
Wings are stamped copper.
☐ Dated
Artist: Linda Sickman
4³⁄₈" H × 2⁹⁄₁₆" W
$16.95   1695QK1134

Mrs. Claus
FOLK ART AMERICANA
COLLECTION
Lantern is copper.
☐ Dated
Artist: Linda Sickman
4⅛" H × 2⁷⁄₁₆" W
$18.95   1895QK1204

Santa's Gifts
FOLK ART AMERICANA
COLLECTION
Brass bells and chain. Wings of
angel are copper.
☐ Dated
Artist: Linda Sickman
4½" H × 2¾" W
$18.95   1895QK1124

Madonna and Child
SACRED MASTERWORKS
COLLECTION
Adapted from a late 19th-century
lithograph published by Marcus
Ward of London after the paint-
ing by Raphael. Historical
Collection, Hallmark Archives.
▨ Dated
Artist: Linda Sickman
3¾" H × 3⁹⁄₁₆" W
$15.95   1595QK1144

Madonna and Child

Praying Madonna
SACRED MASTERWORKS
COLLECTION
Adapted from a late 19th-century
lithograph published by Marcus
Ward of London after the paint-
ing by Sassoferrato. Historical
Collection, Hallmark Archives.
▨ Dated
Artist: Linda Sickman
4" H × 2⁷⁄₁₆" W
$15.95   1595QK1154

Balthasar (Frankincense)
THE MAGI BELLS
COLLECTION
Fine porcelain
▨ Artist: LaDene Votruba
3⅝" H × 1¹³⁄₁₆" W
$13.95   1395QK1174

Melchior (Gold)
THE MAGI BELLS
COLLECTION
Fine porcelain
▨ Artist: LaDene Votruba
3⅝" H × 1¹³⁄₁₆" W
$13.95   1395QK1181

Caspar (Myrrh)
THE MAGI BELLS
COLLECTION
Fine porcelain
▨ Artist: LaDene Votruba
3⅝" H × 1¹³⁄₁₆" W
$13.95   1395QK1184

Clyde
COOKIE JAR FRIENDS
COLLECTION
Porcelain. Lid lifts off.
▨ Dated
Artist: Nina Aubé
3⁷⁄₁₆" H × 2¹⁵⁄₁₆" W
$15.95   1595QK1161

Carmen
COOKIE JAR FRIENDS
COLLECTION
Porcelain. Lid lifts off.
▨ Dated
Artist: Anita Marra Rogers
3½" H × 2¾" W
$15.95   1595QK1164

The Birds' Christmas Tree
NATURE'S SKETCHBOOK
COLLECTION
▨ Dated
Designer: Marjolein Bastin
Artist: Duane Unruh
3¹⁵⁄₁₆" H × 3⅛" W
$18.95   1895QK1114

The Holly Basket
NATURE'S SKETCHBOOK
COLLECTION
▨ Dated
Designer: Marjolein Bastin
Artist: Joyce Lyle
3⅛" H × 3⅞" W
$18.95   1895QK1094

Christmas Bunny
NATURE'S SKETCHBOOK
COLLECTION
▨ Dated
Designer: Marjolein Bastin
Artist: John "Collin" Francis
2¹⁵⁄₁₆" H × 3⅞" W
$18.95   1895QK1104

Praying Madonna

Balthasar (Frankincense)

Melchior (Gold)

Caspar (Myrrh)

Clyde

Carmen

The Birds' Christmas Tree

The Holly Basket

Christmas Bunny

North Pole Volunteers

PEANUTS® Schroeder and Lucy

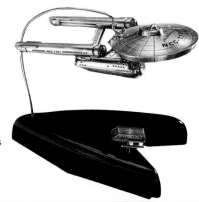
Slippery Day

The Statue of Liberty

SPECIAL EDITION
North Pole Volunteers
Light, motion, and sound. Listen as the bell clangs, the siren wails, and the mascot barks. See Fire Chief Santa pull the cord that makes the bell swing while the wheels of the vintage fire engine turn.
Dated
Artist: Ed Seale
3⅜" H × 5⁵⁄₁₆" W
$42.00   4200QLX7471

Baby's First Christmas

FAMILY
Baby's First Christmas
Light and music. Plays "Brahms' Lullaby" and the star glows.
Dated
Artist: John "Collin" Francis
3⁹⁄₁₆" H × 2¾" W
$22.00   2200QLX7404

COLLECTOR'S CLASSICS
PEANUTS®
Schroeder and Lucy
Music. Plays "Linus and Lucy."
Dated
Artist: Robert Chad
2⅝" H × 3¹⁵⁄₁₆" W
$18.50   1850QLX7394

Slippery Day
Winnie the Pooh
Motion. Figures go around the pond.
Dated
Artist: Bob Siedler
4⅛" H × 3⁹⁄₁₆" W
$24.50   2450QLX7414

The Statue of Liberty
Music and light. Plays "The Star-Spangled Banner." Torch and crown glow. Includes special collector's card.
Dated
Artist: Ed Seale
6⅝" H × 2⁵⁄₁₆" W
$24.50   2450QLX7421

THE JETSONS™
Flickering light. Exhaust clouds flicker and lens glows on bubble-car.
Dated
Artist: Ken Crow
3⁵⁄₁₆" H × 4⅝" W
$28.00   2800QLX7411

Millennium Falcon
STAR WARS™
Light
Dated
1³⁄₁₆" H × 4⁷⁄₁₆" W
$24.00   2400QLX7474

Emerald City
THE WIZARD OF OZ™
Light, motion and music. Plays "We're Off to See the Wizard." Dorothy and her friends spin around on rotating road and the city glows.
Artist: Ken Crow
4⁵⁄₁₆" H × 3⅛" W
$32.00 3200QLX7454

NEW SERIES
Freedom 7
First in Journeys into Space series Celebrates the 35th anniversary of the first American manned spaceflight. Light and sound. Hear an actual countdown from NASA's Mission Control Center in Houston, plus authentic sounds of the rocket's ignition.
Dated
Artist: Ed Seale
6⅛" H × 2⅝" W
$24.00   2400QLX7524

THE JETSONS™

Emerald City

Millennium Falcon

Freedom 7

STAR TREK® 30 Years

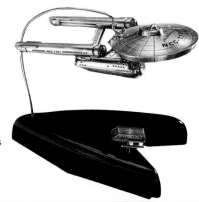
U.S.S. Voyager™

STAR TREK® COLLECTION
STAR TREK®
30 Years
Set of two ornaments with display base. Hear the voice of Captain James T. Kirk™. Battery-operated; batteries included. Die-cast metal.
Dated
U.S.S. Enterprise™ artist: Lynn Norton
Galileo Shuttlecraft™ artist: Dill Rhodus
Base: 5⅜" H × 5⁷⁄₁₆" W
Enterprise: 1¹¹⁄₁₆" H × 5⅜" W
Shuttle: ⁵⁄₁₆" H × 1" W
$45.00   4500QXI7534

U.S.S. Voyager™
STAR TREK®
Light
Dated
Artist: Lynn Norton
1¹⁄₁₆" H × 5³⁄₁₆" W
$24.00   2400QXI7544

Chris Mouse Inn

Tobin Fraley Holiday Carousel

Over the Rooftops

Video Party

ONGOING SERIES
Chris Mouse Inn
12th in the Chris Mouse series
Light. Flame glows.
☐ Dated
Artist: Bob Siedler
3⁹⁄₁₆" H × 2½" W
$14.50   1450QLX7371

FINAL EDITION
Tobin Fraley Holiday Carousel
Third and final in the Tobin Fraley Holiday Carousel series
Light and music.. Plays "On the Beautiful Blue Danube."
☐ Dated
Artist: John "Collin" Francis
5⅜" H × 3³⁄₁₆" W
$32.00   3200QLX7461

GENERAL
Over the Rooftops
Light
☐ Dated
Artist: Ed Seale
3¼" H × 3⅜" W
$14.50   1450QLX7374

Video Party
Light and changing scene. Video scene builds snowman automatically and continuously.
☐ Dated
Artist: Bob Siedler
3¼" H × 3⅛" W
$28.00   2800QLX7431

Let Us Adore Him
Light
☐ Dated
Artist: Joyce Lyle
4¼" H × 2¾" W
$16.50   1650QLX7381

Treasured Memories
Light. Represents the Christmas tree of collector Jim Reid, winner of the costume contest at the July 1993 Keepsake Ornament Collector's Club Convention.
☐ Dated
Artist: Linda Sickman
4½" H × 3⁵⁄₁₆" W
$18.50   1850QLX7384

Let Us Adore Him

Sharing a Soda
Lights flicker automatically and continuously, representing "bubbles" in Santa's soda.
☐ Dated
Artist: Ken Crow
3⅞" H × 3³⁄₁₆" W
$24.50   2450QLX7424

Jukebox Party
Light and music. Jukebox glows and plays "Rockin' Around the Christmas Tree" by Brenda Lee.
☐ Dated
Artist: Don Palmiter
3½" H × 2¹⁄₁₆" W
$24.50   2450QLX7339

Chicken Coop Chorus
Music and motion. Plays "Jingle Bells." Tap ornament gently to see chickens' heads bob.
☐ Artist: Ken Crow
3⁹⁄₁₆" H × 3⁷⁄₁₆" W
$24.50   2450QLX7491

Father Time

Treasured Memories

Sharing a Soda

Jukebox Party

Chicken Coop Chorus

Pinball Wonder
Blinking lights, sound, and movement. See the action and hear the sounds of a pinball machine.
☐ Dated
Artist: Ken Crow
3½" H × 3½" W
$28.00   2800QLX7451

Father Time
Real working timepiece. Battery-operated. Battery included.
☐ Dated
Artist: Robert Chad
4¾" H × 2¹¹⁄₁₆" W
$24.50   2450QLX7391

THE OLYMPIC SPIRIT COLLECTION
Lighting the Flame
Flickering light and music. Plays "Bugler's Dream."
☐ Dated
Artist: Duane Unruh
4¹⁵⁄₁₆" H × 2⅝" W
$28.00   2800QXE7444

Pinball Wonder

Lighting the Flame

The Miniature Ornament Collection

1996

During 1996, the Nutcracker Ballet series debuted with a display stage and the first of five ornaments to come. The March of the Teddy Bears, The Night Before Christmas, and Nature's Angels series came to an end, while 11 series continued. **O Holy Night,** a four-piece nativity set, was this year's Special Edition, and the Southern charm of GONE WITH THE WIND™ was evident in a three-piece Collector's Classics set that commemorated the 60th anniversary of Margaret Mitchell's story of the Old South. **Winnie the Pooh and Tigger, A Tree for WOODSTOCK, Baby Tweety,** and **Baby Sylvester** were among the licensed properties, and we "got help" from a six-piece set of **Tiny Christmas Helpers** who were captured in the midst of Christmas decorating.

The Nutcracker Ballet—Clara

The Nutcracker Ballet—Display Stage

NEW SERIES
The Nutcracker Ballet
First of five ornaments in The Nutcracker Ballet series
Ornament and display stage
Dated
Artist and illustrator: LaDene Votruba
Display piece: $8^{5}/_{16}$" H × $5^{7}/_{16}$" W
Clara: $1^{5}/_{16}$" H × $1^{1}/_{16}$" W
$14.75   1475QXM4064

ONGOING SERIES
On the Road
Fourth in the On the Road series
Pressed tin
Artist and illustrator: Linda Sickman
$7/_{16}$" H × $1^{1}/_{4}$" W
$5.75   575QXM4101

On the Road

Christmas Bells
Second in the Christmas Bells series
Handcrafted and metal
Dated
Artist: Ed Seale
$1^{3}/_{8}$" H × $15/_{16}$" W
$4.75   475QXM4071

Christmas Bells

Murray® "Fire Truck"

Santa's Little Big Top

Mad Hatter

Miniature Clothespin Soldier

Murray® "Fire Truck"
Second in the Miniature Kiddie Car Classics series
Cast metal
Dated
Artist: Don Palmiter
$5/_{8}$" H × $1^{3}/_{16}$" W
$6.75   675QXM4031

Santa's Little Big Top
Second in the Santa's Little Big Top series
Turn knob at bottom to watch clowns perform.
Dated
Artist: Ken Crow
$1^{5}/_{8}$" H × $1^{1}/_{16}$" W
$6.75   675QXM4081

Mad Hatter
Second in the Alice in Wonderland series
Dated
Artist: Patricia Andrews
$1^{5}/_{8}$" H × $1^{1}/_{16}$" W
$6.75   675QXM4074

Miniature Clothespin Soldier
Second in the Miniature Clothespin Soldier series
Moveable arms
Artist: Linda Sickman
$7/_{8}$" H × $5/_{8}$" W
$4.75   475QXM4144

Centuries of Santa
Third in the Centuries of Santa series
Dated
Artist: Linda Sickman
$1^{1}/_{4}$" H × $15/_{16}$" W
$5.75   575QXM4091

Nutcracker Guild
Third in the Nutcracker Guild series
Opens and closes like a real nutcracker.
Dated
Artist: Linda Sickman
$1^{3}/_{16}$" H × $1^{1}/_{16}$" W
$5.75   575QXM4084

Centuries of Santa

Nutcracker Guild

Cookie Car
Eighth in the Noel R.R. series
☐ Dated
Artist: Linda Sickman
$13/16"$ H × $1 3/8"$ W
$6.75   675QXM4114

Village Mill
Ninth in the Old English
Village series
☐ Dated
Artist: Dill Rhodus
$15/16"$ H × $1 1/16"$ W
$6.75   675QXM4124

Rocking Horse
Ninth in the Rocking Horse series
☐ Dated
Artist: Linda Sickman
$1 1/8"$ H × $1 3/8"$ W
$4.75   475QXM4121

FINAL EDITIONS
March of the Teddy Bears
Fourth and final in the March of
the Teddy Bears series
☐ Dated
Artist: Duane Unruh
$1 3/16"$ H × $13/16"$ W
$4.75   475QXM4094

The Night Before Christmas
Fifth and final in The Night
Before Christmas series
☐ Dated
Artist: Duane Unruh
$1 1/16"$ H × $1 1/16"$ W
$5.75   575QXM4104

Nature's Angels
Seventh and final in the Nature's
Angels series
Brass halo
☐ Artist: Sharon Pike
$1 1/8"$ H × $13/16"$ W
$4.75   475QXM4111

SPECIAL EDITION
O Holy Night
Four-piece set. Three Keepsake
Miniature Ornaments with dated
display piece.
☐ Artist: Dill Rhodus
Display: $3 1/2"$ H × $3"$ W
Mary: $1 1/16"$ H × $13/16"$ W
Joseph: $1 7/16"$ H × $11/16"$ W
Manger and Baby Jesus: $5/16"$ H
× $11/16"$ W
$24.50   2450QXM4204

COLLECTOR'S CLASSICS
The Vehicles of STAR WARS™
Set of three ornaments
☐ Dated
Artist: Dill Rhodus
AT-AT (walker): $1 1/8"$ H × $1 1/2"$ W
X-Wing: $5/16"$ H × $1 1/8"$ W
TIE fighter: $5/8"$ H × $13/16"$ W
$19.95   1995QXM4024

GONE WITH THE WIND™
Three-piece set. Copy on back of
Tara: "Margaret Mitchell's story of
the Old South 60th Anniversary
1936–1996."
Rhett and Scarlett artist: Patricia
Andrews
☐ Tara artist: Anita Marra Rogers
Tara: $3 7/16"$ H × $5 7/16"$ W
Scarlett: $2"$ H × $1 5/16"$ W
Rhett: $2 1/4"$ H × $11/16"$ W
$19.95   1995QXM4211

Cookie Car

Village Mill

Rocking Horse

March of the Teddy Bears

The Night Before Christmas

Nature's Angels

The Vehicles of STAR WARS™

O Holy Night

GONE WITH THE WIND™

TIE Fighter (the ornament with the hexagonal wings on its sides) in the 1996 Keepsake Miniature Ornament set, **The Vehicles of STAR WARS™,** initially was produced incorrectly with the hook mounted on the bottom side of the sphere in the center of the ornament. A correction was made during production, and it is not known how many ornaments have the hook on the bottom. Correct ornaments have the red-painted "lights" below the dark gray circle at the front of the sphere. The photo on the packaging for the ornament shows the correct hook placement; the 1996 *Dream Book* photo shows an incorrect version.

Cool Delivery Coca-Cola®

Winnie the Pooh and Tigger

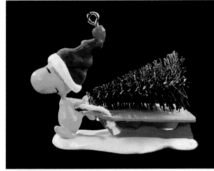

A Tree for WOODSTOCK

Baby Tweety

Baby Sylvester

A Child's Gifts

COLLECTOR'S CLASSICS

Cool Delivery
Coca-Cola®
◻ Artist: Sharon Pike
$^{15}/_{16}$" H × 1$^1/_8$" W
$5.75   575QXM4021

Winnie the Pooh and Tigger
◻ Dated
2$^1/_4$" H × 1" W
$9.75   975QXM4044

A Tree for WOODSTOCK
Complements the A Tree for
SNOOPY Keepsake Ornament.
◻ Dated
Artist: Bob Siedler
1$^1/_{16}$" H × $^5/_8$" W
$5.75   575QXM4767

LOONEY TUNES LOVABLES™

Baby Tweety
◻ Artist: Don Palmiter
$^7/_8$" H × $^9/_{16}$" W
$5.75   575QXM4014

Baby Sylvester
◻ Artist: Don Palmiter
1" H × $^3/_4$" W
$5.75   575QXM4154

GENERAL

A Child's Gifts
◻ Dated
Artist: Patricia Andrews
1$^9/_{16}$" H × $^{11}/_{16}$" W
$6.75   675QXM4234

Tiny Christmas Helpers
Set of six ornaments
◻ Dated
Artist: Ed Seale
Just One More: $^5/_8$" H × $^1/_2$"" W
Just Napping: $^7/_{16}$" H × $^{11}/_{16}$" W
Sprucing Up: 1$^1/_8$" H × 1$^1/_{16}$" W
Starlet: 1$^1/_8$" H × $^1/_2$" W
Helping Santa: $^3/_4$" H × $^9/_{16}$" W
Gifted: $^9/_{16}$" H × $^7/_8$" W
$29.00   2900QXM4261

Tiny Christmas Helpers

Peaceful Christmas

African Elephants

Message for Santa

Long Winter's Nap

Joyous Angel

Hattie Chapeau

Christmas Bear

Peaceful Christmas
▢ Dated
Artist: Duane Unruh
⅝" H × 1" W
$4.75   475QXM4214

African Elephants
Complements "Noah's Ark" Special Edition set introduced in 1994.
▢ Artist: Linda Sickman
¹³⁄₁₆" H × 1⅝" W
$5.75   575QXM4224

Message for Santa
▢ Dated
Artist: Ed Seale
1¹³⁄₁₆" H × ⅝" W
$6.75   675QXM4254

Long Winter's Nap
▢ Dated
Artist: Patricia Andrews
½" H × 1³⁄₁₆" W
$5.75   575QXM4244

Joyous Angel
▢ Dated
Artist: Patricia Andrews
1³⁄₁₆" H × ⁹⁄₁₆" W
$4.75   475QXM4231

Hattie Chapeau
Complements "A Moustershire Christmas" Special Edition introduced in 1995.
▢ Dated
Artist: Dill Rhodus
⅞" H × ¾" W
$4.75   475QXM4251

Christmas Bear
▢ Artist: Ed Seale
⅞" H × ¾" W
$4.75   475QXM4241

Cloisonné Medallion

Cloisonné Medallion
Stylist: Diana McGehee
▢ Dated
1" diameter
$9.75   975QXE4041

PRECIOUS EDITION
Sparkling Crystal Angel
Lead crystal and silver-plate
▢ Dated
Artist: LaDene Votruba
1⅜" H × ¹³⁄₁₆" W
$9.75   975QXM4264

Sparkling Crystal Angel

Easter Ornament Collection

1996

For the first time, the Easter line included two religious ornaments—**Easter Morning** and **Joyful Angels**—designed specifically to help celebrate the Christian Easter observance. Along with **Joyful Angels,** which was first in a series, two more first-in-a-series ornaments debuted—**Locomotive Cottontail Express** and **Peter Rabbit™ Beatrix Potter™.** Peter Rabbit, in particular, sent collectors "hopping" all over the country in search of it! Six series continued, and ornaments based on cute woodland creatures delighted us. And, this year, it was Daffy Duck wearing the bunny suit!

Locomotive Cottontail Express

Joyful Angels

Garden Club

Apple Blossom Lane

Springtime BARBIE™

"Keeping a Secret" Collector's Plate

Peter Rabbit™, Beatrix Potter™

NEW SERIES

Peter Rabbit™, Beatrix Potter™
First in the Storybooks series
▨ Dated
Artist: LaDene Votruba
2½" H × 1" W
$8.95   895QEO8071

Locomotive Cottontail Express
First in the Cottontail Express series
▨ Dated
Artist: Ken Crow
2" H × 2" W
$8.95   895QEO8074

Joyful Angels
First in the Joyful Angels series
▨ Dated
Artist: Joyce Lyle
3" H × 2⅓" W
$8.95   895QEO8184

ONGOING SERIES

Garden Club
Second in the Garden Club series
▨ Dated
Artist: Don Palmiter
1½" H × 1½" W
$7.95   795QEO8091

Apple Blossom Lane
Second in the Apple Blossom Lane series
▨ Dated
Artist: John "Collin" Francis
2½" H × 1½" W
$8.95   895QEO8084

All of the **Peter Rabbit™ Beatrix Potter™** ornaments issued in the 1996 Easter collection mistakenly were marked with the Christmas tree series symbol instead of the Easter egg symbol used for Easter series.

Springtime BARBIE™
Second in the Springtime BARBIE™ series
▨ Dated
Artist: Patricia Andrews
4⁷⁄₁₆" H × 1¼" W
$12.95   1295QEO8081

"Keeping a Secret" Collector's Plate
Third in the Collector's Plate series
Hand-painted. Fine porcelain.
▨ Dated
Artist: LaDene Votruba
3" diameter
$7.95   795QEO8221

Here Comes Easter
Third in the Here Comes Easter series
▨ Dated
Artist: Ken Crow
2" H × 2" W
$7.95   795QEO8094

Springtime Bonnets
Fourth in the Springtime Bonnets series
▨ Dated
Artist: Sharon Pike
2¼" H × 1½" W
$7.95   795QEO8134

Here Comes Easter

Springtime Bonnets

Daffy Duck, LOONEY TUNES™

Strawberry Patch

GENERAL
Daffy Duck
LOONEY TUNES™
Artist: Anita Marra Rogers
2½" H × 1½" W
$8.95   895QEO8154

Strawberry Patch
"STRAWBERRIES PLANT
INSTRUCTIONS—Luscious
Everbearing Strawberries—Plant
by the light of the moon. Make a
wish every night. Watch carefully.
Berries are ready to nibble when
color appears."
Dated
Artist: Ed Seale
3" H × 2" W
$6.95   695QEO8171

Eggstra Special Surprise
Tender Touches
Dated
Artist: Ed Seale
2¼" H × 1¼" W
$8.95   895QEO8161

Hippity Hop Delivery
CRAYOLA® Crayon
Dated
Artist: Ken Crow
2" H × 2" W
$7.95   795QEO8144

Look What I Found!
Dated
Artist: John "Collin" Francis
1½" H × 1" W
$7.95   795QEO8181

Parade Pals, PEANUTS®
Dated
Artist: Dill Rhodus
2¼" H × 1" W
$7.95   795QEO8151

Easter Morning
Dated
Artist: Duane Unruh
2¼" H × 1⅞" W
$7.95   795QEO8164

Pork 'n Beans
Dated
Artist: Robert Chad
2" H × 2" W
$7.95   795QEO8174

Strike Up the Band!
Set of three ornaments
Dated
Artist: Duane Unruh
Bunny: 2¼" H × 1" W
Duck: 1½" H × 1" W
Squirrel: 1½" H × 1" W
$14.95   1495QEO8141

Eggstra Special Surprise, Tender Touches

Hippity Hop Delivery,
CRAYOLA® Crayon

Look What I Found!

Parade Pals, PEANUTS®

Easter Morning

Pork 'n Beans

Strike Up the Band!

1995

In 1995, there was no waiting for later announcements of Special Issues, Premiere-exclusive ornaments or Holiday BARBIE™. The *Dream Book* included everything for the first time!

A new series, Celebration of Angels, debuted, and two new Sports Heroes series—Football Legends (beginning with Joe Montana) and Hoop Stars (beginning with Shaquille O'Neal) caused competition—almost everyone wanted one! We ran to catch **Joe Montana** portrayed in his San Francisco and Kansas City uniforms.

New licensed properties caught our eye, including Thomas the Tank Engine, Nature's Sketchbook by Marjolein Bastin, and Forever Friends Bear by Andrew Brownsword. Other eye-catchers were Mrs. Claus, who shed her apron to water ski with her '90s husband, and the first African-American Nativity set.

Not only was the *Dream Book* inclusive, to a significant degree, so was the entire ornament line. We found African-American, Spanish, Asian, and Caucasian faces or motifs in the designs.

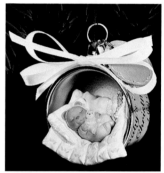

Baby's First Christmas—Baby Boy   Baby's First Christmas—Baby Girl

Baby's First Christmas

Baby's First Christmas

SPECIAL ISSUES

Captain Jean-Luc Picard
STAR TREK®: THE NEXT GENERATION™
☐ Dated
Artist: Anita Marra Rogers
5½" H × 3¹⁵⁄₁₆" W
$13.95   1395QXI5737

Captain James T. Kirk
STAR TREK®
☐ Dated
Artist: Anita Marra Rogers
4¼" H × 2¹³⁄₁₆" W
$13.95   1395QXI5539

BABY

**Baby's First Christmas—
Baby Boy**
"A Baby Boy brightens your world with wonder and joy."
☐ Dated
2⅞" diameter
$5.00   500QX2319

**Baby's First Christmas—
Baby Girl**
"A Baby Girl brightens your world with wonder and joy."
☐ Dated
2⅞" diameter
$5.00   500QX2317

Baby's First Christmas
☐ Dated
Artist: Patricia Andrews
3¹¹⁄₁₆" H × 2⁹⁄₁₆" W
$9.95   995QX5557

Baby's First Christmas
Silver tag for engraving
☐ Dated
Artist: Patricia Andrews
2⅝" H × 2¼" W
$18.95   1895QX5547

Captain James T. Kirk

Captain Jean-Luc Picard

Baby's First Christmas
Photo Holder
▨ Dated
Artist: LaDene Votruba
4⁷⁄₁₆" H × 1¹⁵⁄₁₆" W
$7.95   795QX5549

FAMILY
Mom-to-Be
"Child Bear-ing..."
▨ Dated
Artist: Dill Rhodus
2⁵⁄₁₆" H × 1³⁄₈" W
$7.95   795QX5659

Dad-to-Be
"Le Paws"
▨ Dated
Artist: Dill Rhodus
1¹⁵⁄₁₆" H × 2⁵⁄₁₆" W
$7.95   795QX5667

Packed with Memories
Photo Holder
▨ Dated
Artist: Ed Seale
3⁵⁄₈" H × 2⁹⁄₁₆" W
$7.95   795QX5639

Baby's First Christmas

THE TEDDY BEAR
YEARS COLLECTION
Baby's First Christmas
▨ Dated
Artist: Ken Crow
2³⁄₁₆" H × 1⁵⁄₈" W
$7.95   795QX5559

Baby's Second Christmas
▨ Dated
Artist: Ken Crow
2³⁄₈" H × 2" W
$7.95   795QX5567

Child's Third Christmas
▨ Dated
Artist: Ken Crow
2⁹⁄₁₆" H × 2¹⁄₁₆" W
$7.95   795QX5627

Child's Fourth Christmas
▨ Dated
Artist: John "Collin" Francis
3" H × 2" W
$6.95   695QX5629

Child's Fifth Christmas
▨ Dated
Artist: Dill Rhodus
2³⁄₈" H × 3 ½" W
$6.95   695QX5637

Mom-to-Be

Dad-to-Be

Packed with Memories

Baby's First Christmas

Baby's Second Christmas

Child's Third Christmas

Child's Fourth Christmas

Child's Fifth Christmas

Mom

Dad

Mom and Dad

Sister to Sister

Son

Daughter

Sister

Brother

Special Dog

Special Cat

<u>FAMILY</u>

Mom
▢ Dated
Artist: Bob Siedler
1¾" H × 1¹¹⁄₁₆" W
$7.95   795QX5647

Dad
Bottle brush tree
▢ Dated
Artist: Bob Siedler
1¹³⁄₁₆" H × 2½" W
$7.95   795QX5649

Mom and Dad
Snowmen have flitter.
▢ Dated
Artist: Anita Marra Rogers
2⁹⁄₁₆" H × 2⁵⁄₁₆" W
$9.95   995QX5657

Sister to Sister
"Sisters add spice to the holidays."
▢ Dated
Artist: LaDene Votruba
2¾" H × 2⅛" W
$8.95   895QX5689

Son
"Super Sharp Son"
▢ Dated
Artist: Don Palmiter
2¹³⁄₁₆" H × 1¹³⁄₁₆" W
$6.95   695QX5669

Daughter
"Extra Sharp Daughter"
▢ Dated
Artist: Don Palmiter
2¾" H × 1¹³⁄₁₆" W
$6.95   695QX5677

Sister
▢ Dated
Artist: Joyce Lyle
2⅝" H × 1⅛" W
$6.95   695QX5687

Brother
▢ Dated
Artist: Joyce Lyle
2⁹⁄₁₆" H × 1⁵⁄₁₆" W
$6.95   695QX5679

Special Dog
Photo Holder
"Good Doggies"
▢ Dated
Artist: Robert Chad
2¼" H × 2³⁄₁₆" W
$7.95   795QX5719

Special Cat
Photo Holder
"Good Kitties"
▢ Dated
Artist: Robert Chad
2¼" H × 2⅛" W
$7.95   795QX5717

Our Family
Photo Holder
"Christmas is meant to be shared."
▢ Dated
Artist: Robert Chad
3⁵⁄₁₆" H × 3⁷⁄₁₆" W
$7.95   795QX5709

Our Family

Godchild

Godparent

Godchild
Brass halo
☐ Dated
Artist: Don Palmiter
2³⁄₁₆" H × 1¹³⁄₁₆" W
$7.95   795QX5707

Godparent
Dated
☐ Artist: LaDene Votruba
2⅞" diameter
$5.00 500QX2417

GRANDPARENTS
Grandchild's First Christmas
☐ Dated
Artist: John "Collin" Francis
1⁷⁄₁₆" H × 2⅝" W
$7.95   795QX5777

For My Grandma
Photo Holder
Can be signed.
☐ Dated
Artist: Don Palmiter
4¹⁄₁₆" H × 2⅞" W
$6.95   695QX5729

Grandson
☐ Dated
Artist: Anita Marra Rogers
2⁷⁄₁₆" H × 2⅛" W
$6.95   695QX5787

Granddaughter
☐ Dated
Artist: Anita Marra Rogers
2⁵⁄₁₆" H × 2⅜" W
$6.95   695QX5779

Grandparents
"MERRY CHRISTMAS.
Grandparents warm our hearts
and our lives with their love."
☐ Dated
Artist: Joyce Lyle
2⅞" diameter
$5.00   500QX2419

Grandmother
☐ Dated
Artist: Patricia Andrews
1¹⁵⁄₁₆" H × 2⁵⁄₁₆" W
$7.95   795QX5767

Grandpa
☐ Dated
Artist: Ken Crow
3¹⁄₁₆" H × 1⅝" W
$8.95   895QX5769

Grandchild's First Christmas

For My Grandma

Grandson

Granddaughter

Grandparents

Grandmother

Grandpa

Bugs Bunny

Sylvester and Tweety

Thomas the Tank Engine—No. 1

The Olympic Spirit

Simba, Pumbaa and Timon

Wheel of Fortune®

Sylvester and Tweety
Hang-togethers. Set of
two ornaments.
▨ Artist: Robert Chad
Sylvester: 4⁹/₁₆" H × 2⅛" W
Tweety: 1⅝" H × 1¹/₁₆" W
$13.95   1395QX5017

Bugs Bunny
Artist: Robert Chad
4⅛" H × 2½" W
$8.95   895QX5019

**Thomas the Tank Engine—
No. 1**
▨ Dated
Artist: Dill Rhodus
1¹¹/₁₆" H × 3⁵/₁₆" W
$9.95   995QX5857

The Olympic Spirit
Centennial Games, Atlanta, 1996
▨ 3½" H × 2⅛" W
$7.95   795QX3169

Simba, Pumbaa and Timon
Disney's *The Lion King*
▨ Artist: Ken Crow
3⅛" H × 4¼" W
$12.95   1295QX6159

Wheel of Fortune®
20th ANNIVERSARY EDITION
▨ Artist: Linda Sickman
3¼" H × 3⅞" W
$12.95   1295QX6187

Joy to the World

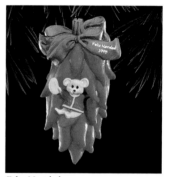
Feliz Navidad

Joy to the World
▨ Dated
Artist: Patricia Andrews
3¹⁵/₁₆" H × 2¹³/₁₆" W
$8.95   895QX5867

Feliz Navidad
▨ Dated
Artist: Dill Rhodus
3¹/₁₆" H × 1¾" W
$7.95   795QX5869

Santa in Paris
Real garland
▨ Dated
Artist: Linda Sickman
3⁹/₁₆" H × 1⁷/₁₆" W
$8.95   895QX5877

Santa in Paris

Happy Wrappers

Rejoice!

Polar Coaster

Waiting Up for Santa

Happy Wrappers
Hang-togethers. Set of
two ornaments.
▢ Dated
Artist: Ken Crow
Elf with package:
2⅛" H × 1¹¹⁄₁₆" W
Elf with bow: 2⅛" H × 1¹⁵⁄₁₆" W
$10.95   1095QX6037

Rejoice!
"A Child is born. The
world rejoices!"
▢ Dated
Artist: Joyce Lyle
3¹⁵⁄₁₆" H × 3¹¹⁄₁₆" W
$10.95   1095QX5987

Polar Coaster
▢ Dated
Artist: Ken Crow
2½" H × 2¹¹⁄₁₆" W
$8.95   895QX6117

Three Wishes

Christmas Morning

Waiting Up for Santa
▢ Dated
Artist: Don Palmiter
2⁹⁄₁₆" H × 1⁷⁄₁₆" W
$8.95   895QX6106

Three Wishes
"LOVE JOY PEACE"
Stars dangle.
▢ Dated
Artist: Patricia Andrews
2⁵⁄₁₆" H × 2⁵⁄₁₆" W
$7.95   795QX5979

Heaven's Gift
Set of two ornaments
▢ Dated
Artist: Patricia Andrews
Joseph: 4⁹⁄₁₆" H × 2¾" W
Mary and Baby:
2¹⁵⁄₁₆" H × 2⁷⁄₁₆" W
$20.00   2000QX6057

Christmas Morning
Represents treasures and
memories of Rhonda Maurer,
winner of the 1993 Keepsake
Ornament Collector's Club
Convention costume contest.
▢ Dated
Artist: John "Collin" Francis
3⁵⁄₁₆" H × 2¾" W
$10.95   1095QX5997

THE POCAHONTAS
COLLECTION
**Pocahontas and
Captain John Smith**
▢ 2⁷⁄₁₆" H × 2¹³⁄₁₆" W
$14.95   1495QXI6197

**Captain John Smith
and Meeko**
▢ 4⁷⁄₁₆" H × 2⅜" W
$12.95   1295QXI6169

Pocahontas
▢ 2⅞" H × 4½" W
$12.95   1295QXI6177

Percy, Flit and Meeko
▢ 2⁷⁄₁₆" H × 2⅜" W
$9.95   995QXI6179

Heaven's Gift

Pocahontas and Captain John Smith

Captain John Smith and Meeko

Pocahontas

Percy, Flit and Meeko

Joe Montana, KANSAS CITY CHIEFS™

Joe Montana, SAN FRANCISCO 49ERS™

Shaquille O'Neal

1956 Ford Truck

A Celebration of Angels

St. Nicholas

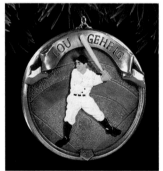

Lou Gehrig

Yuletide Central

Murray® Fire Truck

Solo in the Spotlight BARBIE™

SPORTS HERO
Joe Montana
KANSAS CITY CHIEFS™
A complement to the Football
Legends series
◻ 4⁷⁄₁₆" H × 1¹¹⁄₁₆" W
Artist: Dill Rhodus
$14.95   1495QXI6207

NEW SERIES
Joe Montana
SAN FRANCISCO 49ERS™
First in the Football
Legends series
◻ Artist: Dill Rhodus
4⁷⁄₁₆" H × 1¹¹⁄₁₆" W
$14.95   1495QXI5759

Shaquille O'Neal
First in the Hoop Stars series
5½" H × 3⅛" W
$14.95   1495QXI5517

1956 Ford Truck
First in the All-American
Trucks series
Wheels turn.
◻ Dated
Artist: Don Palmiter
1¾" H × 4³⁄₁₆" W
$13.95   1395QX5527

A Celebration of Angels
First in A Celebration of
Angels series
◻ Dated
Artist: Patricia Andrews
4¾" H × 2¹³⁄₁₆" W
$12.95   1295QX5077

St. Nicholas
First in the Christmas
Visitors series
Staff is brass with satin-brushed
finish.
◻ Dated
Artist: Anita Marra Rogers
4⁹⁄₁₆" H × 2³⁄₁₆" W
$14.95   1495QX5087

ONGOING SERIES
Lou Gehrig
Second in the Baseball
Heroes series
Career highlights featured on
back of ornament.
◻ Dated
Artist: Dill Rhodus
3⅜" diameter
$12.95   1295QX5029

Yuletide Central
Second in the Yuletide
Central series
Pressed tin
◻ Dated
Artist: Linda Sickman
2" H × 2⁷⁄₁₆" W
$18.95   1895QX5079

Murray® Fire Truck
Second in the Kiddie Car
Classics series
Cast metal. Wheels turn.
◻ Dated
Artist: Don Palmiter
1¹⁵⁄₁₆" H × 3⁹⁄₁₆" W
$13.95   1395QX5027

Solo in the Spotlight
BARBIE™
Second in the BARBIE™
Ornament series
◻ Dated
Artist: Patricia Andrews
4⅜" H × 1¹⁵⁄₁₆" W
$14.95   1495QXI5049

Cat Naps

Holiday BARBIE™

Cat Naps
Second in the Cat Naps series
Clip-on
▢ Dated
Artist: Dill Rhodus
1⁹⁄₁₆" H × 3¹⁄₁₆" W
$7.95 795QX5097

Holiday BARBIE™
Third in the Holiday BARBIE™
Ornament series
▢ Dated
Artist: Patricia Andrews
3½" H × 3³⁄₁₆" W
$14.95 1495QXI5057

The PEANUTS® Gang
Third in The PEANUTS®
Gang series
▢ Dated
Artist: Bob Siedler
2⅞" H × 2⅞" W
$9.95 995QX5059

Jack and Jill
Third in the Mother Goose series
Book opens to display verse.
▢ Dated
Artist: Ed Seale
Illustrator: LaDene Votruba
2½" H × 2¹⁄₁₆" W
$13.95 1395QX5099

Puppy Love
Fifth in the Puppy Love series
Brass tag
▢ Dated
Artist: Anita Marra Rogers
2¹⁄₁₆" H × 2¼" W
$7.95 795QX5137

1969 Chevrolet Camaro
Fifth in the Classic American
Cars series
Wheels turn.
▢ Dated
Artist: Don Palmiter
1⁵⁄₁₆" H × 4⅛" W
$12.95 1295QX5239

Fabulous Decade
Sixth in the Fabulous
Decade series
▢ Brass date
Artist: Ed Seale
2⁵⁄₁₆" H × 2½" W
$7.95 795QX5147

Merry Olde Santa
Sixth in the Merry Olde Santa
series
Brass bells on gold cord
▢ Dated
Artist: Patricia Andrews
4⁵⁄₁₆" H × 2⁹⁄₁₆" W
$14.95 1495QX5139

Bright 'n' Sunny Tepee
Seventh in the CRAYOLA®
Crayon series
▢ Dated
Artist: Patricia Andrews
2¹¹⁄₁₆" H × 2⁵⁄₁₆" W
$10.95 1095QX5247

Camellia—Mary's Angels
Eighth in the Mary's Angels series
▢ Designer: Mary Hamilton
Artist: Robert Chad
2⅝" H × 1½" W
$6.95 695QX5149

The PEANUTS® Gang

Jack and Jill

Puppy Love

1969 Chevrolet Camaro

Fabulous Decade

Merry Olde Santa

Bright 'n' Sunny Tepee

Camellia—Mary's Angels

Town Church

Rocking Horse

Frosty Friends

Santa's Roadster

U.S. Christmas Stamps

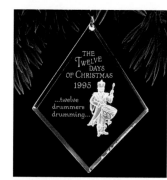

Twelve Drummers Drumming

Pewter Rocking Horse

Tobin Fraley Carousel

Christmas Eve Kiss

15TH ANNIVERSARY EDITION
Pewter Rocking Horse
ANNIVERSARY EDITION
Celebrating 15 years. Pewter.
Dated
Artist: Linda Sickman
3" H × 4" W
$20.00   2000QX6167

ACCESSORIES FOR NOSTALGIC HOUSES AND SHOPS SERIES
Set of three ornaments
Artist: Julia Lee
Street lamp: 1⁹⁄₁₆" H × 1⅛" W
Evergreen tree: 1⁵⁄₁₆" H × 1¹⁄₁₆" W
Roadster: ¹³⁄₁₆" H × 2³⁄₁₆" W
$8.95   895QX5089

ONGING SERIES
Town Church
12th in the Nostalgic Houses and
Shops series
Dated
Artist: Don Palmiter
4¹¹⁄₁₆" H × 2¹³⁄₁₆" W
$14.95   1495QX5159

Rocking Horse
15th in the Rocking Horse series
Dated
Artist: Linda Sickman
3" H × 4" W
$10.95   1095QX5167

Frosty Friends
16th in the Frosty Friends series
Dated
Artist: Ed Seale
2⁹⁄₁₆" H × 2¹³⁄₁₆" W
$10.95   1095QX5169

Santa's Roadster
17th in the Here Comes
Santa series
Dated
Bottle brush tree. Wheels turn.
Artist: Linda Sickman
2¹³⁄₁₆" H × 4⁷⁄₁₆" W
$14.95   1495QX5179

FINAL EDITIONS
U.S. Christmas Stamps
Third and final in the U.S.
Christmas Stamps series
Enamel on copper. Display stand
included. Information about
original commemorative
Christmas stamp appears on back
of ornament.
Dated
3⅜" H × 2⁷⁄₁₆" W
$10.95   1095QX5067

Twelve Drummers Drumming
12th and final in the Twelve Days
of Christmas series
Dated
3⅞" H × 3¹⁄₁₆" W
$6.95   695QX3009

Tobin Fraley Carousel
Fourth and final in the Tobin
Fraley Carousel series
Fine porcelain. Painted by
hand. Display stand included.
Dated
5⅞" H × 3½" W
$28.00   2800QX5069

Christmas Eve Kiss
10th and final in the Mr. and Mrs.
Claus series
Dated
Artist: Duane Unruh
3³⁄₁₆" H × 2¹³⁄₁₆" W
$14.95   1495QX5157

Accessories for Nostalgic Houses and Shops series

PERSONALIZED ORNAMENTS

a. The Champ
☐ Artist: LaDene Votruba
2⁹⁄₁₆" H × 3⅛" W
$12.95   1295QP6127

b. Key Note
☐ Artist: Ed Seale
2⅝" H × 4⁵⁄₁₆" W
$12.95   1295QP6149

c. Computer Cat 'n' Mouse
☐ Artist: Ed Seale
2¾" H × 3¹⁄₁₆" W
$12.95   1295QP6046

d. Reindeer Rooters
☐ Artist: Ken Crow
2¹⁵⁄₁₆" H × 3¹¹⁄₁₆" W
$12.95   1295QP6056

e. Etch A Sketch®
☐ Artist: Ken Crow
2¼" H × 2¹⁵⁄₁₆" W
$12.95   1295QP6015

f. Baby Bear
☐ Artist: Patricia Andrews
2⅝" H × 2³⁄₁₆" W
$12.95   1295QP6157

g. Novel Idea
☐ Artist: LaDene Votruba
2⁷⁄₁₆" H × 3¹³⁄₁₆" W
$12.95   1295QP6066

h. Mailbox Delivery
☐ Artist: Ken Crow
1⅞" H × 2³⁄₁₆" W
$14.95   1495QP6015

i. On the Billboard
☐ Artist: Ken Crow
2⅛" H × 2⅞" W
$12.95   1295QP6022

j. Playing Ball
☐ Artist: John "Collin" Francis
3¹¹⁄₁₆" H × 2⅛" W
$12.95   1295QP6032

k. From the Heart
☐ Artist: Dill Rhodus
1¹⁵⁄₁₆" H × 2¼" W
$14.95   1495QP6036

l. Cookie Time
☐ Artist: LaDene Votruba
3⅛" H × 2⁷⁄₁₆" W
$12.95   1295QP6073

All Personalized store display ornaments in 1994 were personalized with the names of Keepsake Ornament staff members and their family members. For example, **From the Heart** was personalized for Duane Unruh's wife, Barbara, and **Computer Cat 'n' Mouse** was personalized for Ed Seale and his wife, Gail.

Personalized Ornaments: The Champ, Key Note, Computer Cat 'n' Mouse, Reindeer Rooters, Etch A Sketch®, Baby Bear, Novel Idea, Mailbox Delivery, On the Billboard, Playing Ball, From the Heart, Cookie Time

Barrel-Back Rider

Our Little Blessings

Fetching the Firewood

Guiding Santa

Fishing Party

Learning to Skate

Sweet Song

Jolly Santa

Victorian Home Teapot

European Castle Teapot

Ken Crow sculpted
Our Little Blessings
for the 1995 line
based on a photo of
his son and daughter.

Cozy Cottage Teapot

ARTISTS' FAVORITES
Barrel-Back Rider
Will swing back and forth when
hung on branch.
▢ Dated
Artist: John "Collin" Francis
2⁵⁄₁₆" H × 2⁷⁄₁₆" W
$9.95   995QX5189

Our Little Blessings
▢ Dated
Artist: Ken Crow
3⁹⁄₁₆" H × 2⁵⁄₈" W
$12.95   1295QX5209

SHOWCASE ORNAMENTS
Fetching the Firewood
FOLK ART AMERICANA
COLLECTION
▢ Dated
Artist: Linda Sickman
2³⁄₈" H × 3⁹⁄₁₆" W
$15.95   1595QK1057

Guiding Santa
FOLK ART AMERICANA
COLLECTION
▢ Dated
Artist: Linda Sickman
3³⁄₈" H × 2¹⁵⁄₁₆" W
$18.95   1895QK1037

Fishing Party
FOLK ART AMERICANA
COLLECTION
▢ Dated
Artist: Linda Sickman
1⁷⁄₈" H × 3¹⁄₄" W
$15.95   1595QK1039

Learning to Skate
FOLK ART AMERICANA
COLLECTION
▢ Dated
Artist: Linda Sickman
2¹⁄₄" H × 2³⁄₄" W
$14.95   1495QK1047

Sweet Song
SYMBOLS OF
CHRISTMAS COLLECTION
▢ Dated
Artist: Patricia Andrews
2¹⁵⁄₁₆" H × 2" W
$15.95   1595QK1089

Jolly Santa
SYMBOLS OF
CHRISTMAS COLLECTION
▢ Dated
Artist: Patricia Andrews
3¹⁄₁₆" H × 2³⁄₈" W
$15.95   1595QK1087

Victorian Home Teapot
INVITATION TO
TEA COLLECTION
Lid lifts off.
▢ Dated
Artist: Patricia Andrews
2⁷⁄₁₆" H × 3⁵⁄₁₆" W
$15.95   1595QK1119

European Castle Teapot
INVITATION TO
TEA COLLECTION
Lid lifts off.
▢ Dated
Artist: Patricia Andrews
3⁵⁄₁₆" H × 3¹⁄₄" W
$15.95   1595QK1129

Cozy Cottage Teapot
INVITATION TO
TEA COLLECTION
Lid lifts off.
▢ Dated
Artist: Patricia Andrews
2⁷⁄₁₆" H × 3¹⁄₂" W
$15.95   1595QK1127

Angel of Light

Gentle Lullaby

Angel of Light
ALL IS BRIGHT COLLECTION
▦ Dated
Artist: Patricia Andrews
$4^9/_{16}$" H × $1^{15}/_{16}$" W
$11.95   1195QK1159

Gentle Lullaby
ALL IS BRIGHT COLLECTION
▦ Dated
Artist: Patricia Andrews
$4^5/_{16}$" H × 2" W
$11.95   1195QK1157

Following the Star
HOLIDAY ENCHANTMENT
COLLECTION
"We have seen His star in the East
and are come to worship Him."
Matthew 2:2
Fine porcelain with gold cord
▦ Dated
Artist: LaDene Votruba
$3^7/_{16}$" diameter
$13.95   1395QK1099

Away in a Manger
HOLIDAY ENCHANTMENT
COLLECTION
"...the little Lord Jesus, asleep on
the hay."
Fine porcelain with gold cord
▦ Dated
$4^5/_{16}$" H × $4^5/_{16}$" W
$13.95   1395QK1097

NEW SHOWCASE SERIES
The Fireman
First in the Turn-of-the-Century
Parade series
Die-cast metal. Brass bell with red
ribbon. Wheels turn. Bell rings.
▦ Dated
Artist: Ken Crow
$3^1/_8$" H × $3^{13}/_{16}$" W
$16.95
1695QK1027

Following the Star

Away in a Manger

Carole
ANGEL BELLS COLLECTION
Fine bisque porcelain. Feet are
the clapper for bell.
▦ Dated
Artist: LaDene Votruba
$3^9/_{16}$" H × $1^{13}/_{16}$" W
$12.95   1295QK1147

Joy
ANGEL BELLS COLLECTION
Fine bisque porcelain. Feet are
the clapper for bell.
▦ Dated
Artist: LaDene Votruba
$3^1/_2$" H × $1^{11}/_{16}$" W
$12.95   1295QK1137

Noelle
ANGEL BELLS COLLECTION
Fine bisque porcelain. Feet are
the clapper for bell.
▦ Dated
Artist: LaDene Votruba
$3^5/_8$" H × $1^5/_8$" W
$12.95   1295QK1139

Raising a Family
NATURE'S SKETCHBOOK
COLLECTION
▦ Dated
Designer: Marjolein Bastin
Artist: Joyce Lyle
$3^5/_8$" diameter
$18.95   1895QK1067

Violets and Butterflies
NATURE'S SKETCHBOOK
COLLECTION
▦ Dated
Designer: Marjolein Bastin
Artist: Joyce Lyle
$4^1/_8$" H × $2^7/_8$" W
$16.95   1695QK1079

Backyard Orchard
NATURE'S SKETCHBOOK
COLLECTION
▦ Dated
Designer: Marjolein Bastin
Artist: John "Collin" Francis
$3^3/_{16}$" H × $4^1/_{16}$" W
$18.95   1895QK1069

Christmas Cardinal
NATURE'S SKETCHBOOK
COLLECTION
▦ Dated
Designer: Marjolein Bastin
Artist: Joyce Lyle
$3^5/_8$" H × $3^3/_4$" W
$18.95   1895QK1077

The Fireman

Carole

Joy

Noelle

Raising a Family

Violets and Butterflies

Backyard Orchard

Christmas Cardinal

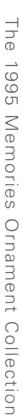

Tobin Fraley Holiday Carousel

Chris Mouse Tree

Forest Frolics

PEANUTS®

Romulan Warbird™

SPECIAL ISSUE
Romulan Warbird™
STAR TREK®: THE
NEXT GENERATION™
Light
▪ Dated
Artist: Lynn Norton
1⅞" H × 5¹³⁄₁₆" W
$24.00   2400QX17267

ONGOING SERIES
**Tobin Fraley Holiday
Carousel**
Second in the Tobin Fraley
Holiday Carousel series
Light and music. Plays "Over
the Waves." Push button to
hear music.
▪ Dated
5⁹⁄₁₆" H × 3⁵⁄₁₆" W
$32.00   3200QLX7269

Chris Mouse Tree
11th in the Chris Mouse series
Light. Tree glows.
▪ Dated
Artist: Anita Marra Rogers
3⅝" H × 1¹³⁄₁₆" W
$12.50   1250QLX7307

FINAL EDITIONS
Forest Frolics
Seventh and final in the Forest
Frolics series
Animals swing back and
forth. On/off switch for motion.
▪ Dated
Artist: Sharon Pike
4⅛" H × 3⁹⁄₁₆" W
$28.00   2800QLX7299

PEANUTS®
Fifth and final in the PEANUTS®
series
Light and motion
SNOOPY spins. On/off switch
for motion.
▪ Dated
Artist: Dill Rhodus
4⅛" H × 3⁹⁄₁₆" W
$24.50   2450QLX7277

GENERAL
Coming to See Santa
Light, motion and voice
Santa moves to and fro and says,
"Ho! Ho! Ho!" On/off switch
for motion. Push button to
hear voice.
▪ Dated
Artist: Don Palmiter
3¹¹⁄₁₆" H × 3¹⁄₁₆" W
$32.00   3200QLX7369

Baby's First Christmas
Light and music
Rocking chair rocks as "Rock-a-
Bye, Baby" music plays. Press but-
ton to hear music.
▪ Dated
Artist: Ken Crow
4⁷⁄₁₆" H × 2³⁄₁₆" W
$22.00   2200QLX7317

My First HOT WHEELS™
Light and motion
Tree lights up and car goes
around track. On/off switch
for motion.
▪ Dated
Artist: Ken Crow
4⅛" H × 3⁹⁄₁₆" W
$28.00   2800QLX7279

Fred and Dino
THE FLINTSTONES®
Light, motion and sound
Star glows. Dino chases Fred
while Fred calls out the holiday
message, "Yabba-Dabba-Doo!
Down, Dino, Down! Have a
Happy Holiday." On/off switch
for motion. Push button to
hear voice.
▪ Dated
Artist: Dill Rhodus
4¹¹⁄₁₆" H × 3⁹⁄₁₆" W
$28.00   2800QLX7289

Victorian Toy Box

Coming to See Santa

SPECIAL EDITION
Victorian Toy Box
Light, motion and music
Christmas tree glows, jack-in-the-
box goes up and down, top spins
and Santa wobbles. On/off switch
for motion. Push button to hear
music. Plays "Toyland."
Artist: Joyce Lyle
4⁵⁄₁₆" H × 4½" W
$42.00   4200QLX7357

Baby's First Christmas

My First HOT WHEELS™

Fred and Dino

Winnie the Pooh—Too Much Hunny
Motion
Friends help push Pooh through hole. On/off switch for motion.
▢ Dated
Artist: Bob Siedler
4⅛" H × 3¼" W
$24.50 2450QLX7297

Wee Little Christmas
Light
Tree glows. See surprise Christmas scene behind wall.
▢ Dated
Artist: Ken Crow
3" H × 2⅞" W
$22.00 2200QLX7329

Friends Share Fun
Flickering light
Light in fire flickers. Clip-on.
▢ Dated
Artist: Anita Marra Rogers
2¹⁄₁₆" H × 3" W
$16.50 1650QLX7349

Space Shuttle
Stringer ornament
Light
Commemorates the first Earth-orbiting flight of the U.S. Space Shuttle *Columbia* and the 30th anniversary of the first U.S. space-walk. Cargo door opens to lift out astronaut and satellite.
▢ Dated
Artist: Ken Crow
2⅛" H × 4¹¹⁄₁₆" W
$24.50 2450QLX7396

Santa's Diner
Light
Sign glows.
▢ Dated
Artist: LaDene Votruba
2" H × 4⅜" W
$24.50 2450QLX7337

Headin' Home
Blinking lights
Inside of airplane glows while lights on wings blink.
▢ Dated
Artist: Julia Lee
1¹³⁄₁₆" H × 4½" W
$22.00 2200QLX7327

Jumping for Joy
Light and motion
Tree and lamp post light up as two mice jump barrels. On/off switch for motion.
▢ Dated
Artist: John "Collin" Francis
4⅛" H × 3¼" W
$28.00 2800QLX7347

Superman™
Light and motion
Sign on the telephone booth glows. Clark Kent turns into Superman™. On/off switch for motion.
▢ Dated
Artist: Robert Chad
5⅛" H × 2⁷⁄₁₆" W
$28.00 2800QLX7309

Goody Gumballs!
Light
Globe of gumball machine glows.
▢ Dated
Artist: Bob Siedler
2⅞" H × 2⁵⁄₁₆" W
$12.50 1250QLX7367

Holiday Swim
Light
Aquarium glows.
▢ Dated
Artist: Anita Marra Rogers
3⁹⁄₁₆" H × 2¹³⁄₁₆" W
$18.50 1850QLX7319

Winnie the Pooh—Too Much Hunny

Wee Little Christmas

Friends Share Fun

Space Shuttle

Santa's Diner

Headin' Home

Jumping for Joy

Superman™

Goody Gumballs!

Holiday Swim

The Miniature Ornament Collection

1995

A significant "first" for the Miniature Ornament Collection occurred during 1995 with the advent of lighted miniature ornaments. **Starlit Nativity** and **Santa's Visit** both glowed beautifully (batteries included!).

Two of my favorite miniature series—Alice in Wonderland and Miniature Kiddie Car Classics—began, along with three other new series—Santa's Little Big Top, Miniature Clothespin Soldier and Christmas Bells. Nine series continued, a six-piece set of tiny make-up artists called **Tiny Treasures** looked ready to help us look our best for a holiday party, and a four-piece Special Edition set acquainted us with **A Moustershire Christmas.** Last but not least, three more Tiny Toon Adventures "tooned" in.

NEW SERIES

Murray® "Champion"
First in the Miniature Kiddie Car Classics series
Cast metal
☐ Dated
Artist: Don Palmiter
9/16" H × 15/16" W
$5.75   575QXM4079

Alice in Wonderland
First in the Alice in Wonderland series
☐ Dated
Artist: Patricia Andrews
1 7/16" H × 15/16" W
$6.75   675QXM4777

Santa's Little Big Top
First in the Santa's Little Big Top series
Turn knob at bottom to watch animals perform.
☐ Dated
Artist: Ken Crow
1 5/8" H × 1 1/16" W
$6.75   675QXM4779

Christmas Bells
First in the Christmas Bells series
Handcrafted and metal
☐ Dated
Artist: Ed Seale
1 1/4" H × 7/8" W
$4.75   475QXM4007

Murray® "Champion"

Miniature Clothespin Soldier
First in the Miniature Clothespin Soldier series. Left arm moves and hat is flocked.
☐ Artist: Linda Sickman
1 1/8" H × 7/8" W
$3.75   375QXM4097

ONGOING SERIES

Centuries of Santa
Second in the Centuries of Santa series
☐ Dated
Artist: Linda Sickman
1 1/4" H × 7/8" W
$5.75   575QXM4789

Nutcracker Guild
Second in the Nutcracker Guild series
Opens and closes like a real nutcracker.
☐ Dated
Artist: Linda Sickman
1 1/8" H × 7/8" W
$5.75   575QXM4787

March of the Teddy Bears
Third in the March of the Teddy Bears series
☐ Dated
Artist: Duane Unruh
1 5/16" H × 1" W
$4.75   475QXM4799

Alice in Wonderland

Santa's Little Big Top

Christmas Bells

Miniature Clothespin Soldier

Centuries of Santa

Nutcracker Guild

March of the Teddy Bears

On the Road
Third in the On the Road series
Pressed tin
☐ Dated
Artist: Linda Sickman
$^{7}/_{16}$" H × $1^{1}/_{4}$" W
$5.75   575QXM4797

The Night Before Christmas
Fourth in The Night Before
Christmas series
☐ Dated
Artist: Duane Unruh
$1^{1}/_{4}$" H × $^{7}/_{8}$" W
$4.75   475QXM4807

Nature's Angels
Sixth in the Nature's
Angels series
Brass halo
☐ Artist: Patricia Andrews
$1^{1}/_{8}$" H × $^{9}/_{16}$" W
$4.75   475QXM4809

Milk Tank Car
Seventh in the Noel R.R. series
☐ Dated
Artist: Linda Sickman
$^{13}/_{16}$" H × $1^{5}/_{16}$" W
$6.75   675QXM4817

Tudor House
Eighth in the Old English
Village series
☐ Dated
Artist: Julia Lee
1" H × $1^{3}/_{16}$" W
$6.75   675QXM4819

Rocking Horse
Eighth in the Rocking Horse
Miniature Ornament series
☐ Dated
Artist: Linda Sickman
$1^{1}/_{8}$" H × $1^{3}/_{8}$" W
$4.75   475QXM4827

TINY TOON ADVENTURES
Furrball
☐ Artist: Anita Marra Rogers
$^{7}/_{8}$" H × $^{15}/_{16}$" W
$5.75   575QXM4459

Little Beeper
☐ Artist: Anita Marra Rogers
$^{3}/_{4}$" H × $1^{3}/_{8}$" W
$5.75   575QXM4469

Calamity Coyote
☐ Artist: Anita Marra Rogers
$1^{7}/_{16}$" H × $1^{1}/_{2}$" W
$6.75   675QXM4467

SPECIAL EDITION
A Moustershire Christmas
Four-piece set. Display piece
with three miniature
ornament characters.
☐ Display piece is dated.
Artist: Dill Rhodus
House: $2^{5}/_{8}$" H × $3^{5}/_{16}$" W
Robin: $^{13}/_{16}$" H × $^{3}/_{4}$" W
Violet: $^{13}/_{16}$" H × $^{3}/_{4}$" W
Dunne: $^{7}/_{8}$" H × $1^{1}/_{16}$" W
$24.50   2450QXM4839

On the Road

The Night Before Christmas

Nature's Angels

Milk Tank Car

Tudor House

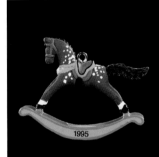
Rocking Horse

Furrball

Little Beeper

Calamity Coyote

A Moustershire Christmas

Tiny Treasures

Baby's First Christmas

Friendship Duet

Grandpa's Gift

GENERAL
Tiny Treasures
Set of six ornaments
☐ Dated
Artist: Ed Seale
Precious Gem: 1³⁄₈" H × 1¹⁄₁₆" W
All Tied Up: ⁵⁄₈" H × ⁹⁄₁₆" W
Smelling Sweet: ³⁄₄" H × ⁷⁄₈" W
Powder Puff Pal: ³⁄₄" H × ⁵⁄₈" W
Glamour Girl: ¹¹⁄₁₆" H × ⁷⁄₁₆" W
Just Reflecting: 1" H × ⁵⁄₈" W
$29.00   2900QXM4009

PRECIOUS EDITION
Cloisonné Partridge
Cloisonné
☐ Artist: LaDene Votruba
1" diameter
$9.75   975QXM4017

Cloisonné Partridge

Downhill Double

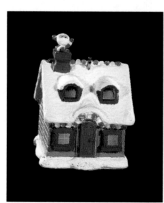

Starlit Nativity

SPECIAL PEOPLE
Baby's First Christmas
☐ Dated
Artist: Ed Seale
1¹⁄₁₆" H × ¹⁵⁄₁₆" W
$4.75   475QXM4027

Friendship Duet
☐ Dated
Artist: Duane Unruh
1¹⁄₄" H × 1¹⁄₁₆" W
$4.75   475QXM4019

ARTISTS' FAVORITES
Grandpa's Gift
☐ Dated
Artist: Anita Marra Rogers
1" H × ¹⁵⁄₁₆" W
$5.75   575QXM4829

Downhill Double
☐ Dated
Artist: Don Palmiter
⁵⁄₈" H × 1¹⁄₈" W
$4.75   475QXM4837

LIGHTED MINIATURES
Starlit Nativity
Light
Press down on button to
illuminate. Battery included.
☐ Dated
Artist: Duane Unruh
1⁷⁄₁₆" H × 1⁵⁄₁₆" W
$7.75   775QXM4039

Santa's Visit
Light
Press down on Santa to
illuminate. Batteries included.
☐ Dated
Artist: Ken Crow
1⁷⁄₁₆" H × 1¹⁄₈" W
$7.75   775QXM4047

Santa's Visit

GENERAL

Heavenly Praises
▫ Dated
Artist: Patricia Andrews
1 5/16" H × 1" W
$5.75   575QXM4037

Precious Creations
Animals representing sea, earth and sky can be turned.
▫ Dated
Artist: Linda Sickman
1 1/4" H × 15/16" W
$9.75   975QXM4077

Pebbles and Bamm-Bamm
THE FLINTSTONES®
▫ Artist: Dill Rhodus
1 1/8" H × 1 1/4" W
$9.75   975QXM4757

Merry Walruses
Complements the "Noah's Ark" Special Edition set introduced in 1994.
▫ Artist: Linda Sickman
9/16" H × 1 1/16" W
$5.75   575QXM4057

Heavenly Praises

Playful Penguins
Complements the "Noah's Ark" Special Edition set introduced in 1994.
▫ Artist: Linda Sickman
11/16" H × 15/16" W
$5.75   575QXM4059

Tunnel of Love
▫ Dated
Artist: Ken Crow
13/16" H × 1 1/16" W
$4.75   475QXM4029

Joyful Santa
▫ Dated
Artist: Duane Unruh
1 1/8" H × 13/16" W
$4.75   475QXM4089

Sugarplum Dreams
Turn dial with your thumb to see the child's Christmas dreams.
▫ Dated
Artist: Ken Crow
15/16" H × 1 1/8" W
$4.75   475QXM4099

Christmas Wishes
▫ Dated
Artist: Ed Seale
1 1/16" H × 1 1/8" W
$3.75   375QXM4087

The Ships of STAR TREK®
Set of three Miniature Ornaments that are reminiscent of Keepsake Magic Ornaments from past years. The "Starship Enterprise™" from the original television program is featured with the "U.S.S. Enterprise™" and "Klingon Bird of Prey™" from STAR TREK®: THE NEXT GENERATION™
▫ Dated
Artist: Lynn Norton
Starship Enterprise™:
9/16" H × 1 9/16" W
U.S.S. Enterprise™:
3/8" H × 1 3/8" W
Klingon Bird of Prey™:
5/8" H × 1 3/4" W
$19.95   1995QXI4109

Precious Creations

Pebbles and Bamm-Bamm

Merry Walruses

Playful Penguins

Tunnel of Love

Joyful Santa

Sugarplum Dreams

Christmas Wishes

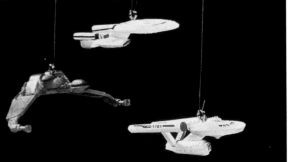
The Ships of STAR TREK®

The Easter Ornament Collection
1995

The first in the Springtime BARBIE™ series sashayed in during 1995, as did two other series—Apple Blossom Lane and Garden Club. In **Bugs Bunny LOONEY TUNES™**, Bugs became an Easter Bunny who preferred to paint carrots rather than eggs, and in **PEANUTS™**, SNOOPY became the Easter beagle again—with rabbit ears!

Among the darling spring creatures in the line were **Flowerpot Friends,** a set of three tiny "potted" animals complete with window box.

Springtime BARBIE™

NEW SERIES
Springtime BARBIE™
First in the Springtime BARBIE™ series
▢ Dated
Artist: Patricia Andrews
4⁷⁄₁₆" H × 1¼" W
$12.95   1295QEO8069

Apple Blossom Lane
First in the Apple Blossom Lane series
▢ Dated
Artist: John "Collin" Francis
2½" H × 1½" W
$8.95   895QEO8207

Garden Club
First in the Garden Club series
▢ Dated
Artist: Linda Sickman
2" H × 2" W
$7.95   795QEO8209

ONGOING SERIES
Collector's Plate
"Catching the Breeze"
Second in the Collector's Plate series
▢ Dated
Artist: LaDene Votruba
3" diameter
$7.95   795QEO8219

Here Comes Easter
Second in the Here Comes Easter series
▢ Dated
Artist: Ken Crow
2½" H × 1½" W
$7.95   795QEO8217

Springtime Bonnets
Third in the Springtime Bonnets series
▢ Dated
Artist: Duane Unruh
2¼" H × 1" W
$7.95   795QEO8227

GENERAL
Baby's First Easter
▢ Dated
Artist: Don Palmiter
1½" H × 1" W
$7.95   795QEO8237

Flowerpot Friends
Set of three ornaments with window box
▢ Dated
Artist: Patricia Andrews
Lambkin: 2" H × 1¼" W
Chicks: 2" H × 1¼" W
Bunny: 2¼" H × 1¼" W
$14.95   1495QEO8229

Apple Blossom Lane

Garden Club

Collector's Plate

Here Comes Easter

Springtime Bonnets

Baby's First Easter

Flowerpot Friends

Daughter

Son

Picture Perfect

April Shower

Daughter
Dated
Artist: Anita Marra Rogers
1⅞" H × 1½" W
$5.95   595QEO8239

Son
Dated
Artist: Anita Marra Rogers
1⅞" H × 1½" W
$5.95   595QEO8247

Picture Perfect
Dated
Artist: Ken Crow
2¼" H × 2" W
$7.95   795QEO8249

April Shower
Dated
Artist: Bob Siedler
2¼" H × 1¼" W
$6.95   695QEO8253

PEANUTS®
Dated
Artist: Dill Rhodus
2¼" H × 1" W
$7.95   795QEO8257

High Hopes, Tender Touches
Dated
Artist: Ed Seale
2¼" H × 1" W
$8.95   895QEO8259

Elegant Lily
Brass
Artist: LaDene Votruba
2" H × 1½" W
$6.95   695QEO8267

Easter Eggspress
Dated
Artist: Bob Siedler
1½" H × 1½" W
$4.95   495QEO8269

Ham 'n Eggs
Artist: Robert Chad
2" H × 2" W
$7.95   795QEO8277

Bugs Bunny LOONEY TUNES™
Artist: Robert Chad
2⅝" H × 2½" W
$8.95   1895QEO8279

PEANUTS®

High Hopes, Tender Touches

Elegant Lily

Easter Eggspress

Ham 'n Eggs

Bugs Bunny, LOONEY TUNES™

The Memories and Magic Ornament Collection

1994

In 1994, Hallmark introduced ornaments based on Disney's *The Lion King*—a hint of ornaments to come. We greeted new series, including Yuletide Central, Kiddie Car Classics, Baseball Heroes and Cat Naps in the Memories line; and Tobin Fraley Holiday Carousel in the Magic line. Retiring series were Owliver, Betsey's Country Christmas and Heart of Christmas. We also were enthralled with **Barney™, STAR TREK™ Klingon Bird of Prey** and **BARBIE™**—nostalgic and holiday designs.

In the Showcase Collection, four ornaments sparkled in silver, four lit up in porcelain bisque and four shimmered with pottery glaze. Five outstanding Folk Art Americana designs completed the Showcase group.

The "Fab Four"—**The Beatles Gift Set**—marked 30 years since Beatlemania came to America, and the "Fab Four" from The Wizard of Oz™ Collection appeared ready to trek down the yellow brick road.

Personalized Ornaments returned, and 19 different licensed properties rounded out the year.

CHILD

Baby's First Christmas
Hand-painted fine porcelain and brass. Brass tag and bell
☐ Dated
Artist: Duane Unruh
2⁹⁄₁₆" H × 2⁷⁄₁₆" W
$18.95   1895QX5633

Baby's First Christmas
Pull the safety pin to open the front panel. Can be signed.
☐ Dated
Artist: Ed Seale
1⁷⁄₈" H × 2¹⁄₁₆" W
$12.95   1295QX5743

Baby's First Christmas—Baby Boy
☐ Dated
2⁷⁄₈" diameter
$5.00   500QX2436

Baby's First Christmas—Baby Girl
☐ Dated
2⁷⁄₈" diameter
$5.00   500QX2433

Baby's First Christmas
Photo Holder
☐ Dated
Artist: LaDene Votruba
3⁵⁄₁₆" H × 2⁵⁄₈" W
$7.95   795QX5636

Grandchild's First Christmas
Clip-on
☐ Dated
Artist: Duane Unruh
3" H × 2³⁄₈" W
$7.95   795QX5676

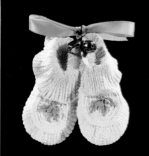

Baby's First Christmas

Baby's First Christmas

Baby's First Christmas—Baby Boy

Baby's First Christmas—Baby Girl

Baby's First Christmas

Grandchild's First Christmas

Dad-to-Be
▨ Dated
Artist: Sharon Pike
2⁹⁄₁₆" H × 1⁹⁄₁₆" W
$7.95   795QX5473

Mom-to-Be
▨ Dated
Artist: Sharon Pike
2½" H × 1¾" W
$7.95   795QX5506

For My Grandma
Photo Holder
Can be signed.
▨ Dated
Artist: Donna Lee
3⁹⁄₁₆" H × 2⅝" W
$6.95   695QX5613

Grandpa
▨ Dated
Artist: Duane Unruh
2⁷⁄₁₆" H × 2¹⁄₁₆" W
$7.95   795QX5616

Dad-to-Be

Mom-to-Be

THE TEDDY BEAR YEARS
COLLECTION
Baby's First Christmas
▨ Dated
Artist: Ken Crow
2³⁄₁₆" H × 1⅝" W
$7.95   795QX5713

Baby's Second Christmas
▨ Dated
Artist: Ken Crow
2⅜" H × 2" W
$7.95   795QX5716

Child's Third Christmas
▨ Dated
Artist: John "Collin" Francis
2½" H × 2⅜" W
$6.95   695QX5723

Child's Fourth Christmas
▨ Dated
Artist: John "Collin" Francis
3" H × 2" W
$6.95   695QX5726

Child's Fifth Christmas
▨ Dated
Artist: Dill Rhodus
2⅜" H × 3½" W
$6.95   695QX5733

For My Grandma

Grandpa

Baby's First Christmas

Baby's Second Christmas

Child's Fourth Christmas

Child's Fifth Christmas

Baby's Second Christmas   Child's Third Christmas

Mom and Dad

Mom

Dad

Son

Daughter

Sister

Brother

Sister to Sister

Our Family

Nephew

Niece

FAMILY

Mom and Dad
⬚ Dated
Artist: Bob Siedler
2¹⁵⁄₁₆" H × 2⅛" W
$9.95   995QX5666

Mom
⬚ Dated
Artist: Anita Marra Rogers
2⁵⁄₁₆" H × 2¼" W
$7.95   795QX5466

Dad
⬚ Dated
Artist: Anita Marra Rogers
2⁵⁄₁₆" H × 2⅛" W
$7.95   795QX5463

Son
⬚ Dated
Artist: Patricia Andrews
3³⁄₁₆" H × 2³⁄₁₆" W
$6.95   695QX5626

Daughter
⬚ Dated
Artist: Patricia Andrews
2¹³⁄₁₆" H × 1⅞" W
$6.95   695QX5623

Sister
⬚ Dated
Artist: Sharon Pike
2⅛" H × 1⅝" W
$6.95   695QX5513

Brother
⬚ Dated
Artist: Sharon Pike
1¹⁵⁄₁₆" H × 2½" W
$6.95   695QX5516

Sister to Sister
⬚ Dated
Artist: Dill Rhodus
3¼" H × 2¼" W
$9.95   995QX5533

Our Family
Photo Holder
⬚ Dated
Artist: Patricia Andrews
3⅝" diameter
$7.95   795QX5576

Nephew
⬚ Dated
Artist: John "Collin" Francis
1¹³⁄₁₆" H × 2½" W
$7.95   795QX5546

Niece
⬚ Dated
Artist: John "Collin" Francis
1½" H × 2⅜" W
$7.95   795QX5543

Grandparents

Grandmother

Grandson

Granddaughter

Godchild

Grandparents
Dated
2⅞" diameter
$5.00   500QX2426

Grandmother
Liner in basket is real fabric.
Dated
Artist: Patricia Andrews
1¹³⁄₁₆" H × 2⁹⁄₁₆" W
$7.95   795QX5673

Grandson
Dated
Artist: Sharon Pike
2⁷⁄₁₆" H × 1⁹⁄₁₆" W
$6.95   695QX5526

Granddaughter
Dated
Artist: Sharon Pike
2¼" H × 1⅝" W
$6.95   695QX5523

Godchild
Push gently and child will swing
from star.
Dated
Artist: Anita Marra Rogers
3½" H × 1¹⁵⁄₁₆" W
$8.95   895QX4453

Godparent
Dated
Designer: Mary Hamilton
2⅞" diameter
$5.00   500QX2423

Special Cat
Photo Holder
Dated
Artist: Dill Rhodus
3¼" H × 3½" W
$7.95   795QX5606

Special Dog
Photo Holder
Dated
Artist: Dill Rhodus
1¹³⁄₁₆" H × 3½" W
$7.95   795QX5603

Anniversary Year
Photo Holder
Brass and chrome. Personalize 10
ways to mark anniversaries for 5,
10, 20, 25, 30, 35, 40, 45, 50, and
60 years.
Dated
Artist: Ron Bishop
3¹³⁄₁₆" H × 2½" W
$10.95   1095QX5683

LOVE
Our First Christmas Together
Photo Holder
Dated
Artist: Don Palmiter
3¾" H × 3⅝" W
$8.95   895QX5653

Our First Christmas Together
Acrylic
Dated
Artist: LaDene Votruba
3³⁄₁₆"H × 3⁹⁄₁₆" W
$6.95   695QX3186

Godparent

Special Cat

Special Dog

Anniversary Year

Our First Christmas Together

Our First Christmas Together

Our First Christmas Together

Our First Christmas Together

Our First Christmas Together

Tou Can Love

Thick 'n' Thin

Friendly Push

Secret Santa

Across the Miles

New Home

Out of This World Teacher

LOVE

Our First Christmas Together
Brass runners. Blanket, scarves and hats are real fabric.
▨ Dated
Artist: Patricia Andrews
3⅛" H × 3¼" W
$18.95   1895QX5706

Our First Christmas Together
▨ Dated
Artist: Ron Bishop
2⁵⁄₁₆" H × 2⅜" W
$9.95   995QX5643

Our Christmas Together
Clip-on. Birds are flocked.
▨ Dated
Artist: Anita Marra Rogers
2⅜" H × 2⅝" W
$9.95   995QX4816

Tou Can Love
▨ Dated
Artist: Anita Marra Rogers
3" H × 1⅝" W
$8.95   895QX5646

FRIENDSHIP

Thick 'n' Thin
Clip-on
▨ Dated
Artist: Anita Marra Rogers
2" H × 2⁹⁄₁₆" W
$10.95   1095QX5693

Friendly Push
▨ Dated
Artist: Bob Siedler
3⅛" H × 2½" W
$8.95   895QX5686

Secret Santa
▨ Dated
Artist: Duane Unruh
2⅝" H × 2" W
$7.95   795QX5736

Across the Miles
▨ Dated
Artist: Patricia Andrews
2⁹⁄₁₆" H × 2⅛" W
$8.95   895QX5656

New Home
▨ Dated
Artist: Patricia Andrews
2⁵⁄₁₆" H × 2¼" W
$8.95   895QX5663

Out of This World Teacher
▨ Dated
Artist: Duane Unruh
3½" H × 1⅝" W
$7.95   795QX5766

Champion Teacher
☐ Dated
Artist: Bob Siedler
1¹¹⁄₁₆" H × 1¹⁵⁄₁₆" W
$6.95   695QX5836

Coach
☐ Dated
Artist: Duane Unruh
3⅛" H × 2" W
$7.95   795QX5933

Child Care Giver
☐ Dated
Artist: LaDene Votruba
2⅛" H × 1⅞" W
$7.95   795QX5906

Stamp of Approval
☐ Dated
Artist: Linda Sickman
1¹⁵⁄₁₆" H × 2¹⁄₁₆" W
$7.95   795QX5703

Open-and-Shut Holiday
Open file to display a
surprise inside.
☐ Dated
Artist: Bob Siedler
3⁵⁄₁₆" H × 2¹³⁄₁₆" W
$9.95   995QX5696

<u>OCCUPATIONS</u>
Caring Doctor
☐ Dated
Artist: Anita Marra Rogers
2⁵⁄₁₆" H × 2⁹⁄₁₆" W
$8.95   895QX5823

Gentle Nurse
☐ Dated
Artist: Joyce Lyle
2⁷⁄₁₆" H × 1⁹⁄₁₆" W
$6.95   695QX5973

Holiday Patrol
☐ Dated
Artist: Dill Rhodus
2½" H × 2" W
$8.95   895QX5826

Extra-Special Delivery
☐ Dated
Artist: Ken Crow
2⅛" H × 1⁷⁄₁₆" W
$7.95   795QX5833

Red Hot Holiday
☐ Dated
Artist: Anita Marra Rogers
2⅝" H × 1⁹⁄₁₆" W
$7.95   795QX5843

Champion Teacher

Coach

Child Care Giver

Stamp of Approval

Open-and-Shut Holiday

Caring Doctor

Gentle Nurse

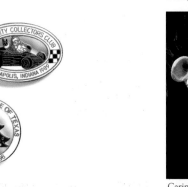

Holiday Patrol

Extra-Special Delivery

Red Hot Holiday

Big Shot

All Pumped Up

Busy Batter

Reindeer Pro

Kickin' Roo

LIFESTYLES

Big Shot
Basketball spins.
☐ Dated
Artist: Bob Siedler
2⅞" H × 1⁷⁄₁₆" W
$7.95   795QX5873

All Pumped Up
☐ Dated
Artist: Dill Rhodus
2⁷⁄₁₆" H × 1¹³⁄₁₆" W
$8.95   895QX5923

Busy Batter
☐ Dated
Artist: Bob Siedler
2⅝" H × 1¼" W
$7.95   795QX5876

Reindeer Pro
☐ Dated
Artist: Dill Rhodus
3³⁄₁₆" H × 1¾" W
$7.95   795QX5926

Kickin' Roo
☐ Dated
Artist: Bob Siedler
2¹¹⁄₁₆" H × 2¹⁄₁₆" W
$7.95   795QX5916

Merry Fishmas
Brass hook
☐ Dated
Artist: Don Palmiter
2⅛" H × 1⅝" W
$8.95   895QX5913

Practice Makes Perfect
☐ Dated
Artist: Don Palmiter
2⁵⁄₁₆" H × 1⅞" W
$8.95   895QX5863

Thrill a Minute
☐ Dated
Artist: Bob Siedler
3¹¹⁄₁₆" H × 2⅛" W
$8.95   895QX5866

It's a Strike
☐ Dated
Artist: Bob Siedler
2¹³⁄₁₆" H × 2⅛" W
$8.95   895QX5856

Kringle's Kayak
☐ Dated
Artist: Ed Seale
1¹³⁄₁₆" H × 2¾" W
$7.95   795QX5886

Colors of Joy
☐ Dated
Artist: Ed Seale
2³⁄₁₆" H × 2⅞" W
$7.95   795QX5893

Merry Fishmas

Practice Makes Perfect

Thrill a Minute

It's a Strike

Kringle's Kayak

Colors of Joy

A Sharp Flat
Front side resembles classical violin. Back side has scene with virtuoso mouse.
☐ Dated
Artist: Ken Crow
3¾" H × 1⅜" W
$10.95   1095QX5773

Follow the Sun
☐ Dated
Artist: Ken Crow
3¹³⁄₁₆" H × 2¹³⁄₁₆" W
$8.95   895QX5846

Ice Show
☐ Dated
Artist: Patricia Andrews
2⅞" H × 1⁷⁄₁₆" W
$7.95   795QX5946

HUMOR
Angel Hare
Brass halo
☐ Artist: Linda Sickman
2½" H × 3⅜" W
$8.95   895QX5896

A Feline of Christmas
Stringer ornament. Designed from Shoebox Greetings.
☐ Dated
Artist: Patricia Andrews
3¹⁄₁₆" H × 2⅜" W
$8.95   895QX5816

Feelin' Groovy
☐ Dated
2¹¹⁄₁₆" H × 1¹⁵⁄₁₆" W
$7.95   795QX5953

Cheery Cyclists
☐ Dated
Artist: Ken Crow
3³⁄₁₆" H × 4⅝" W
$12.95   1295QX5786

Jump-along Jackalope
The artist was able to get a good enough glimpse of a rare and highly elusive jackalope to sculpt this design depicting one of the West's most famous creatures.
☐ Dated
Artist: John "Collin" Francis
3⁷⁄₁₆" H × 1½" W
$8.95   895QX5756

In the Pink
☐ Dated
Artist: Patricia Andrews
2¾" H × 3½" W
$9.95   995QX5763

A Sharp Flat

Follow the Sun

Ice Show

Angel Hare

A Feline of Christmas

Feelin' Groovy

Cheery Cyclists

Jump-along Jackalope   In the Pink

Daffy Duck

Yosemite Sam

Speedy Gonzales

Tasmanian Devil

Road Runner and Wile E. Coyote

LOONEY TUNES COLLECTION

Daffy Duck
Halo is brass.
☐ Artist: Don Palmiter
3" H × 3" W
$8.95   895QX5415

Yosemite Sam
Artist: Don Palmiter
☐ 2⁷⁄₁₆" H × 1¹³⁄₁₆" W
$8.95   895QX5346

Speedy Gonzales
☐ Artist: Don Palmiter
1⁵⁄₈" H × 2¼" W
$8.95   895QX5343

Tasmanian Devil
☐ Artist: Don Palmiter
2³⁄₈" H × 2⁵⁄₈" W
$8.95   895QX5605

Road Runner and Wile E. Coyote
☐ Artist: Robert Chad
3½" H × 2³⁄₁₆" W
$12.95   1295QX5602

COLLECTOR'S CLASSICS
The Tale of Peter Rabbit
BEATRIX POTTER
☐ Dated
2⁷⁄₈" diameter
$5.00   500QX2443

Relaxing Moment
"Coca-Cola®" Santa
☐ Dated
Artist: John "Collin" Francis
2⁹⁄₁₆" H × 4" W
$14.95   1495QX5356

Friendship Sundae
Mice tails are white cording.
Spoon is bright metallic.
☐ Artist: Linda Sickman
3¼" H × 2⁹⁄₁₆" W
$10.95   1095QX4766

Norman Rockwell Art
"Bottom Drawer" cover from
The Saturday Evening Post,
December 29, 1956.
☐ Dated
Artist: Joyce Lyle
2⁷⁄₈" diameter
$5.00   500QX2413

Mary Engelbreit
☐ Dated
2⁷⁄₈" diameter
$5.00   500QX2416

The Tale of Peter Rabbit
—BEATRIX POTTER

Relaxing Moment

Friendship Sundae

Norman Rockwell Art

Mary Engelbreit

Lou Rankin Seal
▨ Clip-on
Artist: Ron Bishop
1⅛" H × 3⁵⁄₁₆" W
$9.95   995QX5456

Winnie the Pooh and Tigger
▨ 2½" H × 3½" W
$12.95   1295QX5746

Fred and Barney
THE FLINTSTONES®
▨ Dated
Artist: Dill Rhodus
2⅝" H × 2¹³⁄₁₆" W
$14.95   1495QX5003

GARFIELD®
▨ Dated
2½"H × 2⅛" W
$12.95   1295QX5753

Lou Rankin Seal

Winnie the Pooh and Tigger

Fred and Barney

Santa's LEGO® Sleigh
▨ Dated
Artist: Ken Crow
1¹³⁄₁₆" H × 2¼" W
$10.95   1095QX5453

Batman
Swings from Batarang.
▨ Artist: Robert Chad
5¹¹⁄₁₆" H × 2¹³⁄₁₆" W
$12.95   1295QX5853

GARFIELD®

Santa's LEGO® Sleigh

THE WIZARD OF OZ™
COLLECTION
Dorothy and Toto
▨ Artist: Joyce Lyle
3⁹⁄₁₆" H × 1¹³⁄₁₆" W
$10.95   1095QX5433

The Scarecrow
▨ Artist: Duane Unruh
3⅞" H × 2⅜" W
$9.95   995QX5436

The Tin Man
▨ Artist: Duane Unruh
3¹³⁄₁₆" H × 2⁹⁄₁₆" W
$9.95   995QX5443

The Cowardly Lion
▨ Artist: Patricia Andrews
3⁹⁄₁₆" H × 1½" W
$9.95   995QX5446

Batman

Dorothy and Toto

The Scarecrow

SPECIAL EDITION
Lucinda and Teddy
Lucinda's dress is made of real fabric. Teddy's tag is brass and tied with real ribbon around his neck.
▨ Dated
Artist: Duane Unruh
2½" H × 2¹¹⁄₁₆" W
$21.75   2175QX4813

The Tin Man

The Cowardly Lion

Lucinda and Teddy

Cheers to You!

The Beatles Gift Set

Cheers to You!
Brass bell. "Fröhliche Weihnacten"—German for "Merry Christmas."
▨ Artist: Ken Crow
3¹/₁₆" H × 1¹⁵/₁₆" W
$10.95 1095QX5796

Feliz Navidad
▨ Dated
Artist: Anita Marra Rogers
2¹³/₁₆" H × 1¹¹/₁₆" W
$8.95 895QX5793

Hearts in Harmony
Hand-painted fine porcelain
▨ Dated
Artist: Patricia Andrews
3" H × 2¹¹/₁₆" W
$10.95 1095QX4406

Feliz Navidad

Hearts in Harmony

Joyous Song

The Beatles Gift Set
Set of five ornaments, plus microphones, stage and drum set. Commemorates 30 years since Beatlemania came to America.
▨ Dated
Artist: Anita Marra Rogers
Paul McCartney:
4⁹/₁₆" H × 3⁵/₁₆"W
John Lennon: 4½" H × 2¾" W
George Harrison:
4⁹/₁₆" H × 2¹³/₁₆" W
Ringo Starr: 3¾" H × 2⅛" W
Drum set: 2¾" H × 2⅝" W
Floor tom-tom: 2¹³/₁₆" H × 1½" W
Top hat cymbal:
2⁷/₁₆" H × ¹³/₁₆" W
Stand with two microphones:
3¹⁵/₁₆" H × ¹¹/₁₆" W
Stage: 2³/₁₆" H × 7⅞" W
$48.00 4800QX5373

Joyous Song
▨ Dated
Artist: Patricia Andrews
3⁹/₁₆" H × 2⁵/₁₆" W
$8.95 895QX4473

Jingle Bell Band
Real jingle bells
▨ Dated
Artist: Ken Crow
4" H × 2⅜" W
$10.95 1095QX5783

Time of Peace
▨ Dated
Artist: Patricia Andrews
2⁹/₁₆" H × 3⅛" W
$7.95 795QX5813

Candy Caper
▨ Dated
Artist: Patricia Andrews
2¹¹/₁₆" H × 1⅝" W
$8.95 895QX5776

Helpful Shepherd
Brass staff
▨ Artist: Robert Chad
2¹¹/₁₆" H × 2" W
$8.95 895QX5536

Magic Carpet Ride
▨ Dated
Artist: Ed Seale
1⅞" H × 3⅛" W
$7.95 795QX5883

Jingle Bell Band

Time of Peace

Candy Caper

Helpful Shepherd

Magic Carpet Ride

THE LION KING COLLECTION

Mufasa and Simba
3" H × 4¼" W
$14.95   1495QX5406

Simba and Nala
Hang-togethers. Set of
two ornaments.
Simba: 2" H × 2¹/₁₆" W
Nala: 2³/₈" H × 1³/₁₆" W
$12.95   1295QX5303

Timon and Pumbaa
2¼" H × 3⅛" W
$8.95   895QX5366

Mufasa and Simba

Simba and Nala

Timon and Pumbaa

GENERAL

Dear Santa Mouse
Hang-togethers. Set of
two ornaments.
Dated
Artist: Ken Crow
Mouse with letter:
2¹⁵/₁₆" H × 1¹¹/₁₆" W
Mouse with ink well:
2³/₁₆" H × 1¹⁵/₁₆" W
$14.95   1495QX5806

Mistletoe Surprise
Hang-togethers. Set of two
ornaments
Dated
Artist: Ed Seale
Chipmunks in chair:
1¹⁵/₁₆" H × 1¹³/₁₆" W
Chipmunk with mistletoe:
1⁹/₁₆" H × 1½" W
$12.95   1295QX5996

Sweet Greeting
Hang-togethers. Set of
two ornaments.
Dated
Artist: Don Palmiter
Kitten with cookie:
1½" H × 1½" W
Kitten with tube of icing:
1¾" H × 1½" W
$10.95   1095QX5803

Dear Santa Mouse

Mistletoe Surprise

Timon and Pumbaa

GARDEN ELVES COLLECTION

Tulip Time
Artist: Robert Chad
2⁵/₁₆" H × 1⁷/₁₆" W
$9.95   995QX5983

Daisy Days
Artist: Robert Chad
2⁷/₈" H × 1¹³/₁₆" W
$9.95   995QX5986

Harvest Joy
Artist: Robert Chad
2¹³/₁₆" H × 1⅜" W
$9.95   995QX5993

Yuletide Cheer
Artist: Robert Chad
2¹³/₁₆" H × 1¹¹/₁₆" W
$9.95   995QX5976

Tulip Time

Daisy Days

Sweet Greeting

Harvest Joy

Yuletide Cheer

A Handwarming Present

Neighborhood Drugstore

Eleven Pipers Piping

Rocking Horse

Frosty Friends

Makin' Tractor Tracks

ONGOING SERIES

A Handwarming Present
Ninth in the Mr. and Mrs.
Claus series
▨ Dated
Artist: Duane Unruh
3¼" H × 2¹⁄₁₆" W
$14.95   1495QX5283

Neighborhood Drugstore
11th in the Nostalgic Houses and
Shops series
▨ Dated
Artist: Donna Lee
4¹⁄₁₆" H × 3" W
$14.95   1495QX5286

Eleven Pipers Piping
11th in the Twelve Days of
Christmas series
▨ Dated
3⅜" H × 2¹¹⁄₁₆" W
$6.95   695QX3183

Rocking Horse
14th in the Rocking Horse series
▨ Dated
Artist: Linda Sickman
3" H × 4" W
$10.95   1095QX5016

Frosty Friends
15th in the Frosty Friends series
Garland wreath
▨ Dated
Artist: Ed Seale
2⅛" H × 2⁹⁄₁₆" W
$9.95   995QX5293

Makin' Tractor Tracks
16th in the Here Comes
Santa series
Wheels turn, and front wheels
swivel left to right.
▨ Dated
Artist: Linda Sickman
2¹¹⁄₁₆" H × 3⅞" W
$14.95   1495QX5296

FINAL EDITIONS

Owliver
Third and final in the
Owliver series
▨ Dated
Artist: Bob Siedler
2⅞" H × 2¼" W
$7.95   795QX5226

Betsey's Country Christmas
Third and final in the Betsey's
Country Christmas series
▨ Dated
2⅞" teardrop
$5.00   500QX2403

Heart of Christmas
Fifth and final in the Heart of
Christmas series
Display the heart open or closed.
▨ Dated
Artist: Ed Seale
2" H × 4½" W (open)
2" H × 2¼" W (closed)
$14.95   1495QX5266

Owliver

Betsey's Country Christmas

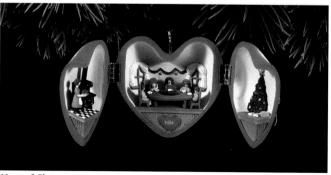
Heart of Christmas

PERSONALIZED ORNAMENTS

a. Goin' Fishin'
Artist: Don Palmiter
3" H × 2½" W
$14.95   1495QP6023

b. From the Heart
Artist: Dill Rhodus
1¹⁵⁄₁₆" H × 2¼" W
$14.95   1495QP6036

c. Computer Cat 'n' Mouse
Artist: Ed Seale
2¾" H × 3¹⁄₁₆" W
$12.95   1295QP6046

d. Reindeer Rooters
Artist: Ken Crow
2¹⁵⁄₁₆" H × 3¹¹⁄₁₆" W
$12.95   1295QP6056

e. Novel Idea
Artist: LaDene Votruba
2⁷⁄₁₆" H × 3¹³⁄₁₆" W
$12.95   1295QP6066

f. Etch A Sketch®
Artist: Ken Crow
2¼" H × 2¹⁵⁄₁₆" W
$12.95   1295QP6006

g. Playing Ball
Artist: John "Collin" Francis
3¹¹⁄₁₆" H × 2⅛" W
$12.95   1295QP6032

h. On the Billboard
Artist: Ken Crow
2⅛" H × 2⅞" W
$12.95   1295QP6022

i. Santa Says
Pull cord and message comes out.
Artist: Ed Seale
2¹⁵⁄₁₆" H × 2⅛" W
$14.95   1495QP6005

j. Going Golfin'
Artist: Don Palmiter
2¹³⁄₁₆" H × 1½" W
$12.95   1295QP6012

k. Cookie Time
Artist: LaDene Votruba
3⅛" H × 2⁷⁄₁₆" W
$12.95   1295QP6073

l. Baby Block
Photo Holder
Artist: John "Collin" Francis
2¹³⁄₁₆" H × 1½" W
$14.95   1495QP6035

m. Festive Album
Photo Holder
Album opens.
Artist: LaDene Votruba
5⁷⁄₁₆" H × 2¾" W
$12.95   1295QP6025

n. Mailbox Delivery
Mailbox opens.
Artist: Ken Crow
1⅞" H × 2³⁄₁₆" W
$14.95   1495QP6015

Personalized Ornaments: Goin' Fishin', From the Heart, Computer Cat 'n' Mouse, Reindeer Rooters

Personalized Ornaments: Novel Idea, Etch A Sketch®, Playing Ball, On the Billboard, Santa Says, Going Golfin', Cookie Time, Baby Block (Photo Holder), Festive Album (Photo Holder), Mailbox Delivery

Silver Bows

Silver Poinsettia

Silver Snowflakes

Silver Bells

Peaceful Dove

Joyful Lamb

Graceful Fawn

Dapper Snowman

Jolly Santa

Peaceful Dove
HOLIDAY FAVORITES
COLLECTION
Includes blue ribbon.
▩ Dated
Artist: LaDene Votruba
1⅝" H × 3⁷⁄₁₆" W
$11.75   1175QK1043

Joyful Lamb
HOLIDAY FAVORITES
COLLECTION
Includes green ribbon.
▩ Dated
Artist: LaDene Votruba
2⁵⁄₁₆" H × 2¹³⁄₁₆" W
$11.75   1175QK1036

Graceful Fawn
HOLIDAY FAVORITES
COLLECTION
Includes blue ribbon.
▩ Dated
Artist: LaDene Votruba
2¹¹⁄₁₆" H × 2¹⁵⁄₁₆" W
$11.75   1175QK1033

Dapper Snowman
HOLIDAY FAVORITES
COLLECTION
Includes blue ribbon.
▩ Dated
Artist: LaDene Votruba
3⅝" H × 2³⁄₁₆" W
$13.75   1375QK1053

Jolly Santa
HOLIDAY FAVORITES
COLLECTION
Includes red ribbon.
▩ Dated
Artist: LaDene Votruba
3¹¹⁄₁₆" H × 2³⁄₁₆" W
$13.75   1375QK1046

SHOWCASE ORNAMENTS
Silver Bows
OLD WORLD
SILVER COLLECTION
Silver-plated. Includes red ribbon.
▩ Dated
Artist: Don Palmiter
3⁹⁄₁₆" H × 1¾" W
$24.75   2475QK1023

Silver Poinsettia
OLD WORLD
SILVER COLLECTION
Silver-plated. Includes red ribbon.
▩ Dated
Artist: Duane Unruh
4" H × 2¾" W
$24.75   2475QK1006

Silver Snowflakes
OLD WORLD
SILVER COLLECTION
Silver-plated. Includes red ribbon.
▩ Dated
Artist: Duane Unruh
3½" H × 1⅞" W
$24.75   2475QK1016

Silver Bells
OLD WORLD
SILVER COLLECTION
Silver-plated. Includes red ribbon.
▩ Dated
3¼" H × 2¼" W
$24.75   2475QK1026

Roundup Time
FOLK ART AMERICANA
COLLECTION
▨ Dated
Artist: Linda Sickman
2¹¹⁄₁₆" H × 3⁵⁄₁₆" W
$16.75   1675QK1176

Catching 40 Winks
FOLK ART AMERICANA
COLLECTION
▨ Dated
Artist: Linda Sickman
1⅞" H × 2⁹⁄₁₆" W
$16.75   1675QK1183

Going to Town
FOLK ART AMERICANA
COLLECTION
▨ Dated
Artist: Linda Sickman
2⁷⁄₁₆" H × 2⅝" W
$15.75   1575QK1166

Racing Through the Snow
FOLK ART AMERICANA
COLLECTION
▨ Dated
Artist: Linda Sickman
3¹⁄₁₆" H × 2⅜" W
$15.75   1575QK1173

Rarin' to Go
FOLK ART AMERICANA
COLLECTION
▨ Dated
Artist: Linda Sickman
2¹¹⁄₁₆" H × 2¹¹⁄₁₆" W
$15.75   1575QK1193

Roundup Time

Catching 40 Winks

Going to Town

Racing Through the Snow

Rarin' to Go

Holiday Hello

MAGIC RECORDABLE
ORNAMENT
Holiday Hello
Battery-operated. Recordable.
The message you record can be
played back for many Christmases
to come.
▨ Artist: Bob Siedler
4½" H × 2¹⁄₁₆" W
$24.95   2495QXR6116

MAGIC SHOWCASE
ORNAMENTS
Peaceful Village
CHRISTMAS LIGHTS
COLLECTION
Lighted. Includes gold ribbon.
▨ Dated
Artist: Robert Chad
2¹³⁄₁₆" H × 3⅜" W
$15.75   1575QK1106

Home for the Holidays
CHRISTMAS LIGHTS
COLLECTION
Lighted. Includes gold ribbon.
▨ Dated
Artist: Don Palmiter
4¹⁄₁₆" H × 3³⁄₁₆" W
$15.75   1575QK1123

Moonbeams
CHRISTMAS LIGHTS
COLLECTION
Lighted. Includes gold ribbon.
▨ Dated
Artist: Patricia Andrews
4⁵⁄₁₆" H × 2⅞" W
$15.75   1575QK1116

Mother and Child
CHRISTMAS LIGHTS
COLLECTION
Lighted. Includes gold ribbon.
▨ Dated
Artist: Anita Marra Rogers
3½" H × 3¹⁄₁₆" W
$15.75   1575QK1126

Peaceful Village

Home for the Holidays

Moonbeams

Mother and Child

Simba, Sarabi and Mufasa

Tobin Fraley Holiday Carousel

THE LION KING COLLECTION
Simba, Sarabi and Mufasa
Two versions were released under the same name.
☐ Light and music. Plays "Circle of Life."
Artist: Ken Crow
4¼" H × 3¹/₁₆" W
$32.00   3200QLX7513
☐ Light only.
Artist: Ken Crow
4¼" H × 3¹/₁₆" W
$20.00   2000QLX7516

NEW SERIES
Tobin Fraley Holiday Carousel
First in the Tobin Fraley Holiday Carousel series
Light and music. Plays "Skater's Waltz."
☐ Dated
Artist: Duane Unruh
4¹⁵/₁₆" H × 3³/₁₆" W
$32.00   3200QLX7496

SPECIAL EDITION
Gingerbread Fantasy
Light, motion and music. Peppermint above top window, gingerbread people and peppermint sticks all turn. Plays "Dance of the Sugar Plum Fairy."
☐ Artist: Don Palmiter
4¼" H × 3⅝" W
$44.00   4400QLX7382

ONGOING SERIES
PEANUTS®
Fourth in the PEANUTS® series
Flickering light. Street lamp flickers.
☐ Dated
Artist: Dill Rhodus
4⅛" H × 2¹⁵/₁₆" W
$20.00   2000QLX7406

Forest Frolics
Sixth in the Forest Frolics series
Light and motion. Animals circle the lighted tree.
☐ Dated
Artist: Sharon Pike
4⅛" H × 3⁹/₁₆" W
$28.00   2800QLX7436

Chris Mouse Jelly
10th in the Chris Mouse series
Light. Clip-on. Lid cover is made of real fabric.
☐ Dated
Artist: Anita Marra Rogers
2¹³/₁₆" H × 2¹⁵/₁₆" W
$12.00   1200QLX7393

SPECIAL ISSUES
Klingon Bird of Prey™
STAR TREK®: THE NEXT GENERATION™
Flickering lights
☐ Dated
Artist: Lynn Norton
2⅛" H × 5³/₁₆" W
$24.00   2400QLX7386

Barney™
Light and motion. Barney and rabbit go around snowman.
☐ Artist: Dill Rhodus
4⅛" H × 3⁹/₁₆" W
$24.00   2400QLX7506

GENERAL
The Eagle Has Landed
Celebrates the 25th anniversary of the first lunar landing. Light and voice.
☐ Dated
Artist: Ed Seale
4½" H × 2¹⁵/₁₆" W
$24.00   2400QLX7486

Winnie the Pooh Parade
Motion and music. Pooh twirls as group parades around him. Tigger spins on his tail. Plays "Winnie the Pooh" song.
☐ Dated
Artist: Ken Crow
4⅛" H × 3¼" W
$32.00   3200QLX7493

White Christmas
Flickering light and music. Fireplace flickers. Plays Irving Berlin's "White Christmas."
☐ Dated
Artist: Donna Lee
3³/₁₆" H × 3" W
$28.00   2800QLX7463

Gingerbread Fantasy

PEANUTS®

Forest Frolics

Chris Mouse Jelly

Klingon Bird of Prey™

Barney™

The Eagle Has Landed

Winnie the Pooh Parade

White Christmas

Santa's Sing-Along

Light and music. Sounds like a real calliope! Plays "Santa Claus is Comin' to Town."
▢ Dated
Artist: Ken Crow
3¹⁵⁄₁₆" H × 3¹⁄₁₆" W
$24.00   2400QLX7473

Maxine

Blinking lights. Character from Shoebox Greetings.
▢ Artist: Linda Sickman
4" H × 2⅜" W
$20.00   2000QLX7503

Baby's First Christmas

Light and music. Plays "Rock-a-Bye Baby."
▢ Dated
Artist: John "Collin" Francis
2¹¹⁄₁₆" H × 2⁷⁄₁₆" W
$20.00   2000QLX7466

Feliz Navidad

Motion and music. Children twirl around sombrero while boy taps bell-shaped piñata with stick. Plays "Feliz Navidad."
▢ Dated
3⅛" H × 3⅞" W
$28.00   2800QLX7433

Conversations with Santa

Motion and voice. Mouth moves as you hear four messages from Santa.
▢ Dated
Artist: Ed Seale
3⅛" H × 2¹⁵⁄₁₆" W
$28.00   2800QLX7426

Very Merry Minutes

Light and motion. Mouse swings back and forth on the pendulum.
▢ Dated
Artist: LaDene Votruba
4⁵⁄₁₆" H × 2½" W
$24.00   2400QLX7443

Country Showtime

Blinking lights and motion. Santa appears to be dancing.
▢ Dated
Artist: Linda Sickman
4³⁄₁₆" H × 3¼" W
$22.00   2200QLX7416

Peekaboo Pup

Motion. Puppy moves up and down in basket, raising lid.
▢ Dated
Artist: Anita Marra Rogers
3⅞" H × 2¹⁵⁄₁₆" W
$20.00   2000QLX7423

Kringle Trolley

Light. Headlight lights up and brass bell jingles.
▢ Dated
Artist: Ken Crow
3⁵⁄₁₆" H × 3⁹⁄₁₆" W
$20.00   2000QLX7413

Rock Candy Miner

Flickering light. Light in lantern flickers.
▢ Dated
Artist: Bob Siedler
2⅝" H × 3½" W
$20.00   2000QLX7403

Candy Cane Lookout

Blinking light. Light on top of lighthouse blinks on and off.
▢ Dated
Artist: John "Collin" Francis
4¼" H × 2⅝" W
$18.00   1800QLX7376

Away in a Manger

Light. Star lights up.
▢ Dated
Artist: Joyce Lyle
3⁷⁄₁₆" H × 3⁹⁄₁₆" W
$16.00   1600QLX7383

Santa's Sing-Along

Maxine

Baby's First Christmas

Feliz Navidad

Conversations with Santa

Very Merry Minutes

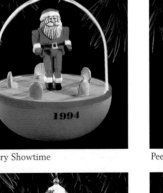

Country Showtime

Peekaboo Pup

Kringle Trolley

Rock Candy Miner

Candy Cane Lookout

Away in a Manger

The Miniature Ornament Collection
1994

The Bearymores made their third and final appearance during 1994, while Noah and his wife floated in as part of the **Noah's Ark** three-piece set. Two new series began—Centuries of Santa and Nutcracker Guild—and six others continued. Licensed properties rendered in miniature included Coca-Cola® in **Pour Some More** and five LOONEY TUNES® characters in the Tiny Toon Adventures group. To round out the year, six tiny mice that together were **Baking Tiny Treats** helped to sweeten our holidays.

March of the Teddy Bears

The Night Before Christmas

NEW SERIES
Centuries of Santa
First in the Centuries of Santa series
☐ Dated
Artist: Linda Sickman
1¼" H × 11⁄16" W
$6.00   600QXM5153

Nutcracker Guild
First in the Nutcracker Guild series
Opens and closes like a real nutcracker.
☐ Dated
Artist: Linda Sickman
1³⁄16" H × ⅝" W
$5.75   575QXM5146

ONGOING SERIES
March of the Teddy Bears
Second in the March of the Teddy Bears series
☐ Dated
Artist: Duane Unruh
1³⁄16" H × ¾" W
$4.50   450QXM5106

The Night Before Christmas
Third of five ornaments in The Night Before Christmas series
☐ Dated
Artist: Duane Unruh
1³⁄16" H × 1¹⁄16" W
$4.50   450QXM5123

Nature's Angels
Fifth in the Nature's Angels series
Brass halo
☐ Artist: LaDene Votruba
1³⁄16" H × 1³⁄16" W
$4.50   450QXM5126

Stock Car
Sixth in the Noel R.R. series
Doors slide open and closed.
☐ Dated
Artist: Linda Sickman
1³⁄16" H × 1⁵⁄16" W
$7.00   700QXM5113

Hat Shop
Seventh in the Old English Village series
☐ Dated
Artist: Patricia Andrews
⅞" H × 1⁵⁄16" W
$7.00   700QXM5143

On the Road
Second in the On the Road series
Pressed tin. Wheels turn.
☐ Dated
Artist: Linda Sickman
⁷⁄16" H × 1¼" W
$5.75   575QXM5103

Rocking Horse
Seventh in the Rocking Horse series
☐ Dated
Artist: Linda Sickman
1⅛" H × 1⅜" W
$4.50   450QXM5116

Nature's Angels

Stock Car

Hat Shop

Centuries of Santa

Nutcracker Guild

On the Road

Rocking Horse

The Bearymores

ARTISTS' FAVORITES
Have a Cookie
Shake gently; cookies
move inside.
▢ Dated
Artist: Donna Lee
⅞" H × 1⅛" W
$5.75   575QXM5166

Scooting Along
▢ Dated
Artist: John "Collin" Francis
1³⁄₁₆" H × 1" W
$6.75   675QXM5173

SPECIAL PEOPLE
Mom
▢ Dated
Artist: Anita Marra Rogers
1" H × 1⅛" W
$4.50   450QXM4013

Friends Need Hugs
▢ Dated
Artist: Joyce Lyle
¹³⁄₁₆" H × 1" W
$4.50   450QXM4016

Baby's First Christmas
▢ Dated
Artist: Joyce Lyle
1¼" H × 1³⁄₁₆" W
$5.75   575QXM4003

PRECIOUS EDITION
Dazzling Reindeer
Green-and-red trim highlights the
harness and bridle.
▢ Artist: LaDene Votruba
1⅜" H × 1¼" W
$9.75   975QXM4026

Dazzling Reindeer

FINAL EDITION
The Bearymores
Third and final in The
Bearymores series
▢ Dated
Artist: Anita Marra Rogers
1⅛" H × ¾" W
$5.75   575QXM5133

SPECIAL EDITION
Noah's Ark
Three-piece set: Noah's Ark
display piece with two Keepsake
Miniature Ornaments. More
animals to follow. Deck lifts off
and ladder lowers.
▢ Artist: Linda Sickman
Ark: 3⅛" H × 4⁵⁄₁₆" W
Bears: ⅝" H × 1¹⁄₁₆" W
Seals: ⅝" H × 1" W
$24.50   2450QXM4106

Mom

GENERAL
Baking Tiny Treats
Set of six ornaments
▢ Artist: Ed Seale
Standin' By (mouse with cookie
cutter): ¾" H × ½" W
Merry Mixer (mouse stirring
cookie dough): 1⅛" H × 1" W
Just Dozin' (mouse snoozing in
bowl—dated): ½" H × 1¹⁄₁₆" W
Scoop (mouse with spatula):
¹¹⁄₁₆" H × ¹³⁄₁₆" W
Rollin' Along (mouse on rolling
pin): ¹³⁄₁₆" H × 1¼" W
Official Taster (mouse on cookie
sheet, nibbling cookie):
⁹⁄₁₆" H × 1" W
$29.00   2900QXM4033

Noah's Ark

Have a Cookie

Scooting Along

Friends Need Hugs

Baby's First Christmas

Baking Tiny Treats: Standin' By, Merry Mixer, Just Dozin',
Scoop, Rollin' Along, Official Taster

Dizzy Devil

Dizzy Devil
Artist: Don Palmiter
$^{15}/_{16}$" H × 1" W
$5.75   575QXM4133

Babs Bunny
Artist: Don Palmiter
1$^5/_{16}$" H × 1$^5/_{16}$" W
$5.75   575QXM4116

Buster Bunny
Artist: Don Palmiter
1$^5/_{16}$" H × 1" W
$5.75   575QXM5163

Plucky Duck
Artist: Don Palmiter
1$^1/_8$" H × $^5/_8$" W
$5.75   575QXM4123

Hamton
Artist: Don Palmiter
1$^1/_{16}$" H × $^{13}/_{16}$" W
$5.75   575QXM4126

GENERAL
Graceful Carousel Horse
Pewter
Dated
Artist: Ron Bishop
1$^1/_4$" H × 1$^3/_8$" W
$7.75   775QXM4056

Melodic Cherub
Dated
Artist: Anita Marra Rogers
1$^5/_{16}$" H × $^{11}/_{16}$" W
$3.75   375QXM4066

Love Was Born
Dated
Artist: Linda Sickman
1$^3/_{16}$" H × $^7/_8$" W
$4.50   450QXM4043

Jolly Visitor
Dated
Artist: Linda Sickman
1" H × $^3/_4$" W
$5.75   575QXM4053

Journey to Bethlehem
Artist: Joyce Lyle
1$^1/_4$" H × 1$^1/_{16}$" W
$5.75   575QXM4036

Babs Bunny   Buster Bunny

Plucky Duck

Hamton

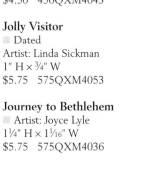

Graceful Carousel Horse   Melodic Cherub

Love Was Born   Jolly Visitor   Journey to Bethlehem

A Merry Flight
Turn dial with thumb, and Santa circles village.
▦ Dated
Artist: Ken Crow
1" H × 1⅛" W
$5.75   575QXM4073

Sweet Dreams
▦ Artist: Ken Crow
¹¹⁄₁₆" H × ⅞" W
$3.00   300QXM4096

Tea with Teddy
▦ Dated
Artist: Anita Marra Rogers
¹⁵⁄₁₆" H × ¹⁵⁄₁₆" W
$7.25   725QXM4046

Jolly Wolly Snowman
Tap gently, and the snowman will wobble.
▦ Dated
Artist: LaDene Votruba
1" H × ¾" W
$3.75   375QXM4093

Hearts A-Sail
▦ Dated
Artist: Ron Bishop
¹⁵⁄₁₆" H × ⅞" W
$5.75   575QXM4006

Beary Perfect Tree
▦ Dated
Artist: Ron Bishop
1³⁄₁₆" H × ¹³⁄₁₆" W
$4.75   475QXM4076

Just My Size
▦ Dated
Artist: Ron Bishop
1⁵⁄₁₆" H × ¹¹⁄₁₆" W
$3.75   375QXM4086

Corny Elf
▦ Artist: Dill Rhodus
1" H × ¹³⁄₁₆" W
$4.50   450QXM4063

Pour Some More
"Enjoy Coca-Cola®"
▦ Artist: Robert Chad
1⁹⁄₁₆" H × 1¼" W
$5.75   575QXM5156

Cute as a Button
▦ Dated
Artist: Ken Crow
¹³⁄₁₆" H × 1" W
$3.75   375QXM4103

A Merry Flight

Sweet Dreams

Tea with Teddy

Jolly Wolly Snowman

Hearts A-Sail

Beary Perfect Tree

Just My Size

Corny Elf

Pour Some More

Cute as a Button

The Easter Ornament Collection
1994

In 1994, an ornament called **Yummy Recipe** came with an added bonus—a carrot cake recipe from Anita Marra Rogers' mom! The Here Comes Easter series rolled in for its first appearance, the Springtime Bonnets series continued, and two series—Eggs in Sports and Easter Parade—took their final bows.

Among the host of beautifully playful spring animals portrayed in this year's line, we find SNOOPY (the Easter beagle!) decorating CHARLIE BROWN's head in lieu of an Easter egg!

Here Comes Easter

NEW SERIES
Here Comes Easter
Egg car
First in the Here Comes Easter series
▨ Dated
Artist: Ken Crow
1¾" H × 1¼" W
$7.75   775QEO8093

Collector's Plate
"Gathering Sunny Memories"
First in the Collector's Plate series
Hand-painted fine porcelain
▨ Dated
Artist: LaDene Votruba
3" diameter
$7.75   775QEO8233

Springtime Bonnets
Second in the Springtime Bonnets series
▨ Dated
Artist: Ron Bishop
2¼" H × 1¼" W
$7.75   775QEO8096

FINAL EDITIONS
Eggs in Sports
Third and final in the Eggs in Sports series
▨ Dated
Artist: Bob Siedler
2" H × 1½" W
$6.75   675QEO8133

Easter Parade
Third and final in the Easter Parade series
▨ Dated
Artist: Dill Rhodus
1¼" H × 1½" W
$6.75   675QEO8136

GENERAL
Daughter
▨ Dated
Artist: Patricia Andrews
2" H × 1¼" W
$5.75   575QEO8156

Son
▨ Dated
Artist: Patricia Andrews
2" H × 1¼" W
$5.75   575QEO8163

Colorful Spring
Bunny in swing made out of CRAYOLA® Crayons.
▨ Dated
Artist: Ken Crow
3" H × 2" W
$7.75   775QEO8166

Collector's Plate

Springtime Bonnets

Eggs in Sport

Easter Parade

Daughter

Son

Colorful Spring

Baby's First Easter
⬜ Dated
Artist: John "Collin" Francis
2" H × 1½" W
$6.75   675QEO8153

Sunny Bunny Garden
Set of three ornaments
⬜ Dated
Artist: Ed Seale
Prize Posey: 1¼" H × 1" W
Top Carrot: 1¼" H × 1" W
Daisies' Friend: 1¼" H × 1" W
$15.00   1500QEO8146

PEANUTS®
⬜ Dated
Artist: Duane Unruh
2¼" H × 1" W
$7.75   775QEO8176

Divine Duet
⬜ Artist: LaDene Votruba
2" H × 1½" W
$6.75   675QEO8183

Sweet as Sugar
Peekaboo Egg
⬜ Dated
Artist: Anita Marra Rogers
2¾" H × 1¾" W
$8.75   875QEO8086

**Sweet Easter Wishes,
Tender Touches**
⬜ Dated
Artist: Ed Seale
2" H × 1½" W
$8.75   875QEO8196

Peeping Out
⬜ Artist: Duane Unruh
1¼" H × 1" W
$6.75   675QEO8203

Treetop Cottage
⬜ Dated
Artist: Linda Sickman
2" H × 1⅜" W
$9.75   975QEO8186

Joyful Lamb
⬜ Artist: Duane Unruh
1¾" H × 1" W
$5.75   575QEO8206

Riding a Breeze
⬜ Dated
Artist: Don Palmiter
2½" H × 1½" W
$5.75   575QEO8213

Easter Art Show
⬜ Dated
Artist: LaDene Votruba
2¼" H × 1½" W
$7.75   775QEO8193

ARTISTS' FAVORITES
Yummy Recipe
Bunny with carrot cake. Recipe
for carrot cake enclosed.
⬜ Dated
Artist: Anita Marra Rogers
2¼" H × 1¼" W
$7.75   775QEO8143

Baby's First Easter

Sunny Bunny Garden: Prize Posey, Top Carrot, Daisies' Friend

Peanuts®

Divine Duet

Sweet as Sugar

Sweet Easter Wishes, Tender Touches

Peeping Out

Treetop Cottage

Joyful Lamb

Riding a Breeze

Easter Art Show

Yummy Recipe

Keepsake Ornament
Collector's Club

1998

Special designs for members of the Hallmark Keepsake Ornament Collector's Club

Exclusive, collectible Keepsake Ornaments that are for Club members only continue to be a benefit of membership in the Hallmark Keepsake Ornament Collector's Club.

Each of the annual membership kits includes Keepsake Ornaments that are referred to as "Keepsake of Membership Ornaments" or simply "Membership Ornaments." These ornaments are beautiful representations of traditional Christmas themes.

Club members also have the opportunity to purchase Club-exclusive ornaments through local Hallmark stores. These Keepsake Ornaments—called "Members-Only Ornaments," "Limited-Edition Ornaments" or, most recently, "Club Edition Ornaments"—often are inspired by popular licensed characters.

Member-Get-Member Gift Bonus ornaments (for Club members who shared the gift of membership with a new member) or Early Renewal Bonus ornaments (for members who renewed early) were part of the Club's offering during some years. From time to time, these extra bonus gifts were not Keepsake Ornaments, but were Merry Miniatures® figurines or special lapel pins. Because this book is dedicated to Keepsake Ornaments, other types of members-only collectibles are not included here.

Club members who attended special Club-sponsored events—EXPO in 1994 and 1995, Artists on Tour in 1996 and 1997, and the 25th Anniversary Celebration in 1998—also had the opportunity to purchase event-exclusive ornaments. Keepsake Ornaments that Club members could purchase during those events are included here; ornaments or other Hallmark products given away in register-to-win drawings as door prizes or as gifts during the events are not included.

Kringle Bells

Making His Way

New Christmas Friend

MEMBERSHIP ORNAMENTS

Kringle Bells
Miniature Ornament
HALLMARK
ARCHIVES COLLECTION
▪ Dated
Artist: Katrina Bricker
1½" H × ¾" W
QXC4486A

Making His Way
Complements the FOLK ART AMERICANA COLLECTION
▪ Dated
Artist: Linda Sickman
4½" H × 3⁵⁄₁₆" W
QXC4523A

New Christmas Friend
HALLMARK ARCHIVES COLLECTION
▪ Dated
Artist: Joanne Eschrich
3½" H × 2¾" W
QXC4516A

Based on the 1990 Happy Holidays®
BARBIE® Doll

1935 Steelcraft by Murray®

Follow the Leader

25TH ANNIVERSARY CELEBRATION EVENT-EXCLUSIVE ORNAMENTS

Christmas Eve Preparations

Studio Edition
Offered exclusively during the 25th Anniversary Celebration event in Kansas City.
■ Dated
A collaborative piece by 21 studio artists.
Sleigh: Duane Unruh
Elf on sleigh: Ed Seale
The base of Christmas Eve Preparations, Santa's leather bag and toys attached to bag: Linda Sickman
Teddy bear peeking over Santa's bag: Sue Tague
Santa's purple lap blanket: Dill Rhodus
The Good Girls and Boys book: Robert Chad
Puppy: Kristina Kline
Police car: Patricia Andrews
Ship: Ken Crow
Airplane: John "Collin" Francis
Nutcracker: Tracy Larsen
Rocking horse: Anita Marra Rogers
Horn: Don Palmiter
Elf loading a package into the sleigh: Nello Williams
Three birds: LaDene Votruba
Elf holding reins: Katrina Bricker
Bunny sitting in front of sleigh: Bob Siedler
Two chipmunks on the side of sleigh: Nina Aubé
Drum and top: Sharon Pike
Victorian doll: Joyce Lyle
Duck and rabbit in back of sleigh: Joanne Eschrich
Sleigh: 3¾" H × 7" W
Boat: 11/16" H × 1¼" W
Nutcracker: 1⅜" H × 9/16" W
Horn: 7/16" H × 3/16" W
Airplane: 11/16" H × 1⅛" W
Rocking Horse: 1" H × 1" W
Car: 9/16" H × 15/16" W
$85.00 8500QXC4506

A Late-Night Snack

Complements the 1998 Keepsake Ornament Studio Edition.
Offered exclusively during the 25th Anniversary Celebration event in Kansas City.
■ Dated
Artists: Robert Chad and Tammy Haddix
4" H × 4⅜" W
$19.95 1995QXC4536

CLUB EDITION ORNAMENTS

Based on the 1990 Happy Holidays® BARBIE® Doll

Third in the Collector's Club series
Complements the Keepsake Ornament Holiday BARBIE™ Collector's series that has depicted Mattel's annual doll since 1993.
■ Dated
Artist: Patricia Andrews
3 9/16" H × 2¾" W
$15.95 1595QXC4493

1935 Steelcraft by Murray®

Based on a 1935 Steelcraft by Murray® pedal car design. This classic pedal car was reproduced as a scale-model Luxury Edition Hallmark Collectible in 1996.
■ Dated
Artist: Don Palmiter
1 15/16" H × 3½" W
$15.95 1595QXC4496

Follow the Leader

Two-piece set
■ Dated
Artist: Bob Siedler
Lucy, Linus and Snoopy: 2 5/16" H × 2 15/16" W
Charlie Brown: 2 5/16" H × 1 5/16" W
$16.95 1695QXC4503

A Late-Night Snack

Christmas Eve Preparations

1997

Based on the 1989 Happy Holidays®
BARBIE® Doll

Farmer's Market, Tender Touches

1937 Steelcraft Airflow by Murray®

CLUB EDITION ORNAMENTS

Based on the 1989 Happy Holidays® BARBIE® Doll

Second in the Collector's
Club series
Complements the Keepsake
Ornament Holiday BARBIE™
Collector's series that has
depicted Mattel's annual doll
since 1993.
■ Dated
Artist: Patricia Andrews
3¾" H × 3⁵⁄₁₆" W
$15.95   1595QXC5162

Farmer's Market, Tender Touches

Complements Bumper Crop, a
three-piece ornament set from
the 1997 Spring Keepsake
Ornament Collection.
■ Dated
Artist: Ed Seale
2¾" H × 2⁹⁄₁₆" W
$15.00   1500QXC5182

1937 Steelcraft Airflow by Murray®

■ Dated
Artist: Don Palmiter
1⅞" H × 3⅝" L × 1½" W
$15.95   1595QXC5185

Happy Christmas to All!

Away to the Window

Jolly Old Santa

Ready for Santa

Mrs. Claus's Story

Trimming Santa's Tree

ARTISTS ON TOUR EVENT-EXCLUSIVE ORNAMENTS

Mrs. Claus's Story

Complements the 1997 Keepsake
Studio Edition. Offered exclu-
sively during 10 regional Artists
on Tour events.
■ Dated
Mrs. Claus: Joanne Eschrich
Cat, chair, floor, and braided rug:
Kristina Kline
3⅜" H × 2¼" W
$14.95

Trimming Santa's Tree

Studio Edition
One Keepsake Miniature
Ornament with display piece
offered exclusively during 10
regional Artists On Tour events.
■ Dated
A collaborative piece by 19
studio artists.
Christmas tree: Robert Chad
Angel topper: Joyce Lyle
Santa moon design, playful kitten
Anita Marra Rogers
Candy cane; Teddy bear with a
heart; and designs resembling
the Clothespin Soldier, Here
Comes Santa, Tin Locomotive,
Nostalgic Houses and Shops
and Rocking Horse collector's
series: Linda Sickman
Chipmunk: Ed Seale
Dollhouse: Ken Crow
Horse pull toy: LaDene Votruba
Puppy peeking out of gift box:
Katrina Bricker
Creche: John "Collin" Francis
Dragon in the wagon: Nina Aubé
Wagon: Tracy Larsen
Roadster: Don Palmiter
Bear sitting in roadster: Nello
Williams
Elf on top of ladder: Sue Tague
Elf assisting below: Sharon Pike
Packages surrounding Sharon's elf:
Patricia Andrews
Elf wrapping: Bob Siedler
Ladder with holly leaf carvings:
Duane Unruh
Floor and braided rug: Dill
Rhodus
Christmas tree: 6⅛" H × 4¼" W
Roadster: 1¹⁄₁₆" H × 1⅞" W
$60.00   6000QXC5175

KEEPSAKE OF MEMBERSHIP ORNAMENTS

Happy Christmas to All!

■ Dated
Artist: Nello Williams
3⁷⁄₁₆" H × 3" W
QXC5132

Away to the Window

■ Dated
Artist: Nello Williams
4¼" H × 2⅝" W
QXC5135

Jolly Old Santa

Miniature Ornament
■ Dated
Artist: Nello Williams
1" H × ¹³⁄₁₆" W
QXC5145

Ready for Santa

Miniature Ornament
■ Dated
Artist: Nello Williams
1" H × ¹¹⁄₁₆" W
QXC5142

Santa

Rudolph® The Red-Nosed Reindeer

Rudolph®'s Helper

KEEPSAKE OF MEMBERSHIP ORNAMENTS

Santa
☐ Dated
Artist: Bob Siedler
4¹³⁄₁₆" H × 2⅝" W
QXC4164

Rudolph®
The Red-Nosed Reindeer
Keepsake Magic Ornament.
Light. Rudolph's nose glows.
This exclusive Keepsake of
Membership Ornament is
based on the styling made
famous by the
Robert L. May Co.
☐ Dated
Artist: Bob Siedler
4¹⁄₁₆" H × 2⅝" W
QXC7341

Rudolph®'s Helper
Miniature Ornament
☐ Dated
Artist: Bob Siedler
1¹¹⁄₁₆" H × 1⅛" W
QXC4171

ARTISTS ON TOUR EVENT-EXCLUSIVE ORNAMENTS

Miniature Gold-plated Rocking Horse
Offered exclusively during eight
regional Artists On Tour events.
24 karat gold-plated
☐ Dated
Artist: Linda Sickman
1⅛" H × 1½" W
$12.95

Toy Shop Santa

Santa's Toy Shop

Rocking Horse

ARTISTS ON TOUR EVENT-EXCLUSIVE ORNAMENTS

Toy Shop Santa
Complements the 1996 Keepsake
Signature Collection piece offered
exclusively during eight regional
Artist On Tour events.
☐ Dated
Artist: Duane Unruh
3¾" H × 2½" W
$14.95

Santa's Toy Shop
Keepsake Signature Collection
Two Keepsake Miniature
Ornaments with display piece
offered exclusively during eight
regional Artists On Tour events.
☐ Dated
A collaborative piece by 17
studio artists.
Jack-in-box: John "Collin" Francis
Rag doll: Anita Marra Rogers
Toy shop: Linda Sickman
Dog: Dill Rhodus
Table: Robert Chad
Sweeping elf: LaDene Votruba
Clock: Ken Crow
Sweeping mouse, airplane, and
paint buckets: Patricia Andrews
Sewing elf: Sue Tague
Painting elf: Nina Aubé
Race car: Bob Siedler
Teddy bear: Joyce Lyle
Mouse with dustpan: Sharon Pike
Standing elf: Don Palmiter
Chair and stool: Ed Seale
Tools: Duane Unruh
Cat: Katrina Bricker
Toy shop: 5½" H × 6½" W
Jack-in-box: 1¼" H × ⅞" W
Doll: ¹⁵⁄₁₆" H × ¹¹⁄₁₆" W
$60.00   6000QXC4201

CLUB EDITION ORNAMENTS

Based on the 1988 Happy Holidays® BARBIE® Doll
First in the new Collector's Club
series
Complements the Keepsake
Ornament Holiday BARBIE™
Collector's series that has depict-
ed Mattel's annual doll since
1993.
☐ Dated
Artist: Patricia Andrews
3⁹⁄₁₆" H × 3¼" W
$14.95   1495QXC4181

1937 Steelcraft Auburn by Murray®
Die-cast metal. Based on a 1935
Auburn pedal car design.
Complements the Keepsake
Ornament Kiddie Car
Classics series.
☐ Dated
Artist: Don Palmiter
1⅞" H × 3¹⁵⁄₁₆" W
$15.95   1595QXC4174

Based on the 1988 Happy Holidays®
BARBIE® Doll

The Wizard of Oz™

1937 Steelcraft Auburn by Murray®

The Wizard of Oz™
Based on a memorable scene from
the motion picture classic *The
Wizard of Oz™*.
☐ Artist: Anita Marra Rogers
4¹⁵⁄₁₆" H × 2⁵⁄₁₆" W
$12.95   1295QXC4161

MEMBER-GET-MEMBER ORNAMENT

Airmail for Santa
Gift membership bonus ornament
available only to current Club
members who enrolled a new
member during 1996.
☐ Dated
Artist: Anita Marra Rogers
2⁷⁄₁₆" H × 2¼" W
QXC4194

Holiday Bunny

EARLY RENEWAL BONUS

Holiday Bunny
Miniature
☐ Artist: John "Collin" Francis
1³⁄₁₆" diameter
QXC4191

Airmail for Santa

1995

Collecting Memories

A Gift from Rodney

CLUB EDITION ORNAMENTS

1958 Ford Edsel Citation Convertible
Complements the Classic American Car series.
☐ Dated
Artist: Don Palmiter
1⅜" H × 4¹³⁄₁₆" W
$12.95   1295QXC4167

Home from the Woods
Complements the FOLK ART AMERICANA COLLECTION.
☐ Dated
Artist: Linda Sickman
3¾" H × 3¹⁄₁₆" W
$15.95   1595QXC1059

Brunette Debut—1959 BARBIE™
☐ Dated
Artist: Patricia Andrews
4⁷⁄₁₆" H × 1¼" W
$14.95   1495QXC5397

1958 Ford Edsel Citation Convertible

KEEPSAKE OF MEMBERSHIP ORNAMENTS

Collecting Memories
☐ Dated
Artist: Bob Siedler
3⅞" H × 2⁵⁄₁₆" W
QXC4117

A Gift from Rodney
Keepsake Miniature Ornament
☐ Dated
Artist: Linda Sickman
1⅛" H × 1¹⁄₁₆" W
QXC4129

Cool Santa
Coca-Cola® Keepsake Miniature Ornament
☐ Artist: John "Collin" Francis
1³⁄₁₆" H × ⅞" W
QXC4457

Fishing for Fun
☐ Dated
Artist: Ed Seale
3¹⁄₁₆" H × 2¾" W
QXC5207

Cool Santa

Fishing for Fun

Home from the Woods

Brunette Debut—1959 BARBIE™

Christmas Eve Bake-Off®

EXPO EVENT-EXCLUSIVE ORNAMENTS

The following ornaments were available exclusively during eight regional EXPO events.

Christmas Eve Bake-Off®
Keepsake Signature Collection Keepsake Ornament with display piece.
☐ Dated
A collaborative piece by 14 studio artists.
Mrs. Claus ornament: Anita Marra Rogers
Stove: Duane Unruh
Teapot: LaDene Votruba

Cookie jar: Patricia Andrews
Salt and pepper shakers: Ken Crow
Pie: Bob Siedler
Coal bucket: Dill Rhodus
Coffeepot: Linda Sickman
Muffins: Robert Chad
Elf holding cookbook: John "Collin" Francis
Elf with cookie sheet: Ed Seale
Dog: Julia Lee
Cat and milk: Joyce Lyle
Milk can: Don Palmiter
Mrs. Claus: 2¹⁵⁄₁₆" H × 1⁵⁄₁₆" W
Stove: 5⅛" H × 5⁷⁄₁₆" W
$60.00   6000QXC4049

1995

**Miniature Pewter
Rocking Horse**
◻ Dated
Artist: Linda Sickman
1⅛" H × 1½" W
$9.75

Artists' Caricatures
◻ 3¼" diameter
$7.95

Miniature Pewter Rocking Horse

Artists' Caricatures

RENEWAL BONUS
Cozy Christmas
"Santa's Club Soda"
◻ Artist: John "Collin" Francis
1³⁄₁₆" diameter
QXC4119

Cozy Christmas

Holiday Pursuit

Sweet Bouquet

Holiday Pursuit
◻ Dated
Artist: John "Collin" Francis
2⅞" H × 2¹⁄₁₆" W
QXC4823

Sweet Bouquet
Keepsake Miniature Ornament
"Santa's Club Soda"
◻ Artist: John "Collin" Francis
1³⁄₁₆" diameter
QXC4806

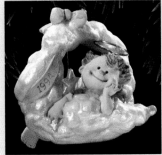

On Cloud Nine

Majestic Deer

CLUB EDITION ORNAMENTS
On Cloud Nine
◻ Dated
Artist: Donna Lee
2¹⁄₁₆" H × 1¹⁵⁄₁₆" W
$12.00   1200QXC4853

Majestic Deer
Hand-painted fine porcelain and
pewter. Wood display stand
included.
◻ Artist: Duane Unruh
3¾" H × 4⅜" W
$25.00   2500QXC4836

Jolly Holly Santa
Handcrafted and hand-painted.
Wood display stand included.
◻ Artist: Joyce Lyle
3⅛" H × 3³⁄₁₆" W
$22.00   2200QXC4833

MEMBERS ONLY ORNAMENT
May Flower
Can be displayed with April
Shower from the 1995 Easter
Keepsake Ornament collection.
◻ Dated
Artist: Bob Siedler
1¹⁄₁₆" H × 1⅛" W
$4.95   495QXC8246

MEMBER-GET-MEMBER
ORNAMENT
First Hello
Gift membership bonus ornament
available only to current Club
members who enrolled a new
member during 1994.
◻ Dated
Artist: Anita Marra Rogers
2" H × 1¼" W
QXC4846

Jolly Holly Santa

May Flower

First Hello

1994 EXPO COLLECTION

The following six ornaments were available exclusively during eight regional EXPO events—two of the six ornaments were sold during each event. Individually cast and plated in 22-karat gold. Fabric ribbon hangers.

Golden Stars and Holly

Golden Sleigh

Mrs. Claus' Cupboard

Golden Santa

Golden Bow

EXPO EVENT-EXCLUSIVE ORNAMENTS

Mrs. Claus' Cupboard
Keepsake Signature Collection
10 Keepsake Miniature Ornaments with display piece. Handcrafted and wood. Offered exclusively during eight regional EXPO events.
A collaborative piece by 14 studio artists.
Hutch, packages and polar bear: Linda Sickman
Elf: Robert Chad
Basket of pinecones: Don Palmiter
Garland and dog: Anita Marra Rogers
Cat: Dill Rhodus
Church: Julia Lee
Creche: John "Collin" Francis
Collector's plate: LaDene Votruba
Mice with books: Ed Seale
Angel: Patricia Andrews
Traditional Santa: Duane Unruh
Victorian Santa: Joyce Lyle
Ark: Ken Crow
Christmas tree: Bob Siedler
Hutch: 6" H × 5^{11}/16" W
Traditional Santa:
^{15}/16" H × ^{11}/16" W
Ark: ^{7}/8" H × 1^{3}/16" W
Victorian Santa: ^{15}/16" H × ^{7}/8" W
Angel: ^{15}/16" H × ^{9}/16" W
Polar bear: ^{13}/16" H × 1^{1}/16" W
Church: 1^{1}/8" H × ^{3}/4" W
Nativity: ^{13}/16" H × ^{13}/16" W
Tree: 1^{9}/16" H × ^{15}/16" W
Mice with books:
^{13}/16" H × 1^{7}/16" W
Collector's plate: ^{7}/8" H × ^{13}/16" W
$55.00 5500QXC4843

Golden Stars and Holly
Artist: Don Palmiter
3^{1}/16" tall
$10.00

Golden Sleigh
Artist: Don Palmiter
3^{1}/8" tall
$10.00

Golden Santa
Artist: Duane Unruh
3^{5}/16" tall
$10.00

Golden Bow
Artist: Don Palmiter
3^{5}/8" tall
$10.00

Golden Dove
Artist: Don Palmiter
3^{3}/16" tall
$10.00

Golden Poinsettia
Artist: Duane Unruh
4" tall
$10.00

Golden Dove

Golden Poinsettia

Added Attractions

This section is designed to help you identify Hallmark ornaments that were made and marketed between 1994 and 1998 as part of promotional programs. These ornaments were not a part of the Keepsake Ornament line. However, they were offered for a limited time period, making them quite collectible.

1998 BARBIE™ COLLECTION
These Keepsake Ornaments were part of the BARBIE™ Collectibles group that also included figurines, dolls, plates and cards.

Holiday Voyage™ BARBIE™
Holiday Homecoming Collection
Inspired by the Hallmark-exclusive Holiday Voyage™ BARBIE® doll.
Artist: Anita Marra Rogers
4" H × 2^{3}/8" W
$14.95 1495QHB6016

Holiday Memories™ BARBIE™
Victorian Christmas Collection
Inspired by the Hallmark-exclusive Holiday Memories™ BARBIE® doll.
Artist: Patricia Andrews
2^{5}/16" H × 4^{1}/16" W
$14.95 1495QHB6020

Holiday Voyage™ BARBIE™

Holiday Memories™ BARBIE™

Decorating Maxine-Style

Decorating Maxine-Style
Character designer: John Wagner
5" H × 2¼" W
$10.95   1095QXE6883

These Keepsake Ornaments were part of the BARBIE™ Collectibles group that also included figurines, dolls, plates and cards.

Holiday Traditions BARBIE™ Ornament
Holiday Homecoming Collection
Inspired by the Hallmark-exclusive Holiday Traditions™ BARBIE® doll.
   Artist: Anita Marra Rogers
4" H × 2½" W
$14.95   1495QHB6002

Victorian Elegance™ BARBIE™ Ornament
Victorian Christmas Collection
Inspired by the Hallmark-exclusive Victorian Elegance™ BARBIE® doll.
   Artist: Patricia Andrews
2⁵⁄₁₆" H × 4¹⁄₁₆" W
$14.95   1495QHB6004

Gift of Friendship, Winnie the Pooh
3¼" diameter
$12.95   1295QXE6835

The Perfect Tree, Tender Touches
   Dated
Artist: Ed Seale
2³⁄₁₆" H × 2¾" W
$15.00   1500QX6572

Welcome Sign, Tender Touches
   Dated
Artist: Ed Seale
2⁹⁄₁₆" H × 2⁷⁄₁₆" W
$15.00   1500QX6331

Filled with Memories
Get Hooked on Collecting Starter Set included a book describing the joys of collecting and starting traditions with Keepsake Ornaments, along with this ornament.
   Dated
Artist: Joyce Lyle
3⁷⁄₁₆" H × 2³⁄₁₆" W
$7.99   799XPR837

Holiday Traditions BARBIE™ Ornament

Wish List, Tender Touches
   Dated
Artist: Ed Seale
2³⁄₈" H × 2⁵⁄₈" W
$15.00   1500QX5859

Happy Holiday Album
Photo Holder
Album opens.
   Artist: Ed Seale
5⁷⁄₁₆" H × 2¾" W
$2.95   295QX6307

A CHARLIE BROWN CHRISTMAS
30th Anniversary Collection
Hallmark stores that participated in the 1995 REACH advertising program offered these four Keepsake Ornaments and a display base.

Snow Scene
PEANUTS®
Tabletop display
   Dated
"A Charlie Brown Christmas television special
Happy 30th anniversary
1965–1995"
   Artist: Anita Marra Rogers
3⁵⁄₁₆" H × 6¹¹⁄₁₆" W
$3.95   395QRP4227
Linus
PEANUTS®
   Artist: Anita Marra Rogers
2½" H × 1⅛" W
$3.95   395QRP4217
Lucy
PEANUTS®
   Artist: Bob Siedler
2½" H × 1¼" W
$3.95   395QRP4209
Charlie Brown
PEANUTS®
   Artist: Bob Siedler
2¹³⁄₁₆" H × 2³⁄₁₆" W
$3.95   395QRP4207
Snoopy
PEANUTS®
   Artist: Anita Marra Rogers
2³⁄₁₆" H × 1½" W
$3.95   395QRP4219

Victorian Elegance™ BARBIE™ Ornament

Gift of Friendship, Winnie the Pooh

The Perfect Tree
Tender Touches

Welcome Sign
Tender Touches

Filled with
Memories

Wish List, Tender Touches

Happy Holiday Album

A CHARLIE BROWN CHRISTMAS

Eager for Christmas, Tender Touches

Eager for Christmas Tender Touches
   Dated
Artist: Ed Seale
2⅞" H × 2½" W
$15.00   1500QX5336

The Collectible Series

A collectible series consists of ornaments that share a theme or motif. Series ornaments are issued one per year for a minimum of three years and are among the most popular with collectors. Two of the longest-running and most-popular series are Here Comes Santa and Frosty Friends.

Beginning in 1982, series ornaments began to be identified with the words, "(number) in a series" or with a tree-shaped symbol with the edition number inside. The Keepsake Easter/Spring series ornaments carry an egg-shaped symbol with the edition number.

This section of the guide chronicles all of the ornaments in Hallmark Keepsake Ornament series that started, continued or ended from 1994 through 1998. If a series ended before 1994, it does not appear in this volume but would be found in the sixth edition of *Hallmark Keepsake Ornaments: A Collector's Guide*.

African-American Holiday BARBIE™: 1998

African-American Holiday BARBIE™
☐ 1998   1595QX6936

A Pony for Christmas
☐ 1998   1095QX6316

Spotlight on SNOOPY
☐ 1998   995QX6453
 Joe Cool

Snow Buddies
☐ 1998   795QX6853

A Pony for Christmas: 1998

Spotlight on SNOOPY: 1998

Snow Buddies: 1998

Disney Unforgettable Villains
☐ 1998   1495QXD4063
Cruella de Vil

Madame Alexander® Holiday Angels
☐ 1998   1495QX6493
Glorious Angel

Disney Unforgettable Villains: 1998

Madame Alexander® Holiday Angels: 1998

Old West: 1998

Winnie the Pooh: 1998

The Old West
☐ 1998   1395QX6323
Pony Express Rider

Winnie the Pooh
☐ 1998   1395QXD4086
A Visit from Piglet

Disney Romantic Vacations
☐ 1998   1495QXD4103
Donald and Daisy in Venice

Disney Romantic Vacations: 1998

Scarlett O'Hara™
- 1998   1495QX6336
- 1997   1495QX6125

Sky's the Limit
- 1998   1495QX6286
   1917 Curtiss JN–4D "Jenny"
- 1997   1495QX5574
   The Flight at Kitty Hawk

Stock Car Champions
- 1998   1595QXI4143
   Richard Petty
- 1997   1595QXI6165
   Jeff Gordon

STAR WARS™
- 1998   1395QXI4026
   Princess Leia™
- 1997   1395QXI5484
   Luke Skywalker™

Marilyn Monroe
- 1998   1495QX6333
- 1997   1495QX5704

Scarlett O'Hara™: 1998, 1997

Sky's the Limit: 1998, 1997

Stock Car Champions: 1998, 1997

STAR WARS™: 1998, 1997

Marilyn Monroe: 1998, 1997

Hockey Greats: 1998, 1997

The Clauses on Vacation: 1998, 1997

Hockey Greats
☐ 1998   1595QXI6476
   Mario Lemieux
☐ 1997   1595QXI6275
   Wayne Gretzky

The Clauses on Vacation
☐ 1998   1495QX6276
☐ 1997   1495QX6112

Majestic Wilderness
☐ 1998   1295QX6273
   Timber Wolves at Play
☐ 1997   1295QX5694
   Snowshoe Rabbits in Winter

Majestic Wilderness: 1998, 1997

Thomas Kinkade
- 1998   1095QX6343
  Victorian Christmas II
- 1997   1095QXI6135
  Victorian Christmas

Mickey's Holiday Parade
- 1998   1395QXD4106
  Minnie Plays the Flute
- 1997   1395QXD4022
  Bandleader Mickey

Thomas Kinkade: 1998, 1997

Enchanted Memories Collection
- 1998   1495QXD4056
  Walt Disney's Snow White
- 1997   1495QXD4045
  Walt Disney's Cinderella

Hallmark Archives
- 1998   1295QXD4006
  Ready for Christmas
- 1997   1295QXD4025
  Donald's Surprising Gift

Enchanted Memories Collection: 1998, 1997

Mickey's Holiday Parade: 1998, 1997

Hallmark Archives: 1998, 1997

The Language of Flowers: 1998, 1997, 1996

All God's Children®: 1998, 1997, 1996

The Language of Flowers
- 1998   1595QX6156
  Iris Angel
- 1997   1595QX1095
  Snowdrop Angel
- 1996   1595QK1171
  Pansy

All God's Children®
- 1998   1295QX6363
  Ricky
- 1997   1295QX6142
  Nikki
- 1996   1295QX5564
  Christy

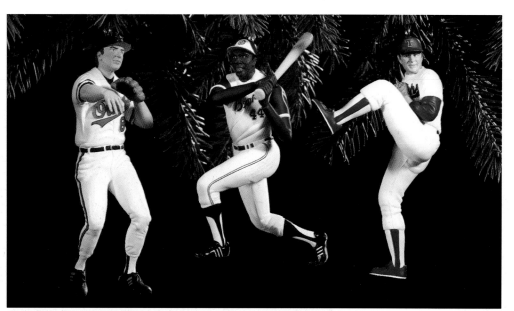

At the Ballpark: 1998, 1997, 1996

Madame Alexander™: 1998, 1997, 1996

"Dolls of the World": 1998, 1997, 1996

At the Ballpark
1998   1495QXI4033
Cal Ripken Jr.
1997   1495QXI6152
Hank Aaron
1996   1495QXI5711
Nolan Ryan

Madame Alexander™
1998   1495QX6353
Mop Top Wendy
1997   1495QX6155
Little Red Riding Hood
1996   1495QX6311
Cinderella—1995

"Dolls of the World"
1998   1495QX6356
Mexican BARBIE™
1997   1495QX6162
Chinese BARBIE™
1996   1495QX5561
Native American BARBIE™

A Celebration of Angels
- 1998 1395QX6366
- 1997 1395QX6175
- 1996 1295QX5634
- 1995 1295QX5077

LIONEL® Train
- 1998 1895QX6346
  Pennsylvania GG–1
  Locomotive
- 1997 1895QX6145
  1950 Santa Fe F3 Diesel
  Locomotive
- 1996 1895QX5531
  700E Hudson Steam
  Locomotive

A Celebration of Angels: 1998, 1997, 1996, 1995

LIONEL® Train: 1998, 1997, 1996

Football Legends

1998 1495QXI4036
Emmitt Smith
1997 1495QXI6182
Joe Namath
1996 1495QXI5021
Troy Aikman
1995 1495QXI5759
Joe Montana

Football Legends: 1998, 1997, 1996, 1995

Hoop Stars

1998 1495QXI6846
Grant Hill
1997 1495QXI6832
Magic Johnson
1996 1495QX15014
Larry Bird
1995 1495QXI5517
Shaquille O'Neal

Hoop Stars: 1998, 1997, 1996, 1995

All-American Trucks

1998 1395QX6263
1937 Ford V–8
1997 1395QX6105
1953 GMC
1996 1395QX5241
1955 Chevrolet Cameo
1995 1395QX5527
1956 Ford Truck

All-American Trucks: 1998, 1997, 1996, 1995

Turn-of-the-Century Parade: 1997, 1996, 1995

Christmas Visitors: 1997, 1996, 1995

Cat Naps: 1998, 1997, 1996, 1995, 1994

Turn-of-the-Century Parade
- 1997 1695QX1215
  Santa Claus
- 1996 1695QK1084
  Uncle Sam
- 1995 1695QK1027
  The Fireman

Christmas Visitors
- 1997 1495QX6172
  Kolyada
- 1996 1495QX5631
  Christkindl
- 1995 1495QX5087
  St. Nicholas

Cat Naps
- 1998 895QX6383
- 1997 895QX6205
- 1996 795QX5641
- 1995 795QX5097
- 1994 795QX5313

Baseball Heroes: 1997, 1996, 1995, 1994

Baseball Heroes
1997   1295QX6202
Jackie Robinson
1996   1295QX5304
Satchel Paige
1995   1295QX5029
Lou Gehrig
1994   1295QX5323
Babe Ruth

BARBIE™
1998   1595QXI4043
Silken Flame™
1997   1595QXI6812
Wedding Day 1959–1962
1996   1495QXI6541
Featuring the Enchanted
Evening BARBIE® Doll
1995   1495QXI5049
Solo in the Spotlight
1994   1495QX5006
Debut 1959

Yuletide Central
1998   1895QX6373
1997   1895QX5812
1996   1895QX5011
1995   1895QX5079
1994   1895QX5316

BARBIE™: 1998, 1997, 1996, 1995, 1994

Yuletide Central: 1998, 1997, 1996, 1995, 1994

Mother Goose: 1997, 1996, 1995, 1994, 1993

Mother Goose
- 1997 1395QX6215
  Little Boy Blue
- 1996 1395QX5644
  Mary Had a Little Lamb
- 1995 1395QX5099
  Jack and Jill
- 1994 1395QX5213
  Hey Diddle, Diddle
- 1993 1395QX528-2
  Humpty-Dumpty

Kiddie Car Classics: 1998, 1997, 1996, 1995, 1994

Holiday BARBIE™
- 1998 1595QXI4023
- 1997 1595QXI6212
- 1996 1495QXI5371
- 1995 1495QXI5057
- 1994 1495QX5216
- 1993 1475QX572-5

Kiddie Car Classics
- 1998 1695QX6376
  1955 Murray® Tractor
  and Trailer
- 1997 1395QX6195
  Murray® Dump Truck
- 1996 1395QX5364
  Murray® Airplane
- 1995 1395QX5027
  Murray® Fire Truck
- 1994 1395QX5426
  Murray® "Champion"

Holiday BARBIE™: 1998, 1997, 1996, 1995, 1994, 1993

U.S. Christmas Stamps: 1995, 1994, 1993

The PEANUTS® Gang: 1996, 1995, 1994, 1993

Tobin Fraley Carousel: 1995, 1994, 1993, 1992

Owliver: 1994, 1993, 1992

Betsey's Country Christmas: 1994, 1993, 1992

Owliver
- 1994   795QX5226
- 1993   775QX542-5
- 1992   775QX454-4

Betsey's Country Christmas
- 1994   500QX2403
- 1993   500QX206-2
- 1992   500QX210-4

Classic American Cars
- 1998   1395QX6256
  1970 Plymouth® Hemi 'Cuda
- 1997   1395QX6102
  1969 Hurst Oldsmobile 442
- 1996   1295QX5384
  1959 Cadillac De Ville
- 1995   1295QX5239
  1969 Chevrolet Camaro
- 1994   1295QX5422
  1957 Chevrolet Bel Air
- 1993   1275QX527-5
  1956 Thunderbird
- 1992   1275QX428-4
  1966 Mustang
- 1991   1275QX431-9
  1957 Corvette

Classic American Cars: 1998, 1997, 1996, 1995,

Classic American Cars: 1994, 1993, 1992, 1991

Puppy Love
1998	795QX6163
1997	795QX6222
1996	795QX5651
1995	795QX5137
1994	795QX5253
1993	775QX504-5
1992	775QX448-4
1991	775QX537-9

Merry Olde Santa
1998	1595QX6386
1997	1495QX6225
1996	1495QX5654
1995	1495QX5139
1994	1495QX5256
1993	1475QX484-2
1992	1475QX441-4
1991	1475QX435-9
1990	1475QX473-6

Puppy Love: 1998, 1997, 1996, 1995, 1994, 1993, 1992, 1991

Merry Olde Santa: 1998, 1997, 1996, 1995

Merry Olde Santa: 1994, 1993, 1992, 1991, 1990

Fabulous Decade
	1998	795QX6393
	1997	795QX6232
	1996	795QX5661
	1995	795QX5147
	1994	795QX5263
	1993	775QX447-5
	1992	775QX424-4
	1991	775QX411-9
	1990	775QX446-6

Heart of Christmas
	1994	1495QX5266
	1993	1475QX448-2
	1992	1375QX441-1
	1991	1375QX435-7
	1990	1375QX472-6

Fabulous Decade: 1998, 1997, 1996, 1995, 1994, 1993, 1992, 1991, 1990

Heart of Christmas: Top row—1994, 1992, 1990; bottom row—1993, 1991

CRAYOLA® Crayon

- 1998 1295QX6166
  Bright Sledding Colors
- 1997 1295QX6235
  Bright Rocking Colors
- 1996 1095QX5391
  Bright Flying Colors
- 1995 1095QX5247
  Bright 'n' Sunny Tepee
- 1994 1095QX5273
  Bright Playful Colors
- 1993 1075QX442-2
  Bright Shining Castle
- 1992 975QX426-4
  Bright Blazing Colors
- 1991 975QX421-9
  Bright Vibrant Colors
- 1990 875QX458-6
  Bright Moving Colors
- 1989 875QX435-2
  Bright Journey

CRAYOLA® Crayon: 1998

CRAYOLA® Crayon: 1997, 1996

CRAYOLA® Crayon: 1995, 1994, 1993

CRAYOLA® Crayon: 1992, 1991, 1990

CRAYOLA® Crayon: 1989

Mary's Angels: 1998, 1997

Mary's Angels: 1996

Mary's Angels

- 1998 795QX6153
  Daphne
- 1997 795QX6242
  Daisy
- 1996 695QX5664
  Violet
- 1995 695QX5149
  Camellia
- 1994 695QX5276
  Jasmine
- 1993 675QX428-2
  Ivy
- 1992 675QX427-4
  Lily
- 1991 675QX427-9
  Iris
- 1990 575QX442-3
  Rosebud
- 1989 575QX454-5
  Bluebell
- 1988 500QX407-4
  Buttercup

Mary's Angels: 1995

Mary's Angels: 1994, 1993

Mary's Angels: 1992, 1991, 1990

Mary's Angels: 1989, 1988

Mr. and Mrs. Claus

- 1995 1495QX5157
  Christmas Eve Kiss
- 1994 1495QX5283
  A Handwarming Present
- 1993 1475QX420-2
  A Fitting Moment
- 1992 1475QX429-4
  Gift Exchange
- 1991 1375QX433-9
  Checking His List
- 1990 1375QX439-3
  Popcorn Party
- 1989 1325QX457-5
  Holiday Duet
- 1988 1300QX401-1
  Shall We Dance
- 1987 1325QX483-7
  Home Cooking
- 1986 1300QX402-6
  Merry Mistletoe Time

Mr. and Mrs. Claus: 1995, 1994

Mr. and Mrs. Claus: 1993, 1992

Mr. and Mrs. Claus: 1991

Mr. and Mrs. Claus: 1990, 1989

Mr. and Mrs. Claus: 1988, 1987, 1986

Twelve Days of Christmas: 1995, 1994

Twelve Days of Christmas: 1993

Twelve Days of Christmas

- 1995 695QX3009
Twelve Drummers
Drumming
- 1994 695QX3183
Eleven Pipers Piping
- 1993 675QX301-2
Ten Lords A-Leaping
- 1992 675QX303-1
Nine Ladies Dancing
- 1991 675QX308-9
Eight Maids A-Milking
- 1990 675QX303-3
Seven Swans A-Swimming
- 1989 675QX381-2
Six Geese A-Laying
- 1988 650QX371-4
Five Golden Rings
- 1987 650QX370-9
Four Colly Birds
- 1986 650QX378-6
Three French Hens
- 1985 650QX371-2
Two Turtle Doves
- 1984 600QX348-4
Partridge in a Pear Tree

Twelve Days of Christmas: 1992, 1991, 1990

Twelve Days of Christmas: 1989, 1988, 1987

Twelve Days of Christmas: 1986

Twelve Days of Christmas: 1985, 1984

Nostalgic Houses and Shops: 1998, 1997, 1996

Nostalgic Houses and Shops: 1995

Nostalgic Houses and Shops

- 1998   1695QX6266
  Grocery Store
- 1997   1695QX6245
  Cafe
- 1996   1495QX5671
  Victorian Painted Lady
- 1995   1495QX5159
  Town Church
- 1994   1495QX5286
  Neighborhood Drugstore
- 1993   1475QX417-5
  Cozy Home
- 1992   1475QX425-4
  Five- and Ten-Cent Store
- 1991   1475QX413-9
  Fire Station
- 1990   1475QX469-6
  Holiday Home
- 1989   1425QX458-2
  U.S. Post Office
- 1988   1450QX401-4
  Hall Bro's Card Shop
- 1987   1400QX483-9
  House on Main St.
- 1986   1375QX403-3
  Christmas Candy Shoppe
- 1985   1375QX497-5
  Old-Fashioned Toy Shop
- 1984   1300QX448-1
  Victorian Dollhouse

Nostalgic Houses and Shops: 1994, 1993, 1992, 1991, 1990

Nostalgic Houses and Shops: 1989

Nostalgic Houses and Shops: 1988, 1987, 1986, 1985, 1984

Here Comes Santa: 1998, 1997, 1996, 1995, 1994, 1993

Here Comes Santa
1998 1495QX6283
Santa's Bumper Car
1997 1495QX6262
The Claus-Mobile
1996 1495QX5684
Santa's 4×4
1995 1495QX5179
Santa's Roadster
1994 1495QX5296
Makin' Tractor Tracks
1993 1475QX410-2
Happy Haul-idays
1992 1475QX434-1
Kringle Tours
1991 1475QX434-9
Santa's Antique Car
1990 1475QX492-3
Festive Surrey
1989 1475QX458-5
Christmas Caboose
1988 1400QX400-1
Kringle Koach
1987 1400QX484-7
Santa's Woody
1986 1400QX404-3
Kringle's Kool Treats
1985 1400QX496-5
Santa's Fire Engine
1984 1300QX432-4
Santa's Deliveries
1983 1300QX403-7
Santa Express
1982 1500QX464-3
Jolly Trolley
1981 1300QX438-2
Rooftop Deliveries
1980 1200QX143-4
Santa's Express
1979 900QX155-9
Santa's Motorcar

Here Comes Santa: 1992

Here Comes Santa: 1991, 1990, 1989

Here Comes Santa: 1988, 1987, 1986, 1985, 1984

Here Comes Santa: 1983, 1982, 1981, 1980, 1979

Rocking Horse

- 1996 1095QX5674
  Black
- 1995 1095QX5167
  Appaloosa
- 1994 1095QX5016
  Chestnut
- 1993 1075QX416-2
  Gray
- 1992 1075QX426-1
  Spotted Brown
- 1991 1075QX414-7
  Buckskin
- 1990 1075QX464-6
  Appaloosa
- 1989 1075QX462-2
  Bay
- 1988 1075QX402-4
  Dappled Gray
- 1987 1075QX482-9
  White
- 1986 1075QX401-6
  Palomino
- 1985 1075QX493-2
  Pinto
- 1984 1000QX435-4
  Appaloosa
- 1983 1000QX417-7
  Russet
- 1982 1000QX502-3
  Black
- 1981 900QX422-2
  Dappled

Rocking Horse: 1996, 1995, 1994, 1993, 1992

Rocking Horse: 1991, 1990, 1989, 1988, 1987

Rocking Horse: 1986, 1985, 1984, 1983, 1982

Rocking Horse: 1981

Frosty Friends

Frosty Friends: 1998, 1997, 1996, 1995, 1994, 1993

Frosty Friends: 1992

Frosty Friends: 1991, 1990, 1989, 1988, 1987, 1986

Frosty Friends: 1985, 1984, 1983

Frosty Friends: 1982, 1981, 1980

Candlelight Services: 1998

Lighthouse Greetings: 1998, 1997

Journeys into Space: 1998, 1997, 1996

Tobin Fraley Holiday Carousel: 1996, 1995, 1994

Forest Frolics: 1995

Forest Frolics: 1994, 1993, 1992

Forest Frolics: 1991, 1990, 1989

Chris Mouse: 1997, 1996, 1995

Chris Mouse: 1994, 1993

Chris Mouse: 1992

Chris Mouse: 1991, 1990

Chris Mouse: 1989

Chris Mouse
- 1997   1495QLX7525
  Chris Mouse Luminaria
- 1996   1450QLX7371
  Chris Mouse Inn
- 1995   1250QLX7307
  Chris Mouse Tree
- 1994   1200QLX7393
  Chris Mouse Jelly
- 1993   1200QLX715-2
  Chris Mouse Flight
- 1992   1200QLX707-4
  Chris Mouse Tales
- 1991   1000QLX720-7
  Chris Mouse Mail
- 1990   1000QLX729-6
  Chris Mouse Wreath
- 1989   950QLX722-5
  Chris Mouse Cookout
- 1988   875QLX715-4
  Chris Mouse Star
- 1987   1100QLX705-7
  Chris Mouse Glow
- 1986   1300QLX705-6
  Chris Mouse Dreams
- 1985   1250QLX703-2
  Chris Mouse

Chris Mouse: 1988, 1987, 1986, 1985

PEANUTS®
- 1995   2450QLX7277
- 1994   2000QLX7406
- 1993   1800QLX715-5
- 1992   1800QLX721-4
- 1991   1800QLX722-9

PEANUTS®: 1995, 1994

PEANUTS®: 1993, 1992, 1991

Kiddie Car Luxury Edition
1998   695QXM4143
   1937 Steelcraft Auburn

The Nativity
1998   995QXM4156

Winter Fun with SNOOPY®
1998   695QXM4243

Antique Tractors
1998   695QXM4166
1997   695QXM4185

Welcome Friends
1998   695QXM4153
1997   695QXM4205

Snowflake Ballet
1998   595QXM4173
1997   595QXM4192

Teddy-Bear Style
1998   595QXM4176
1997   595QXM4215

The Nutcracker Ballet
1998   595QXM4146
   Nutcracker
1997   595QXM4135
   Herr Drosselmeyer
1996   1475QXM4064
   Clara and Display Piece

Kiddie Car Luxury Edition: 1998   The Nativity: 1998   Winter Fun with SNOOPY®: 1998

Antique Tractors: 1998, 1997   Welcome Friends: 1998, 1997

Snowflake Ballet: 1998, 1997   Teddy-Bear Style: 1998, 1997

The Nutcracker Ballet: 1996, 1997, 1998

Alice in Wonderland: 1998, 1996, 1997, 1995

Miniature Kiddie Car Classics: 1998, 1997, 1996, 1995

Miniature Clothespin Soldier: 1998, 1997, 1996, 1995

Christmas Bells: 1998, 1997, 1996, 1995

Alice in Wonderland
- 1998 695QXM4186
  Cheshire Cat
- 1997 695QXM4142
  White Rabbit
- 1996 675QXM4074
  Mad Hatter
- 1995 675QXM4777
  Alice in Wonderland

Miniature Kiddie Car Classics
- 1998 695QXM4183
  Murray Inc.® Dump Truck
- 1997 695QXM4132
  Murray Inc.® "Pursuit"
- 1996 675QXM4031
  Murray® "Fire Truck"
- 1995 575QXM4079
  Murray® "Champion"

Miniature Clothespin Soldier
- 1998 495QXM4193
- 1997 495QXM4155
- 1996 475QXM4144
- 1995 375QXM4097

Christmas Bells
- 1998 495QXM4196
- 1997 495QXM4162
- 1996 475QXM4071
- 1995 475QXM4007

Santa's Little Big Top
- 1997 695QXM4152
- 1996 675QXM4081
- 1995 675QXM4779

Nutcracker Guild
- 1998 695QXM4203
- 1997 695QXM4165
- 1996 575QXM4084
- 1995 575QXM4787
- 1994 575QXM5146

Centuries of Santa
- 1998 595QXM4206
- 1997 595QXM4295
- 1996 575QXM4091
- 1995 575QXM4789
- 1994 600QXM5153

Santa's Little Big Top: 1997, 1996, 1995

Nutcracker Guild: 1998, 1997, 1996, 1995, 1994

Centuries of Santa: 1998, 1997, 1996, 1995, 1994

On the Road: 1998, 1997, 1996, 1995, 1994, 1993

March of the Teddy Bears: 1996, 1995, 1994, 1993

The Night Before Christmas: 1996, 1995, 1994, 1993, 1992

On the Road
- 1998 595QXM4213
- 1997 595QXM4172
- 1996 575QXM4101
- 1995 575QXM4797
- 1994 575QXM5103
- 1993 575QXM400-2

March of the Teddy Bears
- 1996 475QXM4094
- 1995 475QXM4799
- 1994 450QXM5106
- 1993 450QXM400-5

The Night Before Christmas
- 1996 575QXM4104
  Santa in Sleigh
- 1995 475QXM4807
  Santa and Sack
- 1994 450QXM5123
  Father in Cap
- 1993 450QXM511-5
  Children in Bed
- 1992 1375QXM554-1
  Tin Display House and
  Mouse

The Bearymores
1994 575QXM5133
1993 575QXM512-5
1992 575QXM554-4

Nature's Angels
1996 475QXM4111
1995 475QXM4809
1994 450QXM5126
1993 450QXM512-2
1992 450QXM545-1
1991 450QXM565-7
1990 450QXM573-3

The Bearymores: 1994, 1993, 1992

Nature's Angels: 1996, 1995, 1994, 1993, 1992, 1991, 1990

Noel R.R.
1998 695QXM4216
Caboose
1997 695QXM4175
Candy Car
1996 675QXM4114
Cookie Car
1995 675QXM4817
Milk Tank Car
1994 700QXM5113
Stock Car
1993 700QXM510-5
Flatbed Car
1992 700QXM544-1
Box Car
1991 850QXM564-9
Passenger Car
1990 850QXM575-6
Coal Car
1989 850QXM576-2
Locomotive

Noel R.R.: 1998, 1997, 1996, 1995, 1994

Noel R.R.: 1993, 1992, 1991, 1990, 1989

Old English Village

- 1997   695QXM4182
  Village Depot
- 1996   675QXM4124
  Village Mill
- 1995   675QXM4819
  Tudor House
- 1994   700QXM5143
  Hat Shop
- 1993   700QXM513-2
  Toy Shop
- 1992   700QXM538-4
  Church
- 1991   850QXM562-7
  Inn
- 1990   850QXM576-3
  School
- 1989   850QXM561-5
  Sweet Shop
- 1988   850QXM563-4
  Family Home

Rocking Horse

- 1997   495QXM4302
- 1996   475QXM4121
- 1995   475QXM4827
- 1994   450QXM5116
- 1993   450QXM511-2
- 1992   450QXM545-4
- 1991   450QXM563-7
- 1990   450QXM574-3
- 1989   450QXM560-5
- 1988   450QXM562-4

Old English Village: Top row—1997, 1996, 1994, 1992, 1990, 1988; bottom row—1995, 1993, 1991, 1989

Rocking Horse: 1997, 1996, 1995, 1994, 1993, 1992, 1991, 1990, 1989, 1988

Vintage Roadsters
▦ 1998 1495QEO8416
1931 Ford Model A Roadster

Sidewalk Cruisers
▦ 1998 1295QEO8393
1939 Mobo Horse
▦ 1997 1295QEO8632
1935 Steelcraft Streamline
Velocipede by Murray®

Vintage Roadsters: 1998

Sidewalk Cruisers: 1998, 1997

Children's Collector's Series: 1998, 1997

BEATRIX POTTER™: 1998, 1997, 1996

Children's Collector's Series
▦ 1998 1495QEO8373
Based on the BARBIE® as
Little Bo-Peep doll
▦ 1997 1495QEO8635
Based on the BARBIE® as
Rapunzel doll

BEATRIX POTTER™
▦ 1998 895QEO8383
Benjamin Bunny™
▦ 1997 895QEO8645
Jemima Puddle-duck™
▦ 1996 895QEO8071
Peter Rabbit™

Cottontail Express: 1998, 1997, 1996

Cottontail Express
▦ 1998 995QEO8376
Passenger Car
▦ 1997 895QEO8652
Colorful Coal Car
▦ 1996 895QEO8074
Cottontail Express

Joyful Angels
▦ 1998 1095QEO8386
▦ 1997 1095QEO8655
▦ 1996 895QEO8184

Joyful Angels: 1998, 1997, 1996

The Garden Club: 1998, 1997, 1996, 1995

Springtime BARBIE™: 1997, 1996, 1995

Garden Club
- 1998   785QEO8426
- 1997   795QEO8665
- 1996   795QEO8091
- 1995   795QEO8209

Springtime BARBIE™
- 1997   1295QEO8642
- 1996   1295QEO8081
- 1995   1295QEO8069

Apple Blossom Lane
- 1997   895QEO8662
- 1996   895QEO8084
- 1995   895QEO8207

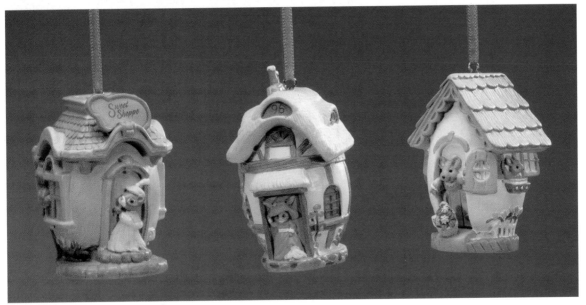

Apple Blossom Lane: 1997, 1996, 1995

Here Comes Easter
- 1997   795QEO8682
- 1996   795QEO8094
- 1995   795QEO8217
- 1994   775QEO8093

Springtime Bonnets
- 1997   795QEO8672
- 1996   795QEO8134
- 1995   795QEO8227
- 1994   775QEO8096
- 1993   775QEO8322

Here Comes Easter: 1997, 1996, 1995, 1994

Springtime Bonnets: 1997, 1996, 1995, 1994, 1993

Collector's Plate: 1997, 1996, 1995, 1994

Easter Parade: 1994, 1993, 1992

Collector's Plate
- 1997   795QEO8675
  "Sunny Sunday Best"
- 1996   795QEO8221
  "Keeping a Secret"
- 1995   795QEO8219
  "Catching the Breeze"
- 1994   775QEO8233
  "Gathering Sunny
  Memories"

Easter Parade
- 1994   675QEO8136
- 1993   675QEO8325
- 1992   675QEO9301

Eggs in Sports
- 1994   675QEO8133
- 1993   675QEO8332
- 1992   675QEO9341

Eggs in Sports: 1994, 1993, 1992

Index

Hallmark